Social Rights in the Welfare State

At a time when the future of the welfare state is the object of heated debate in many European countries, this edited collection explores the relationship between this institution and social rights. Structured around the themes of the politics of social rights, questions of equality and social exclusion/inclusion, and the increasing impact of market imperatives upon social policy, the book explores the effect of transformations in the welfare state upon social rights and their underlying rationalities and logics. Written by a group of international scholars, many of the essays discuss a number of urgent and topical issues within social policy, including: the rights of asylum seekers; the increasing marketization and consumerization of public welfare services; the care of the elderly; and the obligation to work as a condition of access to welfare benefits. International in its scope, and interdisciplinary in its approach, this collection of essays will appeal to scholars and students working in the fields of law and socio-legal studies, sociology, social policy, and politics. It will also be of interest to policy-makers and all those engaged in the debate over the future of the welfare state and social rights.

Toomas Kotkas is Professor of Jurisprudence and Social Law at the University of Eastern Finland, Finland.

Kenneth Veitch is a Senior Lecturer in Law at Sussex Law School, University of Sussex, UK.

Social Rights in the Welfare State

Origins and Transformations

Edited by
Toomas Kotkas and Kenneth Veitch

LONDON AND NEW YORK

First published 2017
by Routledge
2 Park Square, Milton Park, Abingdon, Oxon OX14 4RN

and by Routledge
711 Third Avenue, New York, NY 10017

First issued in paperback 2018

Routledge is an imprint of the Taylor & Francis Group, an informa business

© 2017 selection and editorial matter, Toomas Kotkas and Kenneth Veitch; individual chapters, the contributors

The right of Toomas Kotkas and Kenneth Veitch to be identified as authors of this work has been asserted by them in accordance with sections 77 and 78 of the Copyright, Designs and Patents Act 1988.

All rights reserved. No part of this book may be reprinted or reproduced or utilised in any form or by any electronic, mechanical, or other means, now known or hereafter invented, including photocopying and recording, or in any information storage or retrieval system, without permission in writing from the publishers.

Trademark notice: Product or corporate names may be trademarks or registered trademarks, and are used only for identification and explanation without intent to infringe.

British Library Cataloguing in Publication Data
A catalogue record for this book is available from the British Library

Library of Congress Cataloging in Publication Data
Names: Kotkas, Toomas, 1970- , editor. | Veitch, Kenneth, 1972- , editor.
Title: Social rights in the welfare state: origins and transformations / edited by Toomas Kotkas and Kenneth Veitch.
Description: Abingdon, Oxon; New York, NY : Routledge, 2017. | Includes bibliographical references and index.
Identifiers: LCCN 2016025541 | ISBN 9781138693944 (hbk) |
ISBN 9781315524337 (ebk)
Subjects: LCSH: Social rights–Economic aspects. | Welfare state. | Public welfare–Law and legislation.
Classification: LCC K1700 .S665 2017 | DDC 330–dc23
LC record available at https://lccn.loc.gov/2016025541

ISBN 13: 978-1-138-33343-7 (pbk)
ISBN 13: 978-1-138-69394-4 (hbk)

Typeset in Baskerville
by Taylor & Francis Books

Contents

List of figures	vii
List of contributors	ix

Introduction   1
TOOMAS KOTKAS AND KENNETH VEITCH

PART I
The politics of social rights   13

1   The short and insignificant history of social rights discourse in the
Nordic welfare states   15
TOOMAS KOTKAS

2   The Norwegian welfare state and social rights   35
MALCOLM LANGFORD

3   Unemployment and the obligatory dimension of social rights   58
KENNETH VEITCH

PART II
Social rights, equalities, and inclusions   77

4   Social rights and equality: from universal formalism to
individualized conditionality   79
MAIJA AALTO-HEINILÄ

5   New social risks and new social rights in the French welfare system   99
PHILIPPE MARTIN

vi Contents

6 Asylum seekers, social rights and the rise of new nationalism: from an
   inclusive to exclusive British welfare state?   117
   KATIE BALES

PART III
Social rights and the market   135

7 From social rights to economic incentives? The moral
   (re)construction of welfare capitalism   137
   SABINE FRERICHS

8 Social rights and user charges: resistance or subsumption?   157
   AMIR PAZ-FUCHS

9 European integration and the transformation of the social state:
   from symbiosis to dominance   175
   FERNANDO LOSADA

   Index   195

Figures

2.1	Occupations (number of individuals): 1815–1885	37
2.2	Social expenditure as proportion of GDP	43
2.3	Share of population with large housing payments	47
2.4	Freedom of Speech cases – Supreme Court of Norway: 1837–2010	49

Contributors

Maija Aalto-Heinilä, Senior Lecturer in Philosophy of Law, University of Eastern Finland.

Katie Bales, Lecturer in Law, University of Bristol.

Sabine Frerichs, Professor of Economic Sociology, Vienna University of Economics and Business.

Toomas Kotkas, Professor of Jurisprudence and Social Law, University of Eastern Finland.

Malcolm Langford, Associate Professor, University of Oslo; Co-Director, Centre on Law and Social Transformation, University of Bergen and CMI.

Fernando Losada, Postdoctoral Researcher, University of Helsinki.

Philippe Martin, CNRS Senior Researcher, University of Bordeaux.

Amir Paz-Fuchs, Senior Lecturer in Law, University of Sussex.

Kenneth Veitch, Senior Lecturer in Law, University of Sussex.

Introduction

Toomas Kotkas and Kenneth Veitch

During the last ten years, legal research on social rights has proliferated. A considerable number of monographs, edited volumes and articles in academic journals have been published on the topic of social rights. Within this body of academic literature social rights have, *inter alia*, been "explored", "debated" and "judged". (See, e.g., de Búrca and de Witte (eds) 2005; Langford (ed.) 2008; Gearty and Mantouvalou 2010; Barak-Erez and Gross (eds.) 2011; King 2012; Nolan (ed.) 2014; Dean 2015; Kaltenborn 2015.) What accounts for this recent upsurge in interest in social rights? At least two inter-related explanatory factors can be identified. First, the latest global economic crisis (2008–2012) has brought social rights to the centre of political and legal argumentation. Spontaneous or imposed austerity measures in many countries have given rise to active social rights adjudication and social rights movements that have resorted to social rights argumentation in the campaign against cutbacks and retrenchment. Second, social rights have also gained ground at the institutional level. Social rights have been included in constitutions of individual countries and have also found their way into various international and regional legal instruments, such as the European Union Charter of Fundamental Rights. The coming into force of the Optional Protocol of the International Covenant on Economic, Social and Cultural Rights in 2013 made it possible for individuals to submit communications based on alleged violations of the rights contained in the Covenant. Thus, both the financial crisis and the institutionalization of social rights have led to the growth of social rights jurisprudence at the global, regional and national levels.

As well as charting and analysing the relevant social rights adjudication and case law, recent academic literature on social rights has addressed several interesting theoretical questions too. While these questions are not new, they nevertheless still attract academic attention and occupy the minds of legal scholars. Two questions seem to be of enduring interest. First, is there a categorical difference between social rights, on the one hand, and civil/political rights, on the other? Second, are social rights "real rights" in the sense that they are justiciable in courts? Although affirmative answers to the first question are still given (e.g. Atria 2016), the common view today seems to be that there is no theoretical difference between the two (or three) categories of rights (see e.g. Langford 2008, pp30–1; Gearty and Mantouvalou 2010, p17; Barak-Erez and Gross 2011, p8; King 2012, p1; Garland 2016, p625). Regarding the second question, it has been argued that the proliferation of social rights adjudication in courts alone proves the point that they are, indeed, justiciable (Langford 2008, p4). However, some scholars who agree that no categorical difference between social rights and civil/political rights exists still insist that social rights should not be promoted through courts. Their value, rather, "lies principally in the political arena" (Gearty and Mantouvalou 2010, p1).

What has characterized the recent literature on social rights is that it has mainly focused on *constitutional* social rights and/or social *human* rights – especially from the point of view of adjudication. However, the ambition and focus of this edited collection lie elsewhere. Rather than exploring the question of the justiciability of social rights or adopting the type of legal-normative approach to be found in the current legal literature on social rights, the book addresses social rights in the *context of the changing nature of the welfare state*. This has at least one important implication. We are not interested in social rights as "aspirational rights-claims" (Garland 2016, p624) as they appear in international human rights treaties and national constitutions. Instead, the chapters of this book analyse social rights as "actually-existing rights" (Garland 2016, p624) routinely upheld by welfare state officials.

The relationship between social rights and the welfare state has, of course, been studied before. Even though T. H. Marshall (1964) did not use the term "welfare state" himself, his analysis of the nexus between social rights and social citizenship has marked the study of social rights and the welfare state ever since. It has become a commonplace – almost a necessity – to refer to Marshall when writing on social rights and the welfare state. In a way, this is somewhat paradoxical since Marshall did not engage in any profound theoretical contemplation on the nature of social rights. He primarily used the term "social rights" as a synonym for "social entitlements". This, however, should not be taken to mean that Marshall's seminal work on social rights and social citizenship is no longer of contemporary relevance or a source of inspiration for scholars seeking to make sense of the relationship between social rights and the welfare state today – as several of the contributions to this collection confirm. His work has also garnered the critical interest of scholars seeking to make sense of social rights in the context of the post-national and global reality in which we now live. Dean, for example, has recently advocated a "post-Marshallian theory of social rights" that would conceive of social rights in "social" and not "institutional" terms. In other words, social rights are negotiated, rather than given (Dean 2015, pp148–52).

Marshall's notion of social rights – and social rights in general – was, however, an object of criticism long before the era of globalization and trans-nationalism. Since at least the 1980s, social rights have been discussed in the context of the "crisis of the welfare state". While perhaps the leading figure in those discussions was Jürgen Habermas, the debate also involved other German social theorists and legal scholars, including Gunther Teubner, Ulrich Preuss and Rudolf Wiethölter. They all shared the view that social rights were one of the innate causes of the crisis of the welfare state. Social rights as "distributive rights" not only set unnecessary restrictions on governmental economic policies in times of economic downturn but also had a passivizing effect on individual initiative. Social rights in the form of ever-growing social security legislation also led to the "juridification" of the social sphere and to an increase in administrative power. "Proceduralization of law" and "reflexive law" were offered as solutions to these problems (see Teubner 1986; Preuss 1986; Wiethölter 1986; and Habermas 1987 and 1996).

Habermas, in particular, claimed that T. H. Marshall's description of the linear evolution of the elements of citizenship and concurrent rights was too black and white. According to Habermas, Marshall's analysis "remains insensitive to increases and losses in autonomy". Social entitlements are only *empirically* connected to the idea of political autonomy. In certain circumstances, social rights may advance a "privatistic retreat from the citizen's role [whereby] citizenship is reduced to a client's relationship to administration that provide security, services, and benefits paternalistically" (Habermas 1996, pp77–8). Instead, procedural law, that is, the right to political participation, has a *conceptual* relationship to the individual's political autonomy. This type of dismal account of the potential of social rights has drawn criticism. It has been argued (Tweedy and Hunt 1994), especially in reference to Habermas's critique of social rights, that all rights – including those of the civil and political variety – retain the possibility of limiting individual freedom. Furthermore, social rights are not monolithic and therefore not all social rights imply bureaucratization.

In the context of the French welfare state, Pierre Rosanvallon has touched upon the theme of the crisis of the welfare state and rights. With reference to new forms of social entitlements – especially the *revenu minimum d'insertion* introduced in France in 1988 – Rosanvallon has claimed that these types of procedural rights, "rights to inclusion", offer a way out of the impasses created by the decline of the "insuring society" (Rosanvallon 2000, pp83–4, 88, 104–6). In contrast to Habermas, Rosanvallon's account of procedural rights emphasizes more strongly the substantive dimension of these rights. According to Rosanvallon, what is at stake is not political autonomy but rather the right and obligation to "social usefulness".

Social security systems have, indeed, undergone continuous reforms in Western welfare states during the past 30 years. Austerity measures of different degrees have been imposed, social welfare administration has been streamlined, and the duties of citizens have been strengthened. Some have argued that these reform policies have altered the very nature of social rights. It has been argued, for instance, that social rights have become more "discursive" (Cox 1998). Social rights are no longer perceived as absolute claims. Rather, they are viewed as negotiated claims that need to be balanced against the social rights claims of others. Although there is a certain truth to this argument, historically speaking social rights – like all rights – have always been negotiated. Perhaps the difference between the past and today is that whereas the content and scope of social rights used to be negotiated mainly in the sphere of politics, today, at least in some countries, the negotiations also take place in courts.

Of course, the chapters in this book cannot be, and are not, immune to the foregoing debates on the relationship between social rights and the welfare state. For instance, several chapters engage closely with Marshall's seminal text on social rights and social citizenship, and discussions of the phenomena of juridification and the proceduralization of rights and law can be found here and there. But when discussing such themes, the contributions offered in this collection are less overtly and purely theoretical compared to the literature on the relationship between social rights and the crisis of the welfare state outlined above. Rather, the methodological spirit that animates many of the essays here owes more to historical sociology (Lachmann 2013) and socio-legal studies than it does to legal or political theory. Thus, the aim of the two workshops from which this book emerged was to encourage the contributors to engage with the theme of historical change when approaching the relationship between social rights and the welfare state. What kinds of social, political and economic transformations have impacted upon the nature of the welfare state and how, in turn, has this affected the form and function of social rights today? Why, in some countries with strong welfare states, has the discourse of social rights never, or only rarely or recently, featured in politics or law? As welfare states have developed, what have the implications of the ways in which it has transformed been for ideas intimately and traditionally connected to questions of welfare such as nationalism, equality and inclusion; and how are these related to the form of social rights and their scope or reach? These are the kinds of questions raised and tackled in the chapters of this book. By way of a historical sensibility and attention to the question of transformation, the chapters seek to shed light on how contemporary social rights feature in the context of today's welfare state – what form they take, their scope, their possible functions, and even their potential irrelevance. And those issues are not discussed at a purely abstract or theoretical level, but in many cases are grounded in specific examples (Garland's "actually-existing rights") from various fields of social policy and law – including education, unemployment, health care, and the welfare of asylum seekers.

The collection is divided into three parts, each of which represents a broad theme. What follows is a description of each theme and an overview of the chapters in each part.

The politics of social rights

The book begins by exploring the relationship between politics and social rights. As noted above, all rights – including social rights – are political. The personal and material scope of social rights is subject to continuous political negotiation. But social rights are also political in another sense. Social rights discourse – especially constitutional social rights and social human rights argumentation – is a particular form of politics. Social security systems can be reformed through social rights adjudication. However, from a historical perspective significant social rights adjudication appears to be rare. Social rights, in the sense of social entitlements, have traditionally been promoted through politics rather than through the courts.

Toomas Kotkas explores those themes in this section's opening chapter and argues that the tradition of social rights discourse, at least in Nordic welfare states, has been – and still appears to be today – rather insignificant. Through an analysis of the *travaux préparatoires* of key social security legislation in Finland and Sweden from the 1940s to the 1980s, Kotkas shows how the creation of modern social security schemes as well as social welfare and healthcare services systems, and the consequent emergence of the modern welfare state, took place almost without any explicit discourse on social rights. Instead of individual social rights, the creation of modern social security schemes was legitimized by the need to secure the material well-being of all segments of the population equally. Moreover, he argues that, when explicit social rights discourse emerged in the 1990s, it had, and continues to have, practically no impact upon politics or adjudication. He notes some of the differences between Finland and Sweden: for instance, while social rights were included in the Finnish Constitution in 1995, the "Bill of Rights" of the Swedish Constitution still lacks social rights. They are only referred to as general goals for the legislator.

In his chapter, Malcolm Langford asks if the coterminous rise of neoliberalism and rights in advanced welfare states means that the two phenomena are natural bedfellows. It has been claimed that, since the 1970s, civil rights and social rights have been marshalled by privileged groups in politics, courts and elsewhere to challenge and weaken institutionalized social welfare goods and regulations. Focusing on the Norwegian example, Langford shows that one should take this claim with a grain of salt. First, Langford argues that the long history of 19th-century Norwegian liberalism – including judicial review and constitutionalization – was as much a precursor to the welfare state as an agent of conflict. Second, he suggests that broad-brushed statements about the decline of the social welfare state are misleading because they fail to recognize contradictory trends within contemporary welfare policies. Although conditional forms of social assistance, means-testing and under-funding in programmes have increased, political coalitions have defended and expanded various entitlements and institutions in Norway. One should also keep in mind that social expenditure as a share of gross domestic product (GDP) has been constant or rising across the Nordic states since the 1980s. Third, Langford provides evidence that the renaissance of judicialized civil rights and the entry of social human rights have not necessarily gone hand in glove with neo-liberal attacks on the welfare state. In some individual cases, social rights have been strategically deployed to bolster collective rights, forming a virtuous rather than a vicious circle. All in all, however, the role of constitutional social rights in Norwegian courts has thus far been marginal. In this regard, Norway seems to share the same history with Sweden and Finland analysed by Kotkas in the previous chapter.

The final chapter in this part, by Kenneth Veitch, explores social rights in the welfare state via an analysis of the theme of obligation. The responsibilities and duties of citizenship have become an important focus in third way thinking about social policy, with the discourse of "rights and responsibilities" being central to policy documents, reform proposals and academic literature. But what is the nature of those duties and how, if at all, have they changed since the beginnings of the modern welfare state after World War II? Moreover, what might they reveal about the forms of social relations and political philosophy underpinning social rights at different moments in their history? These are the questions at the heart of Veitch's chapter. Taking the field of unemployment policy as his point of departure, and focusing on William Beveridge's foundational 1942 report *Social Insurance and Allied Services*, T. H. Marshall's seminal essay on citizenship and social class, third-way academic thinking and the contemporary social policy of workfare, Veitch traces the various types of obligation/duty to be found in these sources and how their nature has shifted over time. In undertaking this task, he aims to demonstrate three things. The first is the importance of obligation to an understanding of social rights; indeed, there is a sense in which obligation(s) are prior to (social) rights and that the latter come at the end of a process within which obligations play a central role. Secondly, the duties of citizenship shed light on the *social* dimension of social rights in the sense of the form of social relations that can be considered to underpin them. It allows us, for instance, to ascertain whether the vision of the social at different points in welfare state history is a collective or an individual one, and to determine the extent to which there are continuities in this regard across time. Finally, the types of obligation demanded of the unemployed today resonate at a deeper level – one concerning both the nature of contemporary labour and the transformation of subjectivity.

Social rights, equalities and inclusions

The chapters in the second section of the book revolve around the themes of equality and inclusion. Social rights, in the context of the modern welfare state, have, in one form or another, been closely linked to the ideas of equality amongst citizens and social inclusion. Social rights – social entitlements to be precise – have always meant in practice some form of income transfer to those in need. For instance, social security schemes based on mechanisms of social insurance are founded on the idea of maintaining a reasonable level of income whenever a social risk, such as unemployment, sickness, retirement, or the death of a provider, materializes. Different kinds of social assistance schemes, in turn, are usually funded by tax revenue. But what exactly is the "equality" that modern social rights have aimed at?

Maija Aalto-Heinilä takes up this theme in the opening chapter of this section by asking: in what sense should the welfare state make us equal, and what kinds of social rights are needed for this task? Aalto-Heinilä answers these questions by looking at the concepts of equality at play in the writings of some well-known welfare state scholars and by making more explicit the philosophical underpinnings of these. The chapter is divided into two sections. In the first, Aalto-Heinilä discusses the concept of equality implied by T. H. Marshall's well-known analysis of social rights in post-war welfare states. She claims that the equality with which

Marshall was concerned was primarily equality of *welfare*. However, for Marshall, equality of welfare was by no means a "dead-level equality". Equality was not solely to be measured quantitatively – for example, as equality of income – for equality of welfare also concerns equal opportunities and how citizens make use of those opportunities. Marshallian equality of welfare certainly permitted inequalities of income. Otherwise, we would risk one of the principal values of capitalist welfare democracies, namely freedom. In the second section of her chapter Aalto-Heinilä looks at the kind of egalitarianism that underpins the contemporary discourses of the "social investment state". By analysing the work of three theorists, that of Gøsta Esping-Andersen, Anthony Giddens and Pierre Rosanvallon, she claims that the main difference between the concepts of post-war (Marshall) and contemporary theorists is that the latter are more concerned with a person's *actual* opportunities or capabilities, rather than with mere *formal* equality of opportunity. The strengthening of equal opportunities is a common reaction against the problem of social *exclusion* that plagues modern societies. Differences exist, of course, between the three contemporary theorists.

Philippe Martin analyses transformations in both social rights and social risks in the context of the French welfare state. Martin begins by describing the historical formation of the modern French national social security system that was built on two basic elements: social insurance schemes based on "solidarity between socio-economic groups" (workers) and social assistance benefits based on "national solidarity". He then discusses the limitations of the traditional social security system as a means of responding to the challenges brought about by the new social risks of the post-industrial society. Martin discusses the main new social welfare policies that have been introduced in France in order to tackle these new social risks. He claims that those policies are based on a certain axiology: social action and social work must not only protect vulnerable individuals, but also promote their autonomy, dignity, participation rights and citizenship. Discussing those new policies in the contexts of unemployment and care for the elderly, Martin notes that they are "person oriented", something that marks a substantial change in contrast to the classical approach, which treated recipients of social benefits as an abstract category. This paradigmatic shift has also entailed a conceptual shift in social rights. Today, these rights appear to be more *procedural*, involving such things as assessment procedures, coaching, personalization and individual agreements. Finally, Martin evaluates the extent to which the French welfare system has been transformed by those new social policies and rights, and claims that the "revolution" has only been partial, since the social protection system still remains segmented and bureaucratic.

The last chapter of the book's second section, by Katie Bales, addresses the transformation of the British welfare state from an "inclusive" to an "exclusive" one. Bales's particular focus is on the scope and level of social rights for asylum seekers, which she analyses from the broader perspective of nationalism. By examining the role of nationalism within the post-World War II and contemporary British welfare states, Bales argues that the concept of "nation" has radically altered over the last century. The building of welfare institutions which helped to form a social glue between citizens and non-citizens was one of the central causes of national solidarity during the post-WWII period. Subsequently, this situation changed owing to the partial dismantling of the welfare state that accompanied the introduction of neo-liberal policies beginning in the 1980s. This also had an impact on the idea of nation, which became less inclusive. Bales argues that the changing nature of both welfare and the construct of "new nationalism" have contributed to the marginalization of the asylum seeking community and to the reduction of their social benefits. Though Bales acknowledges that exclusion has always been a pervasive feature of welfare provision, she argues that the realignment of welfare politics from communal to individualistic policies has intensified social divisions amongst communities.

Social rights and the market

Part III explores the impact of the market and market imperatives upon social rights in the context of the welfare state. The increasing importance of economic factors, including a more central role for markets and market-like structures, has been one of the defining features of welfare and social policy in recent decades. Associated with the rise of a neoliberal politics in the West, this phenomenon potentially has wide-reaching implications for social rights both in theory and in practice. The chapters in this section identify, think through and discuss some of those implications.

In the section's opening chapter, Sabine Frerichs deploys an "economic sociology of law" perspective to explore how structural changes in the political economy of welfare capitalism are linked to what she calls "semantic changes in its moral economy". While welfare capitalism involves the integration of a capitalist market economy with a democratic welfare state, and a corresponding balance amongst civil, political and social rights, Frerichs argues that this social compromise is being unsettled today by changes in the revenue and expenditure sides of the welfare state. The shifts in emphasis within the tax state from a contribution to exchange tax mentality, and the movement from a welfare to a debt-fare state, that have accompanied the decline of Keynesianism represent a transformation in the moral economy of welfare capitalism such that "the language of social rights increasingly gives way to the logic of economic incentives". This, for Frerichs, has implications at the level of subjectivity as beneficiaries are no longer taken to be subjects of social rights – that is, social citizens – but subjects of property rights, or market citizens. They are therefore assumed to be able to respond to economic stimuli by altering their behaviour in such a way as to become economically self-sufficient and engaged as "financial" citizens in the credit market. By focusing on transformations at the level of political and moral economy, Frerichs's chapter offers insights into the importance that deeper structures play in affecting the underlying logic, and indeed continued relevance of, social rights in the context of welfare.

The next chapter by Amir Paz-Fuchs can be thought to engage with a specific manifestation of what Frerichs terms the market citizen – namely, the phenomenon of user charges, whereby citizens pay to access government services that were previously provided for free. Focusing on the fields of health and education, Paz-Fuchs explores the implications of user charges in those areas for the role and nature of social rights. Specifically in this regard, he addresses two questions: first, might the rights to health and education function as mechanisms by which to assess the legitimacy and legality of user charges; and, secondly, if user charges, and the market norms they represent, result in a reformulation of the relationship between the citizen and the state such that the citizen becomes the "citizen-consumer" rather than what might be called the social citizen, what will be the consequences for our understanding of social rights? The first question points to the possible inhibitory effect of rights – in this context, their potential to function as a bulwark, or "legal firewall", against the operation of user charges, thereby helping to demarcate, and protect, the public (in the form of public services free from market exigencies) from the private (the incursion of market norms) sphere. In this regard, Paz-Fuchs distinguishes between core and peripheral social services, arguing that the closer we are to the core the more the rights to health and education should function to prevent the imposition of charges for access to those services; conversely, the further we are from the core, the less weight those rights will have in precluding charging for peripheral services. The second question turns the first scenario on its head – in other words, rather than social rights defining the limits of market incursion into publicly funded social services, in the second scenario, and owing to the effects of neoliberalism, those rights are themselves subsumed under, and defined by, market and economic imperatives. Paz-Fuchs argues that this results in the reformulation of the internal logic of social rights, such that their role in protecting free access to core services based on need evaporates as this function is overwhelmed by the all-encompassing shift towards marketization, and the individualization, rather than collectivization, of risk this entails. The consequence is that *all* social rights will become conditional upon having to pay.

The final chapter of this section, by Fernando Losada, traces the changing nature of the relationship between the European integration project and the post-WWII social state – especially its legal incarnation, the Social and Democratic *Rechtsstaat*. Through an analysis of the evolution of the European integration project, Losada argues that this project's original symbiotic relationship with the post-WWII social state has been steadily transformed into one of dominance, in which "social rights are not a priority but a secondary objective subjected to financial stability". This process, Losada argues, has resulted in the uncoupling of the constituent elements of the Social and Democratic *Rechtsstaat* – namely, the rule of law, democracy, and responsiveness to social demands. More specifically, he locates the origins of this uncoupling in the Court of Justice's establishment of European Union law as an autonomous legal order with priority over national legal systems; the Treaty of Maastricht and the constitutionalization of an economic rationale; and, in light of the ongoing global financial crisis, "the adoption of a set of anti-crisis measures [that have] circumvented the European legal order and undermined the democratic principle at both the European and national levels". In this move from symbiosis to dominance, Losada Fraga perceives not merely a deviation from the classical Social and Democratic *Rechtsstaat*, but a rupture that produces a new *economic* governing rationale at the European level to which the social policies of national states must be subject. If the traditional function of social rights was to guarantee social stability via a measure of wealth redistribution, in an era when financial stability via settlement of financial debt is the name of the game, according to Losada social rights now "only figure as an element to be cut off" in the pursuit of this economic end.

Acknowledgements

As noted above, this volume arose from two workshops held at the editors' respective institutions. We would like to thank all of the participants in those workshops for their interesting presentations and the lively and engaging discussions that took place. We are, however, especially grateful to the contributors to this book for all their hard work and enthusiasm over the last couple of years, including their patience during the writing process and latter stages. Finally, we are grateful for the financial support provided by our institutions – the Joensuun yliopiston tukisäätiö at the University of Eastern Finland and the former Centre for Responsibilities, Rights and the Law at the University of Sussex – that enabled the two workshops to take place.

References

ATRIA, F. (2016) Social Rights, Social Contract, Socialism. *Social & Legal Studies.* 24(4). pp598–613.

BARAK-EREZ, B. and GROSS, A. M. (eds) (2011) *Exploring Social Rights: Between Theory and Practice.* Oxford and Portland, OR: Hart.

DE BÚRCA, G. and DE WITTE, G. (eds) (2005) *Social Rights in Europe.* Oxford: Oxford University Press.

COX, R. H. (1998) The Consequences of Welfare Reform: How Conceptions of Social Rights are Changing. *Journal of Social Policy.* 27(1). pp1–16.

DEAN, H. (2015) *Social Rights and Human Welfare.* Abingdon: Routledge.

GARLAND, D. (2016) On the Concept of "Social Rights". *Social & Legal Studies.* 24(4). pp622–628.

GEARTY, C. and MANTOUVALOU, V. (2010) *Debating Social Rights.* Oxford and Portland, OR: Hart.

HABERMAS, J. (1987) *The Theory of Communicative Action, Vol. II.* Cambridge: Polity Press.

HABERMAS, J. (1996) *Between Facts and Norms: Contributions to a Discourse Theory of Law and Democracy.* Cambridge: Polity Press.

KALTENBORN, M. (2015) *Social Rights and International Development: Global Legal Standards for the Post-2015 Development Agenda.* London: Springer.

KING, J. (2012) *Judging Social Rights*. Cambridge: Cambridge University Press.

LACHMANN, R. (2013) *What is Historical Sociology?*. Cambridge: Polity Press.

LANGFORD, M. (ed.) (2008) *Social Rights Jurisprudence: Emerging Trends in International and Comparative Law*. Cambridge: Cambridge University Press.

MARSHALL, T. H. (1964) *Class, Citizenship and Social Development*. New York: Doubleday & Company.

NOLAN, A. (ed.) (2014) *Economic and Social Rights after the Global Financial Crisis*. Cambridge: Cambridge University Press.

PREUSS, U. (1986) The Concept of Rights and the Welfare State. In Teubner, G. (ed.) *Dilemmas of Law in the Welfare State*. Berlin and New York: Walter de Gruyter.

ROSANVALLON, P. (2000) *The New Social Question: Rethinking the Welfare State*. Princeton, NJ: Princeton University Press.

TEUBNER, G. (1986) The Transformation of Law in the Welfare State. In Teubner, G. (ed.). *Dilemmas of Law in the Welfare State*. Berlin and New York: Walter de Gruyter.

TWEEDY, J. and HUNT, A. (1994) The Future of the Welfare State and Social Rights: Reflections on Habermas. *Journal of Law and Society* 21(3). pp228–316.

WIETHÖLTER, R. (1986) Materialization and Proceduralization in Modern Law. In Teubner, G. (ed.). *Dilemmas of Law in the Welfare State*. Berlin and New York: Walter de Gruyter.

Part I

The politics of social rights

Chapter 1

The short and insignificant history of social rights discourse in the Nordic welfare states

Toomas Kotkas

Introduction

The history of Western welfare states goes hand in hand with the history of social rights. Aspirations and policies to secure the social welfare of the people were not, of course, unknown to the liberal states of the early 20th century or even to the absolutist states of previous centuries but it was the legal institutionalization of social rights as distributive rights that gave birth to the *modern* welfare state (Preuss 1986). Welfare states emerged as a result of recognizing citizens' rights to social security and health in national legislation. This took place in Europe after World War II – although at a different pace in different countries. According to T. H. Marshall's (1964, pp71–83) renowned analysis, the recognition of social rights also gave birth to a whole new dimension of citizenship – that is, social citizenship.

Gøsta Esping-Andersen took Marshall's observation as one of the starting points of his seminal work, *The Three Worlds of Welfare Capitalism*. Social citizenship was indeed a result of the recognition of people's social rights. However, Esping-Andersen elaborated Marshall's analysis further. According to Esping-Andersen (1990, pp21–9) the scope and level of social rights, and thus also the nature and extent of social citizenship, varied in different welfare regimes. Citizens were least dependent on the market in the Nordic social democratic welfare regime where social entitlements were universal and their level high. The de-commodifying effect has traditionally been strongest in the Nordic welfare states.

The construction of welfare states with universal social security schemes was "completed" in the Nordic countries by the 1980s. Entitlements to a variety of rather generous income security benefits as well as to social care and healthcare services – that is, extensive social rights – became recognized in social security legislation in Sweden, Denmark, Finland and Norway. One would assume, especially with reference to Marshall's and Esping-Andersen's renowned narratives about the recognition of social rights and the emergence of welfare states in post-war Europe, that these reforms and hence the creation of Nordic welfare states would have been legitimized by an explicit social rights discourse. But was this really the case? This question has not been posed before.

The aim of this chapter is, indeed, to explore the history of social rights discourse in the Nordic welfare states, chiefly Finland and Sweden. By the notion of "social rights discourse" I simply refer to the occurrence and usage of the term "social right" (Finnish: *sosiaalinen oikeus*, Swedish: *social rättighet*) in official law drafting documents. Two questions will be asked. First, when did *explicit discourse on social rights* emerge in Finland and Sweden? Second, what, if any, have been the *practical consequences* of the emergence of an explicit social rights discourse connected to the strengthening of human and constitutional rights discourse in general? The second question relates to the longstanding discussion on the relationship between welfare state regulation and juridification (see e.g. Teubner 1987). The term "juridification" is, of course, equivocal. It has been used to depict a number of interrelated phenomena such as the increased importance of constitutional rights, growing judicial power, more autonomous judicial institutions, more detailed legal regulation, the expansion of legal regulation in new social spheres, and so on (Sinding Aasen et al 2014, p2). I am particularly interested in the question of the relationship between constitutionalization and the emergence of social rights discourse in Sweden and Finland.

The central claim made in this chapter is that the creation of modern social security schemes and social welfare and healthcare services systems, i.e., the emergence of modern welfare states, took place *almost without any explicit discourse on social rights* in the Nordic countries. Instead of individual social rights, the creation of modern social security schemes was legitimized by the need to secure the material well-being of all segments of the population equally. This task was entrusted to the state (i.e. to society, in Nordic parlance). The claim is based on analysis of the *travaux préparatoires* of key social security legislation in Sweden and Finland from the 1940s to the 1980s (section 2). Then, the emergence of explicit social rights discourse will be dated (section 3). Next to be scrutinized will be the consequences of the emergence of an explicit social rights discourse, the relationship between social rights discourse and possible constitutionalisation in particular (section 4). It will further be claimed that the emergence of social rights discourse has thus far had *practically no impact on adjudication*. Lastly, conclusions will be drawn.

The creation of modern social security schemes in Sweden and Finland: the absence of social rights discourse

The construction of modern Nordic welfare states took place in the period between the 1940s and the 1980s, when various social security schemes based on universalism were created. This happened at a slightly different pace in different Nordic countries. For instance, a flat-rate tax-financed national old-age pension scheme with universal coverage was established in Sweden as long ago as 1946. Denmark, Finland and Norway followed the Swedish example in the mid-1950s. A mandatory earnings-related old-age pension scheme was set up in Sweden in 1959, Finland in 1961 and Norway in 1966. In regard to sickness insurance schemes, a mandatory scheme with universal coverage was introduced in Sweden in 1955. The same happened in Norway the following year and in Finland in

1963. However, Denmark was a pioneer in having made membership in a sickness fund obligatory as early as 1933; the public authorities took over the activities of the funds in 1971. In regard to unemployment insurance schemes, Sweden, Denmark and Finland still have the so-called "Ghent system" – that is, the system is based on voluntary membership in trade union-run insurance funds that are state subsidized. Norway operates a state-run unemployment scheme (Kangas and Palme 2005). Finland, Sweden and Denmark also operate a state-funded minimum unemployment benefit system for those who are not members in unemployment funds. For instance, in Finland this was created in 1960.

One characteristic that has distinguished Nordic welfare states from the many Continental welfare states has been the significance of social welfare and healthcare services made available to citizens free of charge or for a small user charge. For instance, in Finland a municipal healthcare system with health centres was established in the 1970s. The first modern social welfare act that granted universal social services was passed in 1982. With the act, the old poor law tradition was finally abolished. In Sweden, modernization of the social services system was carried through a few years earlier with the enactment of the 1980 Social Services Act.

In this section, the *travaux préparatoires* for some of the key Swedish and Finnish post-war social security legislation will be analysed in order to show that they almost entirely lack explicit discourse on abstract individual social rights. Instead, three interrelated themes emerge from these documents. These are:

1 collective social justice;
2 responsibility of the state/society; and
3 rights in a technical meaning.

Each theme will be addressed separately below.

Collective social justice, not individual social rights

The first old-age pension scheme to cover the whole population was created in Sweden in 1913. The scheme consisted of a fully funded contributory pension with means-tested supplements. In 1946, this contribution-based system was abolished and a new tax-financed pay-as-you-go scheme with flat-rate pensions was introduced with the passing of the new National Pension Act (1946: 431) (Kangas and Palme 2005 pp22–4). In turn, an earnings-related old-age pension scheme was introduced in Sweden from 1960 with the General Supplementary Pension Act (1959: 291). The scheme largely followed the design of the Social Democratic Party as a statutory pension that covered all wage earners and entrepreneurs, with pension funds placed under state control. The full pension target was set at 60 per cent of the pensioner's work income. The foundation for a "Scandinavian model" in earnings-related old-age pensions was thus laid (Kangas and Palme 1996).

The aim of the Swedish pension reform of 1946 was to make the old-age pension scheme as comprehensive, equal and sufficient as possible. The idea was to make the level of pension benefits so high that their receivers would not have to resort to various forms of social assistance. With reference to the mandate of the Social Welfare Committee, its report of 1945 stated that:

> In regard to other state measures in the field of social policy, on the one hand it should be investigated if the level of benefits and the prerequisites for their claim are *just* and *fair*, and on the other, how this sort of means could best be extended to cover *groups* that are now excluded [emphasis added].
>
> (Sweden, Socialvårdskommitténs betänkande XI 1945, p8)

The creation of a national pension scheme in Sweden was soon followed by the establishment of the first modern sickness insurance scheme in 1947. This was realized by passing the General Sickness Insurance Act (1947:1). The sickness insurance scheme was made universal and mandatory. In contemplating various alternatives to this scheme – for instance, whether to make the system and premiums compulsory to all segments of the society or not – the Social Welfare Committee stated that:

> But to differentiate *different groups of society* in such a way, i.e., in regard to [their] social responsibilities and rights, would hardly be desirable according to the Committee. [...] It would not satisfy the demands of *social justice* [emphasis added].
>
> (Sweden, Socialvårdskommitténs betänkande VII 1944, p134)

The history of old-age pension schemes in Finland corresponds to a large extent to the development of old-age pension schemes in Sweden. The first old-age pension scheme in Finland was established in the late 1930s. The 1937 National Pension Act (248/1937) created a social insurance scheme that covered the whole population, at least in principle. This scheme was still a savings-related insurance scheme and, as a consequence, it was also more vulnerable to changes in the economic situation. In fact, inflation caused by the war eroded the financial basis of the 1937 scheme. In 1956, the national pension scheme was reformed with a new National Pension Act (347/1956). The reform abolished the savings-relatedness of the national pension, which was transformed into a pay-as-you-go scheme with a flat pension. The reform has been considered a sign of the strong political status of the Agrarian Party. After all, Finnish society remained comparatively agrarian well into the 1960s.

However, the establishment of a national pension system as a universal basic pension soon led to the creation of an earnings-related old-age pension system because labour market organizations saw that the national pension did not provide sufficient pension security for workers. A mandatory earnings-related employee pension system was, indeed, established five years later, in 1961. This was a result of a political union between the social democrats and the conservatives. In contrast to the Agrarian Party, which still favoured flat-rate benefits, both supported an earnings-related pension system that would be financed by employers and run by private insurance companies where both employers' and employees' organizations would be represented (Kangas and Palme 2005, pp22–5).

As in Sweden, so, too, in Finland the biggest concern in the preliminary work for the pension acts seems to have been the just distribution of both pension premiums as well as pension benefits between different segments of the population. For instance, the Government Bill for the 1956 National Pension Act in Finland stated that:

> Because the supplementary allowances of the pensions form a considerable and ever-growing strain on the public economy, there is a reason to carefully consider their *just distribution between different groups of pensioners* [emphasis added].
>
> (Finland, Hallituksen esitys, 1955, p6)

The Pension Committee of 1960, whose task was to evaluate the need for an earnings-related old-age pension system in Finland, used the same kind of rhetoric and argumentation in its report. The committee stated that:

> Although the Committee in accordance with its assignment focuses on the question of pension security of those who are privately employed, the Committee nevertheless wishes to state as its principled stand that *all segments of the population* have, of course, an *equal right* to old-age security and other social security benefits [emphasis added].
>
> (Finland, Eläkekomitean mietintö, 1960, p7)

What characterizes these references is talk about the right of different *groups of the population* to social security benefits. In the documents, justice is a question of social solidarity between different groups and not a question of an individual's right to social security and social welfare. Vahlne Westerhäll (2005, pp375–6) has argued that in comparison to social assistance schemes of previous decades, the social insurance-based schemes were not meant for the lower classes only. Instead, they were to cover the whole population and to level the socio-economic differences between different groups of citizens. This was seen to increase solidarity between groups.

The documents attest, in fact, to a claim by François Ewald in his classic study on the welfare state, *L'État providence*. Ewald (1986, p451) argues that the law in the modern welfare state concerns individuals not so much as isolated actors but rather as members of a group, class or profession. The law of the welfare state is *social* by nature (i.e., *droit social*). The collective nature of social security law is explained by Ewald through the fact that social security in the post-war welfare states was provided and produced through a specific technology (i.e., social insurance). In regard to social insurance and the risks (such as work-related accidents) that it is designed to deal with, it is not so much individuals and their blameworthiness that is relevant. What matters, instead, are socio-professional groups. The idea of individualized social rights is simply not relevant for social insurance as a technology. However, the Nordic welfare states took a step further and extended social insurance schemes to cover the whole population.

Social security as society's responsibility, not an individual's right

The modern social insurance system in Finland was completed in 1963 by establishing a statutory sickness insurance system. Instead of private sickness funds, the administration of sickness allowances was assigned to the Finnish Social Insurance Institution. The first Sickness Insurance Act (364/1963) introduced two main forms of sickness benefit:

1 reimbursement of the cost of medical treatment (examination and treatment from the private sector, prescription medicines and travel costs); and
2 sickness allowance intended to compensate for loss of earnings during a period of incapacity for work, pregnancy or birth of a child.

The scheme covered the entire population and was thus based on the principle of universality. A universal scheme had been on the political agenda of the Agrarian Party ever since the beginning of independence (Mattila 2011, pp69–84).

The need for a sickness insurance scheme was justified in the Government Bill in the following way:

> In a modern society it is in the *responsibility of the public authorities* to ensure that *each citizen's* subsistence is adequately secured. [...] The social security system in Finland is in some respect satisfactory whereas some aspects, first and foremost security against sickness, is seriously lagging behind [emphasis added].
>
> (Finland, Hallituksen esitys 1962, p1)

The Finnish unemployment insurance scheme was reformed in the 1960s, with the labour market organizations playing an important role in the creation of a new system. In 1960, a minority government run by the Agrarian Party proposed the establishment of general mandatory unemployment insurance. However, the employers' central organization (then *STK*, currently *EK*) opposed the proposition because it saw that unemployment in the countryside was structural and could be solved through general economic policy. The employers' central organization was also unwilling to take part in financing a general unemployment insurance scheme. The conflict was resolved by strengthening the status of unemployment funds and creating a tax-funded minimum unemployment benefit scheme. In other words, a two-tier system was then created (Niemelä and Salminen 2006, p13).

The Government Bill for the Unemployment Insurance Act reasoned that:

> By paying a small unemployment insurance premium, even those *segments of the population* whose risk of ending up unemployed is low would thus support

workers whose risk of unemployment is higher and pay *compensation* for the fact that *society* has been able to arrange them a reasonably secure income [emphasis added].

(Finland, Hallituksen esitys, 1960, p5)

The contemporary Finnish public healthcare system started to acquire its contours from the 1950s onwards, when building up a nationwide network of central hospitals began. By the mid-1970s, this goal was achieved. Furthermore, a modern health centre system was created in the early 1970s through enacting the National Health Act (66/1972) in which the obligation to establish health centres was imposed on municipalities. Health centres were to provide the inhabitants of each municipality with healthcare services free of charge (Mattila 2011, pp91–102, 155–8). National health work was defined in the Government Bill as:

... healthcare [services] and medical treatment whose *object* is an *individual* and her living environment, and other related activities whose purpose is to maintain and promote the health of the *population* [emphasis added].

(Finland, Hallituksen esitys, 1971, p2)

Similarly, it has been argued that the basic value of the Swedish healthcare system from the 1950s to the 1980s was not an individual's right to healthcare but, rather, the healthcare authority's responsibility to provide the service (Vahlne Westerhäll 2005, pp379–81).

A modern social care system was finally set up in Finland at the beginning of the 1980s. As early as 1971 a committee report on the principles of social care was published in which citizens' constitutional rights were emphasized (see Finland, Sosiaalihuollon periaatekomitean mietintö, 1971). However, the focus was not laid on social rights but instead on classical civil rights (i.e., the right to individual self-determination, bodily integrity and equality). During the 1970s, a pressing problem was the use of coercive measures in care institutions. The Finnish Social Care Act (710/1982) of 1982 entailed a clear break with the tradition of poor relief. Social care services were now intended for everyone, not only for the worst off. The general aim of the new act was:

... to maintain and promote the social security and living of the *population*. The realization of these goals is increasingly the concern of *society* along with the family and other close communities. On the other hand, these goals cannot simply be achieved with the help of society by making the service system more effective and by increasing economic support. Simultaneously, other means must be used to support the independent coping of individuals and the *solidarity* and sense of responsibility between the citizens must also be strengthened. ... More clearly than before, the goal of social care is to strive for *societal justice* and *equality* [emphasis added].

(Finland, Hallituksen esitys, 1981, p5)

Society's strong position with respect to individuals also becomes evident in the Swedish documents. With the passing of the 1980 Welfare Services Act, individuals' right to means-tested income support became recognized. However, the social welfare reform was not primarily about individuals and their rights. Instead, what was at issue was society at large. Rather than only concentrating on certain population groups and individuals, which was the case with the old poor law tradition, social welfare was now to tackle social problems on a structural level. If social problems were to be eradicated, this was to happen by proactively paying attention to large-scale societal issues such as regional equality, childhood living conditions, schooling and education, employment and working life, income distribution, housing, health and dietary habits, recreational activities, political participation, and immigration (Sweden, Principbetänkande av socialutredning, 1974, pp167–78). At the time, a strong belief in social engineering existed.

The 1974 Committee report did refer to Article 22 ("right to social security") of the Universal Declaration of Human Rights, the Preamble to the Constitution of the WHO ("the enjoyment of the highest attainable standard of health is one of the fundamental rights of every human being") and the European Social Charter. But these regulations and conventions were not referred to in order to argue that the reform should be based on individuals' social rights. Rather, these regulations were merely seen as "general formulations of goals" which the reform should take into account. The 1974 report stated that:

> ... these conventions lend support to the extensive and generally formulated goals that are meaningful for all areas of societal activities. However, it has proven very difficult to derive from these international goal formulations any concrete and single goals for social welfare. [...] The general goals [of social welfare reform] are: democracy, equality, solidarity and security.
> (Sweden, Principbetänkande av socialutredning, 1974, p240)

These examples show that in Sweden and Finland social entitlements were still, in the 1980s, not understood as rights based on which individuals could make claims on the government and authorities. Instead, social entitlements were something that the state granted to individuals – provided that it had the economic means to do so. Society, in the shape of the public authorities, took care of its members automatically as if acting on their behalf, so that the question of the need for individuals to make rights-based claims did not even arise.

Ewald (1986, pp436, 462) asserted that in the welfare state there are no absolute rights. Instead of rights, law is the manifestation of compromises between the collective interests of different groups. Individuals only exist in relation to others, to society as a whole. Vahlne Westerhäll has argued, in the same vein, that the "legal culture" in Sweden in the 1970s and 1980s was "dominated by goal-rational and welfare-oriented argumentation" (Vahlne Westerhäll 2005, p373).

Entitlements to concrete benefits, not abstract rights

Even though the draft law contained very little explicit discourse on rights, the term "right" (Swedish "*rätt*", Finnish "*oikeus*") did occur in the documents in certain connections. For instance, the Committee Report on the Swedish Sickness Insurance Act of 1947 stated that instead of introducing a tax-financed sickness security scheme, an insurance-based model had the advantage that:

> ... those who were in need of help would feel gratification in knowing that they through their own insurance contribution had acquired a *right* to assistance.
> (Sweden, Socialvårdskommitténs betänkande VII, 1944, p117)

The committee (p135) also emphasized the responsibility of each citizen to acquire sickness insurance instead of having an automatic right to it. The right to claim sickness insurance benefits only followed from fulfilment of the responsibility of first arranging insurance. Individual responsibility was also later emphasised in the Government Bill for the 1980 Social Welfare Act in Sweden. Although recognizing individuals' right to income support, the Bill stated that:

> ... society's support is not unconditional. He who can for instance support himself through work in a satisfactory way will not have a right to society's support as an alternative. ... The Social Welfare Act should be amended so that the individual's responsibility will be clearly expressed.
> (Sweden, Regeringens proposition 1979/80:1, 1979, p129)

We are not dealing here with an individual's abstract right to social security and welfare. A "right" is a concrete entitlement to a particular welfare benefit. This becomes even more apparent if we scrutinize individual provisions of social security legislation from the period. For instance, the first Section of the 1961 Finnish Employment Pension Act (395/1961) stated that "[a]n employee has a *right* to old-age and disability pension according to this act". A right is also here understood in a concrete sense: if the requirements of the act are fulfilled, an individual has the right to a particular welfare benefit.

The emergence of explicit social rights discourse

Finland

In Finland, explicit social rights discourse emerged in the *travaux préparatoires* of social security legislation only in the 1990s. However, there was already some talk about constitutional social rights and social human rights in the 1970s but it did not occur in relation to basic social security legislation. Two committees were appointed in the 1970s to consider reforming the constitution of 1919. It was then acknowledged that the absence of economic, social and cultural rights in the constitution was an obvious flaw that needed to be fixed. The temporary report of the first committee stated that:

> ... the realization of economic, social and cultural rights is as important for the well-being and quality of life of citizens as is, for instance, ensuring constitutional political rights.
>
> (Finland, Valtiosääntökomitean välimietintö, 1974, p124)

The committee mentioned as constitutional social rights the right to live a life worthy of human dignity, the right to income security, the right to housing, and the right to protection of health and medical treatment. This list of rights was repeated in the report of the second Constitutional Reform Committee (Finland, Toisen valtiosääntökomitean mietintö, 1975, p121).

However, it took more than two decades before a comprehensive list of social rights was included in the Finnish Constitution. Thus, the system of constitutional rights of the 1919 constitution was only reformed in 1995. The Constitutional Rights Committee that issued its report in 1992 justified the reform with much the same arguments as the two Constitutional Committees 20 years earlier. The Finnish system of constitutional rights was outdated and did not correspond to international human rights treaties. The committee referred, among others, to the International Covenant on Economic, Social and Cultural Rights, the European Social Charter, and several International Labour Organization (ILO) conventions. The inclusion of social rights, in particular, in the constitution was seen as necessary. The Committee Report stated that:

> It is characteristic of Nordic welfare societies and states that all residents have the right to a secure life regardless of their status in working life, family relations or other equivalent factors.
>
> (Finland, Perusoikeuskomitean mietintö, 1992, p333)

Ever since the constitutional rights reform, discourse on constitutional social rights and social human rights has become "part and parcel" of the *travaux préparatoires* of social security legislation in Finland. For example, the Government Bill on the 1992 Patient Act included references to international covenants in which the right of everyone to enjoy the best possible health was recognized (Finland, Hallituksen esitys, 1991, pp5–6). The Government Bill on the 2010 Health Care Act also included a chapter that stressed the importance of constitutional social rights in healthcare. It was recalled that Section 19.3 of the constitution secured for everyone the right to adequate healthcare services and obliged the public authorities to promote the health of the population (Finland, Hallituksen esitys, 2010, pp6–7). In regard to legislation on social care, there, too, social rights discourse has become a permanent part of the *travaux préparatoires*. The Government Bills for the 2012 Elderly Care Act as well as for the 2014 Social Care Act both referred to individuals' constitutional right to adequate health and social care services (Finland, Hallituksen esitys, 2012, pp7–8). The latter document stated that:

> The constitutional and human rights that are secured for *individuals* in the Constitution and international treaties set vital conditions for reform of the social care system. We are dealing with universal, fundamental and inalienable rights that belong to everyone [emphasis added].
>
> (Finland, Hallituksen esitys, 2014, pp10–12)

In Finland, the strengthening of social rights discourse in the *travaux préparatoires* of social security legislation bears witness to the withdrawal of paternalistic ideology from the social political discourse. Clients and patients are no longer merely "objects" of authoritative measures. Instead, clients now have an individualized right to social security – whether income security benefits, social care services or healthcare services. Moreover, clients and patients are expected to actively claim their rights and take part in planning the contents of employment, social care and healthcare services. Clients' right to self-determination has become one of the leitmotifs in social security administration and services.

Sweden

Although the social rights discourse is practically absent in the *travaux préparatoires* for key Swedish social security legislation from the 1940s to the 1980s, constitutional social rights were nevertheless also debated in Sweden early on. As in Finland, this debate took place in relation to various attempts at constitutional reform. The Swedish Constitution dated back to 1809. Even in 1938, a bill was passed in the Swedish Parliament in which a question was raised about including a catalogue of fundamental rights in the constitution. This was the first time that such positive rights as the right to work and the right to subsistence were mentioned in the debate. After the 1938 report, work continued and a few further reports on constitutional reform were drawn up in 1941, 1963 and 1972. The long project came to an end in 1974 when the new constitution (1974: 152) was finally enacted. However, the end result was that social rights were not included in the second chapter of the new constitution (i.e., the Swedish "bill of rights"). Instead, individuals' personal, economic and cultural well-being are mentioned as general "goals". The rights to employment, housing and education are mentioned but not so much as rights; rather, only as general goals for the public authorities to strive for. These "rights" are mentioned along with the obligation of the government to promote social care and security, and favourable conditions for good health (Lind 2009, pp52–76).

At least two reasons may explain why social rights were not included in the constitution of 1974. First, as already implied, in Swedish constitutional doctrine constitutional rights have traditionally been understood more as *guidelines for the legislator* but not so much as individual rights that could be claimed in the courts. It has not been considered reasonable to tie the hands of the legislator with overly detailed rights that the government might not be able to realize in times of scarcity. Second, and in line with the first argument, promoting citizens' social welfare has been seen as an obligation for the state/society to fulfil rather than something that citizens have a right to. It is noteworthy that the Social Democrats, in particular, were against including positive justiciable social rights in the Constitution of 1974 (Lind 2009, pp58–74).

So, individual social rights are still not included in the Swedish Constitution to date. Consequently, the discourse on constitutional social and social human rights has remained rather weak, or even evasive, in later *travaux préparatoires* for Swedish social security and welfare legislation. A telling example is the Final Report of a Committee whose task was to ponder the reform of the 1980 Social Welfare Act (1980:620). The report, from 1999, refers to the distinction between civil and political rights, on the one hand, and social rights, on the other by saying that:

> In order to enforce social and economic rights, the state is dependent on economic resources. In regard to civil and political rights, the state's economic resources are not so decisive for their enforcement as is the state's benevolence.
> (Sweden, Slutbetänkande från Socialtjänstutredningen, 1999, p175)

It seems that a certain kind of indecision still exists about the nature of social rights in Swedish politics. One does not seem to be able to make up one's mind about whether to rely on general goal-oriented provisions and to give the authorities more room for interpretation, or whether to enact rights-based provisions and to improve individuals' legal security. The danger with the first alternative is that it may infringe upon individuals' social rights, and with the latter that it might give rise to unjustified expectations amongst citizens (Sweden, Slutbetänkande från Socialtjänstutredningen, 1999, p175).

Because social rights as justiciable rights have never been included in the Swedish constitution, it is self-evident that there is no case law to which the courts could have referred about constitutional social rights. Of course, other constitutional rights exist, such as the prohibition on using retroactive legislation, the right to property, the right to equality and the right to legitimate expectations that could have been used as arguments in the reasoning of the courts in order to promote social rights indirectly. But the legislator has not given any indication that the courts should actually do so and therefore they have thus far not done so either (Vahlne Westerhäll 2005, p385).

Consequently, the promotion of constitutional social rights in Sweden has been left to legal scholars, among others. It has been argued, for instance, that there is no principled obstacle to extending the constitutional protection of property to cover supplementary pension benefits (Vahlne Westerhäll 1996, pp30–4); that there are no theoretical grounds for juxtaposition between social rights and civil/political rights (Gustafsson 2005); or that when the report (2008:125) of the

Constitutional Committee claimed that reform of the constitutional provision on social rights was not required, the committee ignored the development of social human rights within public international law and EU law (Lind 2009, pp76, 459). However, the academic campaign for constitutional social rights has so far been unsuccessful in Sweden.

Explicit social rights discourse: A sign of "hyper-constitutionalization"?

Based on the above analysis it can be argued that the Nordic welfare states – at least Finland and Sweden – were built on, and citizens' rights to social entitlements recognized, almost without any explicit discourse on individual social rights. More widespread discourse on constitutional social and social human rights emerged in Finland only from the 1990s onwards when fundamental social rights were included in the constitution. In Sweden, the constitution even today lacks a list of social rights, while discourse on constitutional social rights or social human rights is rather vague in the *travaux préparatoires* for social security legislation.

What kind of consequences has explicit social rights discourse brought about in Finland? As already mentioned in the introduction, it is justified to ask if this development has, perhaps, led to "hyper-constitutionalization" (i.e., excessive emphasis on constitutional (and human) social rights). The notion of hyper-constitutionalization has at least two aspects: it refers to juridification of politics, on the one hand, and to politicization of adjudication, on the other (Tuori 2011, pp241–8). Since social rights have not been constitutionalised in Sweden to date, the question of hyper-constitutionalization does not really apply. Therefore I am going to focus on the Finnish case.

We should first ask whether Finnish political decision-making processes, especially in regard to social security policy, have somehow juridified. If we limit the analysis simply to a discursive level, the answer is clear and affirmative. As indicated above, social rights discourse has become an elemental part of general social policy discourse in Finland. However, this does not yet mean that the discourse would have had far-reaching practical consequences on social policy. We must ask further to what extent constitutional social rights have set boundaries to the decision-making of the legislator in the field of social policy. Of course, this question is not easy to answer but we can, in fact, try to approach it by scrutinizing statements by the Parliamentary Constitutional Law Committee.

Finland has no Constitutional Court, as is also the case in the other Nordic countries, too, so that the constitutionality of law is evaluated in advance by the Parliamentary Constitutional Law Committee. A recent analysis (Huhtanen 2013) of statements by the committee from 1995 to 2012 reveals that it has assumed a rather cautious role in questions related to constitutional social rights. For instance, the committee has avoided taking a definite stand on the question of the minimum level of basic income security and has contented itself with evaluating proposed retrenchments to the level of income security on a case by case basis. Usually, the committee has demanded minor correction or specifications to draft provisions so that acts could be passed according to the normal legislative procedure. The committee has thus left decisions concerning social policy to the Parliament.

What about the second aspect of hyper-constitutionalization (i.e., the politicization of adjudication)? To what extent have the courts in Finland taken an active role in deciding cases related to social rights? Very little research has been done on the use of constitutional social rights argumentation in Finnish courts. Administrative decisions concerning income security (e.g., pension, sickness and unemployment benefits) can first be appealed in special appellate boards and then in the Insurance Court, which is the last instance. In turn, decisions concerning social care services and income support may be taken further to administrative courts and eventually to the Supreme Administrative Court. I have quite recently (Kotkas 2013) analysed the constitutional social rights argumentation of the Finnish Supreme Administrative Court in its rulings from 1995 to 2013 (i.e., from the constitutional rights reform onwards). The analysis revealed that references to constitutional social rights in the decisions of the Supreme Administrative Court have been very scarce. During this 19-year period, the court referred to the social rights provision of the constitution (Section 19) only 19 times (i.e., once a year). In most of the cases the argumentation was "decorative": the court had merely referred to social basic rights in order to indicate the constitutional basis of an individual provision in regular law. The cases were decided on the grounds of the provisions of regular law rather than constitutional social rights. Only twice did the court use Section 19 as an "interpretative tool" when determining the meaning of a provision of a particular act. In its practice the court has refrained from making far-reaching decisions concerning, for instance, questions of prioritizing scarce municipal resources. The significance of decisions has been limited to the individual cases at hand. It can thus be argued that at least the Finnish Supreme Administrative Court has certainly not assumed any political role in cases concerning social policy and social security legislation. It is unlikely that the situation in administrative courts, special appellate boards or the Insurance Court would be any different.

All in all, it can thus be concluded that the inclusion of social rights in the Finnish Constitution and the intensification of social rights discourse in general have not really added anything significant to Finnish political or legal culture, and have certainly not led to hyper-constitutionalization. Finally, it must be asked why this is so.

Conclusions: social rights discourse – so what?

The above-analysis of the *travaux préparatoires* for key legislation in the field of social law in Finland and Sweden from the 1940s to the 1980s showed that the social security schemes in both countries were created almost without reference to individuals' social rights. Instead, major social policy reforms were legitimized by using different kinds of rhetoric. Such terms as "solidarity", "social justice" and "rights of groups" appeared in the documents. Even though social rights discourse has intensified from the 1990s onwards in both countries and a provision on fundamental social rights has been included in the Finnish constitution, the consequences of this change seem to have remained somewhat insignificant.

How, then, to account for the insignificant role of (constitutional) social rights both in politics as well as in adjudication in Finland and in Sweden? Malcolm Langford (2009, pp9–11) has claimed that the significance of social rights in any legal jurisdiction is tied to at least four interrelated factors. The first factor has to do with the level and nature of *social organization* of a given society. The stronger and more active social movements are, the more likely it is that social rights are advocated through the courts. Second, judicial receptivity to social rights usually depends on the degree of *political achievement of social rights*. If a failure occurs in realizing social rights through legislation and administration, it is more likely that social rights claims will be tried in the courts. The third factor is related to the *judicial culture* and the overall judicialization of human rights. If courts have traditionally recognized and acknowledged civil and political rights, they are likely also to do so in the case of social rights. The fourth factor is more abstract. The occurrence and success of social rights adjudication is connected to the way in which human rights in general are valued and embedded in a particular society, in its *culture*.

If we apply Langford's thesis to Finland and Sweden, we may, indeed, find an explanation for the practical insignificance of social rights discourse and lack of constitutional social rights argumentation in the Finnish Supreme Administrative Court. First, in regard to the vibrancy of social movements in contemporary Nordic societies, there is no space here to engage in detailed analysis. I will only content myself by noting, on a general level, that *historically* the state and civil society have not been conceived as opposite actors, either in Finland or in Sweden (Kettunen 2003, pp169–74). The tradition of social movements which would have been/are independent of or even antithetical to the state is rather weak. Instead, civil society and the state have formed a unity through which politics have been practised. Rights to different social benefits were, and still are, created and negotiated in the political sphere, broadly defined, in Finland and Sweden.

Second, in regard to the realization of social rights through politics, it has already been shown above that by the 1980s the Finnish and Swedish social security systems and the benefits they included had reached a rather high level and wide coverage, at least by international comparison. Therefore, no need has arisen to promote social rights through the courts, not even during or after the 1990s retrenchment policies. This is perhaps the most important cause of the non-existence of significant social rights adjudication in the two countries.

How about the judicial culture in Finland and Sweden (i.e., the third factor in Langford's explanatory model)? Judicial practice in the Finnish Supreme Administrative Court in general has traditionally been characterized as "reserved", non-activist. The trend has been to avoid giving any principled and far-reaching decisions that would have had implications beyond individual cases and rulings. Judicial practice has been labelled "legalistic" (see e.g. Määttä 2008, pp405–7;

Lavapuro 2010, p124). To resort to constitutional social rights or social human rights argumentation would mean that the courts stepped away from this legalistic tradition because constitutional and human rights are legal principles by their very nature rather than legal rules. However, as already indicated, this has not so far happened. Against this background it is therefore not surprising that the judicial practice of the Finnish Supreme Administrative Court lacks high-profile social rights cases in which it would have actively promoted constitutional social rights and stepped on the toes of the legislator. As to Sweden, it has already been noted that courts have not even engaged in classical civil rights argumentation with the purpose of promoting citizens' right to social entitlements (Vahlne Westerhäll 2005, p385).

Fourth, it is not easy to evaluate the general human rights culture in a country. Finland and Sweden certainly do not rank very high amongst European countries in terms of breaches of the European Convention on Human Rights. However, as has already been shown above, a certain level of mistrust seems to exist toward the possibility of solving social problems by resorting to social human rights and constitutional social rights argumentation. This seems to apply particularly to Sweden, where fundamental social rights are still to date not included in the constitution and where fundamental social rights have traditionally been seen as policy guidelines rather than rights that could be invoked in courts by individuals. To be sure, cases concerning individuals' right to different social benefits and services are tried in administrative courts and appellate boards on a daily basis. However, I dare claim that constitutional social rights are seldom invoked by clients and even more rarely given weight by judges. What is at stake in these cases are such "mundane" legal questions as whether the residence requirement set for a particular benefit is fulfilled or not, whether an individual is unfit to work or not, whether a particular type of income should be taken into account when calculating the amount of income support, whether a person is a disabled person in the meaning of the law, and the like.

The power to make far-reaching decisions concerning groups' or individuals' right to different social entitlements has traditionally resided in the political sphere in the Nordic countries, and still does. Social rights are something to be negotiated in the political sphere. In fact, Sakari Hänninen has argued that the "ethos of Nordic welfare" has always been especially *political* rather than ethical, economic or even social. Hänninen (2001, pp29–30) writes that:

> Nordic welfare ethos cannot be reduced to a social democratic, socialist or, in general, to a leftist project. In fact, it should not be reduced to any single project, plan or programme. This ethos has emerged from instances of struggle whose parties have been able, despite their differences, to communicate with each other by recognizing each other reciprocally.

Hänninen (2001, p29) names solidarity, fairness and worldliness as three distinctive features of Nordic welfare ethos. Solidarity in the Nordic welfare state context

Nordic welfare states and social rights discourse   31

means that even those who are worst off are given a chance to make their contribution without having to feel or show a debt of gratitude to those who have been generous. Fairness, in turn, implies that limitations are set to all forms of excess and people are encouraged to act responsibly. Worldliness refers to a secular view according to which security is valued in the form of a predictable life. Security cannot be based on transcendent notions of an "invisible hand", or the like. Raija Julkunen (2006, pp190–2) has argued that it has been characteristic of the Nordic regime to think that society is responsible for the welfare of its citizens rather than that citizens should be "rights owning individuals".

What kind of conclusions should one draw from the rather insignificant impact of social rights (discourse) in the Nordic welfare states, especially in regard to contemporary debates on the nature of social rights (see e.g. Gearty and Mantouvalou 2008)? Even though theoretical questions such as whether social rights categorically differ from civil and political rights or if social rights should be justiciable have not been the topic of this chapter, I am tempted to argue that the Nordic example in which social rights have almost exclusively been realized through politics without resorting to explicit social rights discourse or adjudication actually endorses the view that there is no categorical difference between social rights, on the one hand, and civil and political rights, on the other. The reason why constitutional social rights discourse or adjudication have not figured in the Nordic welfare states is not because social rights would somehow fundamentally differ from civil and political rights, but *because there simply has not been a need for them.* Entitlements to social benefits have been accomplished through politics rather than through adjudication.

I agree with David Garland who has recently noted "that all legal rights are also *political*", that "[t]hey are the outcome of political struggles, conflicts and settlements, the legal expression of underlying bargains struck between haves and have-nots" (Garland 2016, p626). Social rights discourse is, indeed, also a political discourse but it is not the only form of political discourse. Entitlement to different social benefits can also be pursued through other forms of political discourse. The Nordic welfare states are a clear example of this; instead of social rights, the political discourse has revolved around other discursive themes such as solidarity, equality and democracy. Individual social rights have not been important in the "political parlance and culture" of the Nordic welfare states.

Having said this, it must also be noted that discourses on fundamental rights have made a difference in shaping the social reality of Nordic welfare states. For example, constitutional civil rights and civil human rights did play a role in the field of social welfare law from the 1980s onwards, when practices of institutional care in psychiatric hospitals, old people's homes, children's homes, homes for the disabled, and so on were reformed. Instead of being under limitless institutional power of personnel, individuals' right to bodily integrity, the right to self-determination, to good quality of care, to be heard, the right of appeal, amongst others, began to be recognized in legislation and by the courts. The fact that this change came so late can be at least partly explained by the very same fact why there was no explicit

32 Toomas Kotkas

social rights discourse until the 1990s: it was the responsibility of society to take care of all its members. This was the cornerstone of the Nordic welfare states during their formative years.

References

ATRIA, F. (2016) Social Rights, Social Contract, Socialism. *Social & Legal Studies* 24(4). pp598–613.

BARAK-EREZ, B. and GROSS, A. M. (eds) (2011) *Exploring Social Rights: Between Theory and Practice*. Oxford and Portland, OR: Hart.

ESPING-ANDERSEN, G. (1990) *The Three Worlds of Welfare Capitalism*. Cambridge: Polity Press.

EWALD, F. (1986) *L'État providence*. Paris: Bernard Grasset.

FINLAND (1955) *Hallituksen esitys nro 36. Eduskunnalle kansaneläkelaiksi ja eräiksi siihen liittyviksi laeiksi*. Helsinki.

FINLAND (1960a) *Eläkekomitean mietintö 11 (A)*. Helsinki.

FINLAND (1960b) *Hallituksen esitys nro 5. Eduskunnalle työttömyysvakuutuslaiksi ja eräiksi siihen liittyviksi laeiksi*. Helsinki.

FINLAND (1962) *Hallituksen esitys nro 129. Eduskunnalle sairausvakuutuslaiksi ja eräiksi siihen liittyviksi laeiksi*. Helsinki.

FINLAND (1971a) *Hallituksen esitys nro 98. Eduskunnalle kansanterveystyöstä ja sen voimaanpanosta annettaviksi laeiksi*. Helsinki.

FINLAND (1971b) *Sosiaalihuollon periaatekomitean mietintö A 25*. Helsinki.

FINLAND (1974) *Valtiosääntökomitean välimietintö 27*. Helsinki.

FINLAND (1975) *Toisen valtiosääntökomitean mietintö 88*. Helsinki.

FINLAND (1981) *Hallituksen esitys nro 102. Eduskunnalle sosiaalihuoltolaiksi*. Helsinki.

FINLAND (1991) *Hallituksen esitys nro 185. Eduskunnalle laiksi potilaan asemasta ja oikeuksista*. Helsinki.

FINLAND (1992) *Perusoikeuskomitean mietintö 3*. Helsinki.

FINLAND (2010) *Hallituksen esitys nro 90. Eduskunnalle terveydenhuoltolaiksi sekä laeiksi kansanterveyslain ja erikoissairaanhoitolain muuttamiseksi sekä sosiaali- ja terveydenhuollon asiakasmaksuista annetun lain muuttamiseksi*. Helsinki.

FINLAND (2012) *Hallituksen esitys nro 160. Eduskunnalle laiksi ikääntyneen väestö toimintakyvyn tukemista sekä iäkkäiden sosiaali- ja terveyspalveluista sekä laiksi terveydenhuoltolain 20 §:n kumoamisesta*. Helsinki.

FINLAND (2014) *Hallituksen esitys nro 164. Eduskunnalle sosiaalihuoltolaiksi ja eräiksi siihen liittyviksi laeiksi*. Helsinki.

GARLAND, D. (2016) On the Concept of 'Social Rights'. *Social & Legal Studies* 24(4). pp622–628.

GEARTY, C. and MANTOUVALOU, V. (2008) *Debating Social Rights*. Oxford and Portland, OR: Hart.

GUSTAFSSON, H. (2005) Taking Social Rights Seriously (I). *Tidsskrift for Rettsvitenskap*. (4–5). pp439–490.

HÄNNINEN, S. (2001) Pohjoismaisen hyvinvoinnin poliittinen eetos. *Tiede & edistys*. (1). pp19–33.

HUHTANEN, R. (2013) Sosiaaliset perusoikeudet perustuslakivaliokunnan käytännössä. In Pajukoski, M. et al (eds), *Muuttuva sosiaalioikeus*. Helsinki: Suomalainen lakimiesyhdistys.

Nordic welfare states and social rights discourse   33

JULKUNEN, R. (2006) *Kuka vastaa? Hyvinvointivaltion rajat ja julkinen vastuu.* Helsinki: Stakes.

KANGAS, O. and PALME, J. (1996) The Development of Occupational Pensions in Finland and Sweden: Class Politics and Institutional Feedbacks. In SHALEV, M. (ed.). *The Privatization of Social Policy? Occupational Welfare and the Welfare State in America, Scandinavia and Japan.* Hampshire and New York: Macmillan Press and St. Martin's Press.

KANGAS, O. and PALME, J. (2005) Coming Late – Catching Up: The Formation of a 'Nordic Model'. In KANGAS, O. and PALME, J. (eds). *Social Policy and Economic Development in the Nordic Countries.* Hampshire and New York: Palgrave Macmillan.

KETTUNEN, P. (2003) Yhteiskunta. In HYVÄRINEN, M. et al (eds). *Käsitteet liikkeessä. Suomen poliittisen kulttuurin käsitehistoria.* Tampere: Vastapaino.

KING, J. (2012) *Judging Social Rights.* Cambridge: Cambridge University Press.

KOTKAS, T. (2013) Perustuslain 19 §:n sosiaaliset perusoikeudet korkeimman hallinto-oikeuden lainkäytössä. In PAJUKOSKI, M. et al (eds). *Muuttuva sosiaalioikeus.* Helsinki: Suomalainen lakimiesyhdistys.

LANGFORD, M. (2009) The Justiciability of Social Rights: From Theory to Practice. In LANGFORD, M. (ed.). *Social Rights Jurisprudence: Emerging Trends in International and Comparative Law.* Cambridge: Cambridge University Press.

LAVAPURO, J. (2010) *Uusi perustuslakikontrolli.* Helsinki: Suomalainen lakimiesyhdistys.

LIND, A.-S. (2009) *Sociala rättigheter i förändring. En konstitutionellrättslig studie.* Uppsala: Uppsala universitet.

MÄÄTTÄ, T. (2008) Havaintoja KHO:n sosiaali- ja terveydenhuoltoasioita koskevien vuosikirjapäätösten perusteluista. In MIETTINEN, T. and MUUKKONEN, M. (eds). *Juhlakirja Pentti Arajärvi 1948–2/6–2008.* Joensuu: Oikeustieteiden laitos.

MARSHALL, T. H. (1964) *Class, Citizenship and Social Development.* New York: Doubleday & Company.

MATTILA, Y. (2011) *Suuria käännekohtia vai tasaista kehitystä? Tutkimus Suomen terveydenhuollon suuntaviivoista.* Helsinki: Kelan tutkimusosasto.

NIEMELÄ, H. and SALMINEN, K. (2006) *Social Security in Finland.* Helsinki: Social Insurance Institution & Finnish Centre for Pensions & Finnish Pension Alliance & Ministry of Social Affairs and Health.

PREUSS, U. (1986) The Concept of Rights and the Welfare State. In TEUBNER, G. (ed.). *Dilemmas of Law in the Welfare State.* Berlin and New York: Walter de Gruyter.

SINDING AASEN, H. et al. (eds) (2014) *Juridification and Social Citizenship in the Welfare State.* Cheltenham and Northampton, MA: Edward Elgar.

SINDING AASEN, H. et al. (2014) Introduction. In SINDING AASEN, H., *Juridification and Social Citizenship in the Welfare State.* Cheltenham and Northampton, MA: Edward Elgar.

SWEDEN (1944) *Socialvårdskommitténs betänkande VII. Utredning och förslag angående Lag om allmän sjukförsäkring.* Stockholm: Statens offentliga utredningar: 15.

SWEDEN (1945) *Socialvårdskommitténs betänkande XI. Utredning och förslag angående lag om folkpensionering.* Stockholm: Statens offentliga utredningar: 46.

SWEDEN (1974) *Principbetänkade av socialutredningen.Socialvården. Mål och medel.* Stockholm: Statens offentliga utredningar: 39.

SWEDEN (1979). *Regeringens proposition 1979/80:1 om socialtjänsten.* Stockholm.

SWEDEN (1999) *Slutbetänkande från Socialtjänstutredningen. Socialtjänst i förändring, Del A.* Stockholm: Statens offentliga utredningar: 97.

TEUBNER, G. (ed.) (1987) *Juridification of Social Spheres: A Comparative Analysis in the Areas of Labor, Corporate, Antitrust and Social Welfare Law.* Berlin & New York: Walter de Gruyter.

TUORI, K. (2011) *Ratio and Voluntas: The Tension between Reason and Will in Law*. Surrey and Burlington, VT: Ashgate.

VAHLNE WESTERHÄLL, L. (2005) Om sociala rättigheters funktion och konstruktion. In REGNER, G., ELIASON, M. and VOGEL, H.-H. (eds). *Festskrift till Hans Ragnemalm*. Lund: Juristförlaget i Lund.

VAHLNE WESTERHÄLL, L. (1996) Rättigheter som grund till social trygghet. *Retfaerd*. 75. pp30–34.

Chapter 2

The Norwegian welfare state and social rights

Malcolm Langford

Introduction

Does the coterminous rise of neoliberalism and rights in advanced welfare states mean that the two phenomena are natural bedfellows? Critics have alleged that civil rights (and some social rights) have been marshalled by privileged groups in politics, courts and elsewhere to challenge and weaken institutionalized social welfare goods and regulations. Hirschl (2011, p462) highlights the correlation between the contemporary "shrinkage of the Keynesian welfare state" and the "prevalent conceptualization of rights as essential negative liberties that shield the private sphere from the long arm of the encroaching state". The blame for this development is often sheeted home to top-down premier liberal and neoliberal institutions like the European Court of Human Rights and, particularly, the European Union; although Hirschl also points to the rise of conservative parties that have created political space for judicial review.

Even the contemporary mobilization of positive social rights has been subject to this critique. The current universalist and individualist-inflected social rights discourse is contrasted to the earlier grounded and institutionalized collective social rights which characterized the rise of welfare states (*à la* Marshall 1964). This new atomistic framing of social rights has been blamed for helping to legitimate a minimalist social state and dismember the solidaristic bonds that hold together the universalistic and collective model of social rights (Fischer 2013). D'Souza (2008) also points out that turning to individual social rights often implies accepting the full classical regime of civil rights, particularly property rights.

Does the above twinning of rights with neoliberalism hold in a Nordic welfare state such as Norway? On the one hand, the claim has some resonance. Trade unions have strongly resisted rights-based demands for minimum wages or freedom of association in order to protect powerful collective bargaining institutions; and some alarm has been expressed over the growing individualization and judiciali-zation of health rights, with the fear that they may privilege the middle classes and thus widen, not reduce, disparities.

On the other hand, these critiques require a closer empirical investigation. Both critique and counter-critique must engage, as the critical modernists would say, in the "relentless reviewing of processes and methods" (Redhead 2005, p39).

One must be particularly wary of simplistic historical sociological accounts in which the past (or the future) is always better. We must make sense of social rights in a *particular country* and *historical and global context*. Moreover, accounts of political change that foreground discourse and occlude political contestation and agency should be viewed with some scepticism.

In Norway, the potential problem with the critical narrative of rights and neoliberalism is threefold. First, it seems to gloss over the long history of liberal rights and judicial review as prelude to the social welfare state. Second, it overstates and misstates the degree and nature of "regressive" change in welfare states. Third, it arguably papers over the diverse bottom-up and systemic drivers for individualized social rights in Norway.

The structure of this chapter is divided according to these three *empirical* challenges to the critical narrative. The second section examines the *longue durée* of the rule of law and Norwegian social welfare state in order to understand the role of rights and courts. The third section examines the extent to which neoliberalism has inflected (politically and legally) the Norwegian welfare state and associated social rights. The fourth section analyses the origins and trajectories of the turn(s) to rights from the 1970s, and whether they have weakened, defended or helped perfect the social welfare state.

Rights and the welfare state in the *longue durée*

At first glance, the Nordic states seem curiously devoid of rights, courts and lawyers. They seemingly represent the antithesis of turbocharged American legal adversarialism (Kagan 2001). A typical picture is painted by Hirschl (2011, p458) the Nordic constitutional tradition has been based on "local and national democracy, popular sovereignty, parliamentary supremacy, and majority rule" together with "overall good governance, political and judicial restraint, relative social cohesiveness, a traditional commitment to social democracy, a well-developed welfare state combined with a vibrant market economy". Moreover, the Nordic states have been mostly unenthusiastic "toward the American notion of rights and judicial review", and the number of lawyers remains "relatively low in relation to the size of the population" (pp454, 468).

Is Hirschl correct? Is the trajectory of both political liberalism and the rise of the social welfare state in the Nordic countries a story to be told without rights, courts and lawyers? It might certainly be in the case of Sweden up and until the 1970s (Schaffer 2015) although its historical commitment to both electoral and social democracy is much shorter than Hirschl implies (Schaffer 2016). A common error in Nordic exceptionalism research, however, is the presumption of regional homogeneity. Thus, it is important to return to the 19th century and chart the somewhat different development of the modern Norwegian state.

Norwegian liberal constitutionalism

In 1814, the upstart Norwegian nation and proto-state adopted the most liberal constitution of its time, ushering in a longstanding practice of judicial review and an initially lawyer-dominated parliament and state apparatus. While Norway was forced subsequently into a United Kingdom with Sweden for almost a century, it retained domestic powers and the constitution helped create the conditions for the development of a liberal moderate state. The Swedish king was physically separated from his cabinet, a parliament was introduced, the right to vote was partly expanded, and hermeneutic space was carved out for the recognition of judicial review.

The constitution was also replete with a set of *core civil rights* (Mestad 2014; Michalsen 2015). Inspired by the American and French declarations, the 1812 Spanish constitution, Enlightenment philosophy, and experiences with English liberalism, it included *habeas corpus*, protection against torture, freedom of expression and the right to property. However, some elements of the constitution were clearly illiberal and discriminatory, such as the exclusion of Jews and Jesuits from the Kingdom.

Lawyers and judges were central to the constitutional negotiations but also to the wave of subsequent economic and political reforms which gave life to these constitutional guarantees (Larsen 2013; Mestad 2008; Slagstad 1998). In a short period of time, Norway moved from a mercantilist economy dominated by royal privileges to a liberal market economy, although one partly guided by the state and with a heavy emphasis on the rule of law and other basic freedoms (Slagstad 1998). It was driven by the powerful elite of civil servants (*embetsmenn*) that dominated parliament until the mid-19th century and the running of government until the late 19th century (Seip 1974; Neumann 2010; Myhre 2008). This cast was principally constituted by lawyers, priests and doctors, and partly by military officers; and the "jurists dominated the government totally". As Figure 2.1 shows, the number of permanent judges was relatively stable throughout the 19th century while the population of advocates increased by 500 per cent.

Importantly, law had a double-edged role in this state-building process, represented in the philosophy of the leading politicians, law professors Scheweigaard and Stang (Slagstad 1998, pp26–36). It was viewed intrinsically (promoting rights

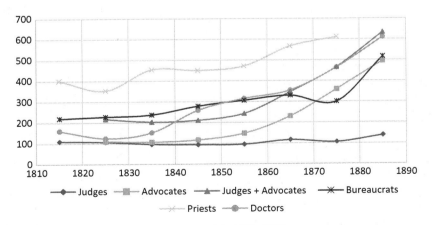

Figure 2.1 Occupations (number of individuals): 1815–1885

and delimiting power)[1] but also instrumentally. Along with technical competence, legal knowledge and techniques were to help modernize one of the poorest and underdeveloped states in Europe – foreshadowing a vision of law to later emerge in the social welfare state.

Like its American cousin, the newly minted Norwegian constitution was ambiguous on the powers of judicial review. Yet, this did not halt the Norwegian Supreme Court in assigning to itself the power to invalidate legislation contravening the constitution (Smith 2010, pp1–2). A mere nineteen years after the 1803 judgment of *Marbury v. Madison*, the court first exercised its power of judicial review. The cancellation without compensation of the rights of certain civil servants in Trondheim to auction copper contravened constitutional rights on property expropriation and non-retroactivity according to the majority of the court (Hølmøyvik and Michalsen 2015, pp334–5). To avoid a formal conflict with parliament, the relevant constitutional provisions were read into the relevant law.

This judgment and its successors were undoubtedly influenced by the American experience but they were equally a product of indigenous factors in Norwegian political and judicial development (for the background, see Slagstad 1995, pp82–4). Initially, the Norwegian Supreme Court largely issued brief formal conclusions although these were the subject of public and legal debate (Slagstad, 1995) and in 1866, in the *Wedel Jarlsberg* judgment, the Chief Justice formally articulated the grounds and method for exercising judicial review. However, the court was not necessarily oppositional or oriented to limiting state power. It increasingly aligned itself with parliamentary conservatives and baulked at defending core civil rights in controversial cases.

Social rights were certainly not part of the above rights discourse; and most definitely were not viewed as something for the courts. Their entrance into Norwegian politics emerged from below. Partly reflecting 1848 movements elsewhere in Europe, a local union of 160 rural and urban workers, under Marcus Thrane's leadership, was established. By 1850 the union had grown into a national organization with a critical and satirical magazine, *Arbeiderforeningernes Blad* (Seip 2002, pp183–206). During that year, the national union delivered a petition with 13,000 member signatures to the king and the parliament demanding an array of civil, political and social rights: universal voting, mandatory military service for all classes of society, equality before the law, better schools, reduction or elimination of custom taxes on staple crops, and cheap loans to poor farmers for land grants. The petition was dismissed and in the following year the union's national conference sought a revolution. While Thrane halted these insurrectionary plans, the authorities seized the opportunity to arrest him and 132 members.

The movement was defended intensely and, paradoxically, by the arch-conservative criminal defence lawyer Bernhard Dunker. When the case came before the Supreme Court in 1855, his final submission lasted nine days and amounted almost to a prosecution of the authorities themselves (Espeli, Næss and Rinde 2008, p97). Yet, the Supreme Court was unmoved and sentenced Thrane to prison for another four years. Support for Thrane lay elsewhere in society:

"The courtroom, court hallways and stairs were full of workers, their wives, children and relatives and in the *Christiania Daily*, Ludwig Kristensen Daa claimed that the whole nation followed every moment" (Østvedt 1940, p50).

It was only towards the end of the 19th century that lawyers mobilized proactively on social issues, although not through courts. Legislation to establish child welfare boards (passed in 1900) was driven by two professional groups – teachers and lawyers: "Many criminal lawyers disliked the practice of putting wayward children in prison" (Aubert 1989, p73). This movement was partly liberal in character but also coloured by a broader sense of social justice that characterized the emerging social liberal state under the leadership of the *Venstre* ("Left") party. It reflected the growing legal positivization, the instrumental use of law for the "optimal pursuit of goals with the most effective means" (Aubert 1989, p72).

The rise of the social welfare state: conflict or evolution?

In the period from the introduction of parliamentarism in 1884 until the early 1970s, the visibility of rights, courts and lawyers began a long and slow decline (Espeli, Næss and Rinde 2008), even if the numbers of lawyers increased dramatically. This demise might be attributed to *conflict* and a social democratic victory over the entrenched classical liberalism of the 19th Century. Norwegian jurists were well aware of the *Lochner* period in the USA, as the American judiciary attempted to hold back social reforms (Helgadóttir 2006); and were deeply divided over whether law should serve as an instrument of the emerging social state or as a firewall.

The rupture came to a head in a major case concerning expropriation of hydro operations after the expiry of a concession. The law was passed by a *Venstre*-led government but drafted by Minister of Justice Castberg, a prominent lawyer from a more left-leaning party. The law was particularly targeted at foreigners who were beginning to invest in Norwegian hydroelectric power. However, Castberg defended the law on a general basis: the right of all Norwegians to benefit. Indeed, it was opposed by the right-wing on principled grounds – as a threat to the market economy. Not only was the *Høyre* ("Right") political party deeply opposed to this, but many lawyers across the country were particularly prominent in denouncing the law. The matter ended in the Supreme Court eight years later in Rt. 1918 s. 403, and a narrow majority (thanks to some branch-stacking by the social liberals) found that the law did not amount to expropriation.

While the general principle of judicial review remained, the case heralded the shift by the Supreme Court to a distinctively deferential model of judicial review (Holmøvik and Michalsen 2015, pp348–59). And it may have helped usher in the conditions that aided the social liberals and social democrats (from the 1940s) to accelerate the development of social welfare. New governing rationalities, in which bureaucratic planning and collective bargaining became pre-eminent, emerged. As Madsen (2015, p3) puts it:

> The Scandinavian welfare state can best be characterized by its core idea of a comprehensive protection of social rights. The key innovation of the Scandinavian welfare State in regard to *rights* was more precisely the State's strong and unrivalled position as sole provider of *basic services* to every citizen, thereby monopolizing social policy as a State enterprise. The consolidation of this position came through the development of a wide-ranging socio-economic service catalogue closely linked to the explicit objective of *equality*, both a social and economic notion in the Scandinavian context. While private business was allowed a degree of freedom of movement, the backbone of the State's expansion was the equally expanding taxation of the citizens that allowed for a comprehensive income redistribution to take place as an integral part of the social and economic policies. Thereby the Scandinavian "interventionist State" was placed as the very guarantor of (social) democracy and (social) justice, as well as it grew to become virtually synonymous with democracy by the internalization of its objectives in the population at large. In the same way, human rights became largely a State business [emphasis in original].

In this new modus of governance, not only were liberal rights no longer central, lawyers lost their pre-eminent status. Indeed, one view of the rise of the second wave of Scandinavian legal realism was that it was strategic. It was a clear attempt to rein in conservative lawyers and naturalistic ideas of rights by legitimating readings of law that focused on literalism, drafting intention, and pragmatism. It thus mirrored the rise of non-justiciability doctrines in the US Supreme Court and elsewhere that sought to stem the use of judicial vetoes over social welfare legislation (King 2012).

A notable example of this welfarist conception of rights is the social right to work. In the 1930s, it was a key mobilizing slogan of the Norwegian labour party and full employment was central to their platform when they gained national power in 1935. In 1953, they secured the insertion of the right to work in the constitution but it was made specifically programmatic; its construction rendered it outside the scope of judicial review (Smith 2009).

However, the shift from classical liberalism to social liberalism/welfarism might be viewed differently – as an *evolutionary* and interdependent movement. On account of the strong entrenchment of political liberalism, Norway could move more easily in a Marshallian direction[2] through to the advancement of expansive political and social rights. This diachronic interdependence of rights was underscored by the experience of the Second World War. The Norwegian Supreme Court refused to bow to the Nazi occupation and Quisling. In 1940, the justices resigned *en masse* and many joined the resistance and its Labour Party-dominated leadership (see generally Graver 2015). On the eve of liberation, the statement of one of the former justices, Berg, captures best this dialectical understanding of the role of law and rights in the Marshallian transition:

> We shall build up again old rule-of-law state, but our times demand that the State does not only have the task of protecting life and property. The State

shall and will be a welfare state that has its task to make life worth living for us all.

(Lødrup 2009)

In this perspective, civil and social rights were not necessarily in opposition but largely complementary. Only occasionally would civil rights, particularly property, need to bend to the new social order. Indeed, the notion that strong support for civil rights and the rule of law is key to the development of strong and effective social welfare states is central to institutional economics.

This compromise and confluence is perhaps best underscored by two examples. First, during the 1920s and 1930s, the power of judicial review was regularly debated in parliament. Motions for its abolition along with rights to property and non-retroactivity were regularly voted on although a majority was never found (Kierulf, 2014). Importantly, while the Labour Party was the most consistent driver of this campaign against judicial review, its own members in the Standing Committee on Constitutional Affairs voted in 1929 to uphold it. One explanation is that the Labour Party found itself on the other side of the debate in a dispute over the reduction of civil servant salaries in 1927. A conservative-agrarian alliance had passed the law but it was successfully challenged in a local court. The Labour Party argued strongly that courts had the competence to review budgetary decisions and act as a guarantee against illegal political action (Kierulf, 2014). Second, in 1952, the Labour-led government moved to give itself full price and ration-setting powers (Espeli, Næss and Rinde 2008, p347). Høyre's leadership reacted by raising the prospect of invoking constitutional rights before the Supreme Court; and commercial-oriented lawyers strongly agitated against this move to "full powers". However, the matter was resolved after the Labour Party withdrew many of the most controversial proposals. Interestingly, the historian Francis Sejerstad has suggested that academic lawyers and a judge associated with the Labour Party had worked behind the scenes to convince the party to scale back some of the absolute powers granted in the law. Such a retreat could be viewed as clear evidence of the "chilling effect" of property rights and judicial review. Yet, the eventual compromise in the shadow of the court could also be read as an entrenchment of the social democratic bargain with capital. It helped to maintain social trust and prevented excessive conflict and capital flight (on this role of judicial review, see Langford 2014).

In any case, the point here is that in Norway, the tension between rights and the welfare state is not always apparent or as problematic as some critics make out. Furthermore, one can go back to the 1840s to find a distinct political ideology that tried to marry consequentialist state-led social and economic planning with the development of a rule of law state. And from emerging sub-altern movements one could find growing demands for the full range of civil, political and social rights. However, one clear tension existed. That concerned the role of the judiciary. Controversial cases, parliamentary antagonism, and the rise of social democratic movement in the early 19th century ushered in a period of judicial deference. Between 1918 and 1976, courts were cautious in exercising judicial review when

42 Malcolm Langford

it concerned civil rights, particularly property rights. Indeed, when the Norwegian Ombudsman was established in 1962 to ensure executive compliance with legislation, it was placed under the parliament.

The welfare state in neoliberal times

The second claim by some critics is that the Nordic welfare states have succumbed to the march of neolibralism. Certainly, it did not spare the Nordic states. Central to the discourse that emerged from the Washington consensus was that sclerotic social welfare states could no longer meet the aspirations of development and even poverty reduction. Even strong welfare states were likely to be vulnerable to new economic ideas and political alignments. As Nonet and Selznick (1978) observed long ago, in "reaching for complex achievement", the *responsive law* of welfare states "makes great demands for competence and resilience in the political community" (pp26, 78).

Economically, the Nordic states faced growing budget deficits and recurrent recessions, strong doubts over the virtues of state-led industrial models and an opening global economy in which knowledge and services provided likely comparative advantage. Politically, neoliberalism was promoted by powerful norm entrepreneurs in the form of the World Bank and the International Monetary Fund (IMF), and, closer to home, the Organisation for Economic Co-operation and Development (OECD). In 1981 the latter reported that "new agents for welfare and well-being (must be) developed; the responsibilities of individuals for themselves and others must be reinforced" (OECD 1981, p12).

Over the next three decades, these discourses were mobilized by both social democratic and conservative parties (Ervik and Lindén 2015; Knutsen 1998); and a series of socio-economic reforms bent in the direction of neo-liberal dictates. However, this trend should not be exaggerated or simplified. Broad-brush statements that "the local version of the Keynesian welfare state" was shelved "in favour of more market-oriented, 'small state' economic policies" (Hirschl 2011, p461) are, to put it bluntly, wrong and misleading. They are wrong because some specific and general aspects of the social welfare state have dramatically expanded. Crisscrossing political coalitions, constituted by robust trade unions, family welfare-focused Christian Democrats, and right-wing populist parties have defended and expanded various entitlements and institutions. They are misleading because such grand narratives of decline miss the more problematic meso-level aspects of the neo-liberal footprint.

A better heuristic of the changes in Norway and the other Nordic states can be captured by specific and contradictory trends in the age of neoliberalism: the decline and expansion of the welfare state and its new cleavages.

Decline and expansion

To be sure, there have been a number of reforms that sought to *cut back* the size and "rigidities" of the welfare state. In Norway, like the other Nordics, there were various adjustments in the 1990s and 2000s to pensions. Initially, the earnings-related component was reduced and restructured while the qualifying conditions were tightened for the universal minimum pension (Kulne 2000, pp213–14). In 2011, a major reform introduced decrementalism, less than full wage indexation (Ervik and Lindén 2015). Moreover, the *state's ownership* of a range of enterprises was gradually reduced to either a controlling majority, a minority stake or none at all; attempts were made to privatize schooling (successful in Sweden but stopped in Norway); and user fees were introduced for some social welfare goods (e.g., individual contribution to a certain maximum in Norway, Sweden and Finland).

Contrariwise, a series of reforms *increased the size* of Nordic welfare states. This is shown clearly in Figure 2.2: social expenditure as a share of gross domestic product (GDP) has been constant or rising across the Nordic states since the 1980s. Most of the changes in this graph have been ascribed to shifts in the denominator (GDP) rather than major reductions or increases in social expenditure. The story is one of a gradual rise since the onset of neoliberalism.

This increased expenditure is especially noticeable in social security and particular social services. The reasons for this resistance to neoliberal macroeconomic logic can be seen once we move to specific policies. The sickness insurance benefit levels and universal child allowances have been maintained, a larger number of people have access to disability pensions, parental level schemes were significantly expanded, expenditures on childcare dramatically increased and in Norway, there was a significant increase in the level of the old age pension (in 1998). This rise in social outlays correlates with the dramatic rise in proportion of public sector employees. In 1990, government employment in the Nordics represented 26.9 per cent of total employment and increased to 29.4 per cent in 1995 (this is to be contrasted with a stable average of 19 per cent in continental Europe) (Kulne 2000, p218). More than a decade later, some Nordic countries were markedly above the

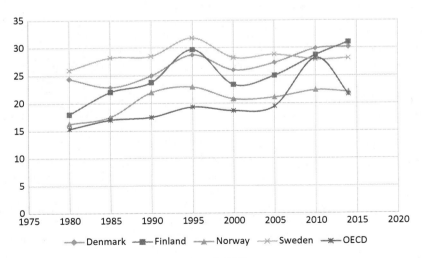

Figure 2.2 Social expenditure as proportion of GDP

previous average. In 2013, it was 34 per cent in Norway and 35 per cent in Denmark (OECD 2015). The Norwegian pension reform reveals in particular the power of trade unions and public sector employees and the limits of the neoliberal retrenchment agenda: most of the burden of the reform fell on private-sector employees and earlier retirement possibilities were expanded not constricted. And, despite a reduction in state ownership of enterprises, the governments of both Norway and Finland continue to invest heavily in particular enterprises. In Norway, a remarkable 25 per cent of gross national income (GNI) comes from oil and telecoms sales, assets and market values (Kowalski et al 2013); not only is this the highest in Europe, it does not include state-owned enterprises in hydroelectricity, forestry and aviation, etc.

In some instances, these two heuristics have been merged in a single reform: flexicurity. Here we have a classic corporatist deal (trading job security for generous wage-based unemployment benefits) which managed to marry both growth and social concerns. The result is less labour market regulation but states expand welfare state spending as a form of compensation.

Cleavage

The next heuristic concerns the reforms at the meso-level of *policy design and implementation*. It is here that neoliberalism has possibly made its most distinctive ideological mark in the Nordics and Norway; and it is here that Norway shares similar vectors to other states in the neoliberal age. First, *performativity* has emerged as the normative lodestar of the welfare state: it must justify itself by its efficiency and output (Edgeworth 2003, p123).

Second, notions of fairness and desert beyond solidarity form part of the public discourse (King 2016). Such notions undergird the renaissance of the distinction between the deserving and undeserving poor; and the rise of downwards envy, in which particular social benefits for marginalized groups are viewed sceptically. However, whether this rise of welfare envy is driven solely by neoliberalism is doubtful. Social democratic welfare policies are politically based on the conditional reciprocity of a pragmatic contract designed to promote individual autonomy (Barker 2012; Rothstein 1998).

Third, there is a rise in *intra-state welfare conflict*: "competition for resources within the overall state budget" (King 2016, p109). Sometimes this conflict may be sectoral rather than class-based (e.g. between public- and private-sector workers; families and single persons; urban and rural). More troublesome are those intra-state welfare conflicts in which a cleavage emerges between classes. The result is that in Norway and other Nordic states we find the following dichotomy:

> The big, expensive, welfare programmes, health care and health-related income transfers and old age pensions, are the most popular welfare programmes. Programmes for social assistance, housing benefits and unemployment benefits are less popular.
>
> (Kulne 2000, p218)

What is notable about these three vectors is that they challenge central aspects of social rights that Marshall (1964) identified in nascent welfare states. The current reforms partly embrace greater commodification yet a distinctive feature of welfare states was that they sought greater de-commodification: the "economic value of the individual claimant" should not determine their social citizenship.[3] Accordingly, social rights could not be provided in a manner which evoked stigma (such as Britain's poor relief laws), which required the concomitant loss of other rights, or entrenched rather than alleviated or abated social inequalities. Although some reciprocity might be demanded: social rights could be conditional on the discharge of the general duties of citizenship.[4]

Further, the reforms represent a waning commitment to the objective of achieving equality of status. For Marshall, the whole project was the progressive reduction of disparities that undermined equality of status: "I mean the whole range, from the right to a modicum of economic welfare and security to the right to share to the full in the social heritage and to live the life of a civilized being" (Marshall 1964, p72). While he acknowledges the importance of first addressing the basic minimum (the "basement of the social edifice") and that achievement of full social citizenship need not be immediate (it is dependent on resources) (Marshall 1964, p86), he cautions that any minimalistic endeavours must be part a movement towards full social citizenship (not simply making the "class system less vulnerable to attack by alleviating its less defensible consequences" (Marshall 1964, p86). As is well traversed, such equality of status also implies a preference for forms of social provision and regulation that are universal and inclusive rather than targeted and means-tested. Even if such an approach can be regressive in income terms (e.g., social insurance schemes which disproportionately reward higher-paid workers), Marshall asserts that they build social integration and thus equality of status (Marshall 1964, pp102–3). Notably, Marshall does not make universal-based provision an axiomatic end in itself, as is often assumed, but rather a means to ensuring equality of status.

Let us take some vignettes of social rights in Norway that demonstrate the emergence of these vectors of performativity, downwards envy and conflict, and thus challenge some of the central tenets of social welfare state ideology.

The first concerns job activation policy and the conditions for social assistance. Workfare-like policies first emerged in Norwegian state policy in the early to mid-1990s (Nilssen 2014, p31). The Social Assistance Act of 1993 provided that municipalities could impose work requirements on recipients while a series of government and parliamentary reports embraced the new "work line" philosophy. These policies were intensified and expanded in the comprehensive "NAV reform in the mid-2000s". For long-term social assistance recipients, a range of employment-related measures were developed, ranging from skills and motivational training through to direct job supports. Participation in the programme, however, was voluntary.

However, the system built in clear incentives to participate in such programmes. The first was to make access to other benefits conditional on participation: these included the consolidated WWA benefit that includes medical rehabilitation, vocational rehabilitation and temporary disability (Nilssen 2014, p33). The second was to ensure that social assistance was effectively below the poverty line in order to incentivize recipients to find work or join the different programmes (Khan 2016). Despite a range of reports from various official and non-governmental organization (NGO) bodies criticizing the level of benefits as well as the arbitrary nature of their disbursal in many municipalities, little has happened (Harborg 2011). They resonate with performativity and the sensitivities of the large middle class: it demonstrates that the social welfare system is focused on employment outcomes and that individual beneficiaries are required to perform to certain standards. While the normative debate on the extent to which conditionalities are consistent with both Marshallian and human rights-based understanding continues, there is certainly a distinct neoliberal shift in this area.

Another example comes from housing policy. Already in 1987, the housing sector in Norway was described as the "wobbly pillar" of the Norwegian welfare state (Torgersen 1987). The sector was traditionally subject to heavy regulation in order to meet the government's goal, set in 1945, that housing expenses should not exceed 20 per cent of the income of a standard wage-earner. Moreover, there was significant state support for housing co-operatives that dramatically expanded the housing stock and accessibility for working class communities. However, rent controls and heavy restrictions on sale encouraged illegal practices by average citizens. As the value of houses far exceeded their sale and rental potential, under-the-table payments became widespread. In the 1980s, the sector was subject to widespread liberalization.

However, the state continues to significantly subsidise mortgage payments, which contributes to Norway having the highest home ownership rates in the world. At least 77 per cent of Norwegian homes are privately owned: with 63 per cent fully privately owned and 14 per cent owned through a housing co-operative (which have generally taken on a more private character over time). A further 4 per cent live in public or municipal housing and the remaining 17 per cent rent.

Two things are notable about this shift in policy. The first is that from the mid-1990s it was no longer a state goal that housing should be affordable (Annaniassen 2006, p124). Instead, the overall policy was the vague aim that everyone should be able to live safely and well.[5] The second is that universalist approaches were gradually replaced by means-tested models. In 1996, the function of the state-financed Housing Bank was altered from supporting everyone to supporting those in "difficult situations".[6] A range of targeted policies were targeted at poorer and excluded citizens and permanent residents, which sought to ensure that this group could progressively own their own home.

This new cocktail of policies has not been a particular success for low-income earners who do not own a home or struggle with repayments. In 1973, only 12 per cent used more than a quarter of their disposable income on housing. Two decades later, the figure doubled. As Figure 2.3 demonstrates, single parents ("*eneforeldre*") use now 35 per cent of disposable income. One result is that the costs

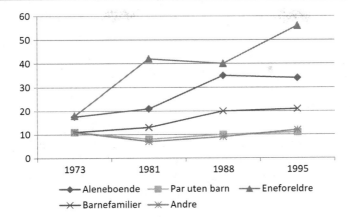

Figure 2.3 Share of population with large housing payments
Raw data taken from Boforholdsundersøkelsene (1973, 1981, 1988 and 1995)

of housing are much higher in Norway than in the rest of Europe – 10th out of 24 countries (Normann 2010; Normann et al 2009). When taking into account available national resources, Norway falls to 13th and 15th place, respectively, for high housing costs and very high housing costs; and from 17th to 22nd for those who reported housing payment problems (Langford and Nilsen 2011). Moreover, levels of homelessness have been consistent and persistent over time. In 2009, a report found that 6091 individuals were homeless in 2008 (2.36 homeless persons per 1000 residents in large cities),[7] representing an increase since 1996 (Dyb and Johannessen 2008, p14).

In 2008, the Government Auditor issued a scathing report. He strongly criticized municipalities, departments and the Housing Bank for their lack of effort in supporting the most marginalized groups in the housing market.[8] With the election of the Centre-Left Government in 2007, steps were made to address some of the underlying problems in the system – such as the overly strict conditions for housing support and subsidised loans together with the low supply of public and private housing which keeps prices high. However, it is difficult to conclude that these policies were successful and even conservative parties championed the housing issue in the lead-up to the 2013 elections, although have done little since winning power.

Yet, this is not simply a problem of a decline in universalist policies. The *cleavage* between class interests becomes particularly apparent when we examine the policies that benefit home owners with mortgages. The Department of Finance estimated that the tax deductions for interest payments in 2009 amounted to 58 billion Norwegian crowns, complemented by a further 26 million crowns in benefits in land tax through artificial calculations of the value of real property. An alternative calculation puts the total figure at 105.6 billion (Langford and Nilsen 2011). Yet, housing support payments to low-income earners were a mere 2.4 billion in 2010 (State Budget) and, in 2008, support for private actors to rent was 2 billion (Stamsø 2009, p214). Notably, the upper middle classes also derive

48 Malcolm Langford

the most benefit from the system as the subsidies are based on the absolute amount of interest paid.

Contemporary social rights: problem or panacea?

Constitutionalization and judicialization

The above discussion suggests that neoliberalism is a contingent feature of the social welfare landscape in Norway. But are individual rights implicated in this development? The global turn to rights and constitutionalism from the early 1970s has certainly been a feature of contemporary Norwegian politics and law. Yet, this shift cannot be merely explained in simple realist and strategic terms as Hirschl (2011) suggests. While top-down European pressures or the exploitation of the judicial space by empowered conservative actors was important, there were deeper structural and ideational factors at play.

On the demand-side, in the words of Samuel Huntingdon, the late 1960s were a time of "creedal passion" (1981); an "outrage" over the gulf between "egalitarian political creeds" and the "inequalities that stem from contemporary institutional practices" (Kagan 2001, pxix). While the Nordic states' level of rights realization may be high, Nordic states have also engaged in domestic policies and practices that in retrospect can only be described as systematic, large-scale abuses of civil and social rights (see sources in Langford and Schaffer 2016). This was the "dark side" of the efficient, powerful and sometimes paternalistic social welfare state. In the 1930s, Norway enacted sterilization laws and eugenics programs which affected tens of thousands of citizens and were abolished only by the 1970s. Traveller and Roma minorities were the primary target of a broad range of coercive social policies, including forcible sterilization, removal of children from families, and prevention of their traditionally nomadic lifestyle. Children placed in foster care and orphanages have systematically been subject to abuse; and the Sami population in Finland, Norway and Sweden has been subject to more or less coercive assimilation policies. And, in close collaboration with each other and trade unions, Scandinavian governments have engaged in extensive illegal surveillance of citizens suspected of sympathizing with communism.

On the supply-side, politicians "competed to translate" the new demands into "new regulatory programs, anti-discrimination laws, and rights to challenge government decisions and policies in court" (Kagan 2001, pxix). And as social welfare states had achieved a certain maturity, their ranks were filled with highly trained and competent bureaucrats (Kennedy 2006, pp43–4; Larsen 2013), ready to adapt to new techniques in order to respond to such demands.

In this moment, the US Supreme Court offered new heuristics for injecting legal rationalities and modalities in efforts to tackle social exclusion. And related proportionality approaches to law (Teubner 1983) seemed appealing in a society marked by greater complexity and heterogeneity.[9] During the early 1970s, lawyers, scholars and reformists debated the role of courts and law in social reform, often in the shadow of this court's 1954 decision in *Brown v. Board of Education*. In Norway, this rising legal consciousness was soon connected with mobilization. The "1968 generation" drove the establishment of the first student legal centre, *Juss Buss* (1971) at the University of Oslo. Three years later came JURK (legal aid for women, 1974), the *Rettspolitisk forening* (*Law & Politics Society* 1974) and a new journal *Kritisk Juss* (*Critical Law*). While the latter was partly in sync with the emergent American critical legal studies movement, its participants were more open to litigation – whether to advance political ends or to reveal, even via failure, the flaws of democratic capitalism.

This university-centred wave of activity was followed by specialized law firms and individual cause lawyers that took selected rights cases. In the last five years, the Bar Association has turned to strategic litigation in cases on solitary confinement and the rights of asylum seekers (Humlen and Myhre 2015); and NGOs have lobbied for ratification of new human rights instruments and use existing ones to scrutinize and criticize their own governments. The political character of these actors is also consistent with Kennedy's (2006, p61) observation of the shift to rights and courts from the 1970s: "The dominant rhetoric of critique was civil libertarian, and permitted a de facto alliance of left and right".

The first judicial move came in 1976 and drew on the 19th century tradition of judicial review. In *Kløfta*, the Supreme Court signalled by a narrow majority a return to a more robust form of judicial review, especially in cases concerning core civil rights. Notably, while the judgment affirmed that the court would continue to take a deferential approach to the right to property, the complaint against the expropriation process for highway development was successful.

With a rising number of applications, the court moved very slowly over the next few decades in enforcing this new approach but it has made landmark constitutional and statutory decisions. Some of these are clearly positive from a *normative* social welfarist perspective (e.g., asylum seeker rights) while others are more questionable (e.g., striking down of retroactive taxes in the shipping industry). The court was pushed in this direction by a growing caseload. A good illustration is freedom of expression cases: see Figure 2.4. Between 1837 and 2013, there have been 203 judgments with the bulk coming since 1976.

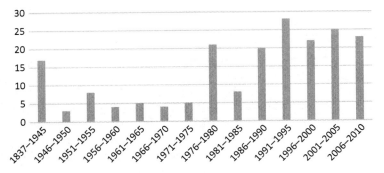

Figure 2.4 Freedom of Speech cases – Supreme Court of Norway: 1837–2010

50 Malcolm Langford

While there remains a divide in the court over its appropriate role, there is significant openness to rights. From the late 1970s, the court has been partly pushed in this direction by the European Court of Human Rights. Between 1980 and 1992, Norwegian lawyers cited Strasbourg jurisprudence in 47 cases before the Norwegian Supreme Court and sent approximately 100 petitions to the European Commission on Human Rights (Espeli, Næss and Rinde 2008, p349). These strategies had little impact until 1992, when Knut Rognlien became the first Norwegian lawyer to win a case in the European Court.

The status of international rights treaties in Norwegian law also became a theme. During the 1990s, the Bar Association proposed the domestic incorporation of key international human rights instruments. Partly through the leadership of the centrist Christian Democrat Party, this came to fruition in 1999 in the form of the Human Rights Act. The European Convention on Human Rights (ECHR) and the International Covenant on Civil and Political Rights (ICCPR) were placed between ordinary legislation and the constitution, with women's rights and child rights conventions added later to the list. While this was a Nordic trend for the ECHR, only Norway and Finland have incorporated such a wide range of United Nations treaties.

Incorporation of human rights was taken to another level with the revision of the bill of rights in the Norwegian Constitution in 2014. This reform was driven by a range of factors: the symbolic (bicentenary of the 1814 constitution); a process of "modernization" (Menneskerettighetersutvalget 2011); and a push from below (various voices championed social rights and centrist liberals called for recognition of ECHR rights such as privacy). While a commission recommended the inclusion of a full set of social rights, *Høyre* shifted position through the negotiations. It aligned with the populist party to slim down the number: only the right to education and social assistance, children's social rights and the programmatic right to work survived. However, parliament also included section 92, which purports on its face to include all international human rights treaties in the Norwegian constitution. Thus, the International Covenant on Economic, Social and Cultural Rights (ICESCR) has arguably been constitutionalized (but it is a subject of ongoing doctrinal debate).

Social rights in politics and courts

What has been the effect of this political and constitutional turn to social rights in the context of the neoliberal challenge to the welfare state? If we turn to constitutional rights, their role has been marginal. The Supreme Court has expressed caution as to whether socio-economic rights in the ICESCR are justiciable.[10] In an early decision, Justice Lund noted that when such treaties are domesticated, without being transformed into a standard statute, the court "must take a position on whether the actual provisions provide individual rights" or instead "express an objective or require states parties to meet a required goal or minimum standard". The provisions in the treaties concerning "more traditional human rights" were

The Norwegian welfare state and social rights 51

deemed concrete enough to generate individual rights but "questions can be asked whether immediate application for example arises for specific provisions in the ICESCR". Notably, the court did not consult international or comparative jurisprudence on the matter which might have suggested a different approach.

In 2011, the Supreme Court received a case that directly raised a social right. It concerned the obligation to live on inherited farm property (which can be bought at a below-market price).[11] After re-expressing its doubt as to justiciability, it noted that in any case the applicant's social rights were not at stake. He could have chosen to sell the farm and live close to his place of employment instead of having to commute. The applicant had an alternative in realizing his social rights. The decision is notable in that it resisted attempts to liberalize rural policy (possibly ineffective at times but certainly solidaristic in function).

The court thus managed to avoid the dangers of an individualist approach and making a decision that would mostly have favoured more privileged urban dwellers. Turning to policy and legislation, it is useful to focus on two areas already mentioned: labour rights and social assistance/housing policy. In the case of *labour rights*, trade unions have been mostly sceptical to the "rights revolution". Norwegian trade unions have retained significant density in most sectors (although slightly lower than their Nordic counterparts). Consequently, they prefer the use of collective agreements to set wages together with clear and strong rights to use collective sanctions such as strikes. The European Court of Justice's *Viking* and *Laval* judgments, in which express economic freedoms were controversially prioritized over an implied right to strike, only strengthened the commitment to this model.[12] Moreover, Norwegian trade unions have joined with their Nordic counterparts to resist attempts by Southern European trade unions to implement a minimum wage; again, on the premise that collective bargaining leads to better outcomes than rights-based models.

However, trade unions have embraced individual social rights tactically. A good illustration concerns the minimum wage in the building industry. With the rise of European free movement, this industry has seen an explosive rise in migrant workers. Yet, with low union density (37 per cent), only 60 per cent of workers are covered by collective agreements (Hardy et al 2012, p357). After significant debate, the relevant trade union *Fellesforbundet* applied for an extension of the collective agreement through a long-dormant law, which had the effect of setting a national minimum wage for the sector (Hardy et al 2012, p357). Notably, and paradoxically, what the union feared most (free-riding by non-members) did not transpire. The *Fellesforbundet* increased membership as the migrants saw that the union attended to their interests. Conversely, the opposite may have occurred in the sea and fish industry. Despite a considerable rise in migrant workers, the relevant union has not sought protections for non-members; and migrants have not engaged with the union (Hardy et al 2012, p355).

This vignette of minimum wages in the construction sector indicates the potential virtuous cycle of individual and collective social rights for welfare states in a globalized world. Another example illustrates the potential use of express social rights litigation when unions are unable to work through political channels.

In 2008, the Seamen's trade union challenged a 62-year age limit in the maritime industry in a complaint to the European Committee on Social Rights.[13] The Supreme Court of Norway affirmed the limit in 2010, noting that it was in line with the ECHR (particularly as the right to work could not be derived from it); and that it was consistent with ICCPR jurisprudence as it was based on "reasonable and objective criteria".[14] However, the European Committee on Social Rights found that there was no empirical evidence for the reasons given by the state for the differential treatment of older seamen (who also suffered in loss of pension rights as a result). It thus found the age-limit to be discriminatory. Two months later, the Norwegian government informed the Committee that the state had amended its legislation.

Turning to *social assistance and housing*, the Norwegian courts have taken a partial lead. The Supreme Court developed a social right to minimum assistance, but through administrative law. In its 1990 *Fusa* judgment, concerning social benefits for an elderly person with a disability, the court found that the state had failed to provide a "minimum core" of social protection.[15] Rejecting originalist methods, the court essentially juridified a minimum threshold of all current social services. However, the debate is ongoing as to the extent to which this applies to all social benefits and services.

Puzzlingly, litigation has not continued on the subject, neither in Norwegian courts nor the European Committee on Social Rights. This is despite the earlier-described swathe of critique from official and non-government organizations on the levels of social assistance and the dysfunctionality of housing policy; and the fact that the Social Assistance Act specifically refers to the individual social rights to an adequate standard of living. These policies affect some of the most socially marginalized groups in society and have been successfully challenged elsewhere. Arguably, it is on these "unpopular" issues that an individualized and even judicialized social rights approach may help. A universal or collectivist solution is most unlikely given there is no mobilization by powerful organized interests (such as trade unions).

The same concerns punitive Nordic policies and laws on homelessness, prostitution and drug use that criss-cross social and civil rights. These policies have been particularly trained on certain migrant groups. The Nordic states have not only vacillated between generous and restrictive migration policies but have partly resurrected repressive modes of criminal law against foreigners living in poverty. This suggests that the dark side of the welfare state has been strengthened by its inherent exclusiveness. The Achilles heel of welfare states and Marshall's theory has always been national centrism (for a discussion see Crowley 1998). Moreover, such an exclusive and punitive modus of law sits comfortably with neoliberalism, on account of its commitment to non-market social control and its agnosticism towards earlier advances in liberalism and autonomous law.

In Norway, the exclusive features of the welfare state have been discursively mobilized to justify exclusive and harsh policies against poor foreigners from Eastern Europe and Africa. For example, in 2013, the Norwegian capital of Oslo passed an absolute ban on sleeping rough. Despite outcry from social organizations, churches rights groups and minor parties it was passed and maintained despite empirical evidence that it is solely, and sometimes brutally, targeted at homeless foreign citizens (NCHR 2015). A similar prohibition together with a begging ban was introduced in Copenhagen (Djuve et al 2015).

Conclusion

This chapter asked whether rights constitute part of the neoliberal hollowing out of the welfare state. In the case of Norway, the answer must be conditional. First, putting the issue in historical perspective, it has argued that the long history of 19th-century Norwegian liberalism (including judicial review and constitutionalization) was as much a precursor to the welfare state as an agent of conflict. Second, it has questioned broad-brushed statements about the decline of the social welfare state and has highlighted instead the neoliberal imprint in the form of growing conditional forms of social assistance, means-testing and under-funding in programmes which do not enjoy middle-class support. Third, it has argued that the renaissance of judicialized civil rights and the entry of social human rights has not necessarily gone hand in glove with neoliberal attacks on the welfare state. In some cases, individual social rights have been strategically used to bolster collective rights, forming a virtuous, rather than a vicious circle.

Notes

1 Both conceptions of law were underscored by an early legal positivism, particularly in the writings of Scheweigaard. Hagerup's attempts to defend a strong German idealism and natural law met with modest success Blandhol and Michalsen (2007).
2 Marshall (1964).
3 Marshall (1964). See also Esping-Andersen (1990, pp21–3).
4 Others have argued though that Marshall set these too lightly due to his historical position: Hemerijck (2000).
5 See Kommunal- regionaldepartementets nettsider:
   www.regjeringen.no/nb/dep/krd/tema/bolig-_og_bygningspolitikk.html?id=943.
6 See Annaniassen (2006, p124) and Parliamentary Report No. 34 (1994–1995).
7 NIBR-rapport (2009, pp14, 17).
8 *Riksrevisjonenes undersøkelse av tilbudet til de vanskeligstilte på boligmarkedet*. Dokument nr. 3:8 (2008).
9 To give a banal but revealing example, legislation long permitted housing co-operatives the absolute power to veto apartment owners from keeping domestic pets. A Supreme Court judgment in the 1990s and legislation in 2000 moved towards a proportionality test: the benefits and costs must be weighed.
10 Rt. 2001–1006, ibid, p1015.
11 Rt. 2011 s.304.
12 *Case C-438/05 International Transport Workers & Or v. Viking Line* Judgment, 11 December 2007, *Case C-341/05 Laval v Svenska Byggnadsarbetareförbundet*, Judgment 18 December 2007. See discussion in Davies (2008).
13 *Fellesforbundet for Sjøfolk (FFFS) v. Norway*, Collective Complaint No. 74/2011, Decision on the merits, 2 July 2013.

54 Malcolm Langford

14 *Kystlink case* Rt (Norwegian Law Reports) −2010–202; § 70.
15 Rt. 1990 s.874.

References

Annaniassen, E. (2006) Én skandinavisk boligmodell? – Historien om et sosialdemokratisk eierland og et sosialdemokratisk leieboerland, *NOVA Temahefte* 1/06.

Ås, D. (1996) Boligstandard og boutgifter 1973–1995: Vinnere og tapere i boligmarkedet, *Samfunnsspeilet*, 4.

Aubert, V. (1989) Law and Social Change in 19th Century Norway. In Starr, J. and Fishburne Collier, J. (eds), *History and Power in the Study of Law: New Directions in Legal Anthropology*. Ithaca: NY: Cornell University Press.

Barker, V. (2012) Nordic Exceptionalism Revisited: Explaining the paradox of a Janus-faced penal regime, *Theoretical Criminology*, 17. pp5–25.

Blandhol, S. and Michalsen, D. (2007) *Rettsforsker, Politker, Internasjonalist: Perspektiver på Francis Hagerup*. Oslo: Unipax.

Crowley, J. (1998) The National Dimension of Citizenship. In Marshall, T. H. (ed) *Citizenship Studies*, 2. pp165–178.

D'Souza, R. (2008) Liberal Theory, Human Rights and Water-Justice: Back to Square One?, *Law, Social Justice & Global Development Journal (LGD)*. p1.

Davies, A. C. L. (2008) One Step Forward, Two Steps Back? The Viking and Laval Cases, *Industrial Law Journal*, 37. pp126–148.

Djuve, A., Friberg, J., Tyldum, G. and Zhang, H. (2015) *When poverty meets affluence: Migrants from Romania on the streets of the Scandinavian capitals*. Oslo: Fafo and Rockwool Foundation.

Dyb, E. and Johannessen, K. (2008) *Bostedsløse i Norge – en kartlegging* (NIBR-rapport 17: Oslo).

Edgeworth, B. (2003) *Law, Modernity, Postmodernity: Legal Change in the Contracting State*. Aldershot: Ashgate.

Ervik, R. and Skogedal Lindén, T. (2015) The Shark Jaw and the Elevator: Arguing the Case for the Necessity, Harmlessness and Fairness of the Norwegian Pension Reform, *Scandinavian Political Studies*, 38. pp386–409.

Espeli, H., Næss, H. E. and Rinde H. (2008) Våpendrager og Veiviser: Advokatenes Historie i Norge. Oslo: Universitetsforlag.

Esping-Andersen, Gøsta. (1990) *The Three Worlds of Welfare Capitalism*. Princeton, NJ: Princeton University Press.

Fischer, A. (2013) The Political within the Depoliticised. In Langford, M., Sumner, A. and Ely Yamin, A. (eds), *The MDGs and Human Rights: Past, Present and Future*. Cambridge: Cambridge University Press.

Graver, H. P. (2015) *Dommernes Krig*. Oslo: Pax Forlag.

Harborg, H. (2011) *Valgfri Protokoll til ØSK – Mulige Virkninger av Tilslutning*. Oslo: Norwegian Ministry of Foreign Affairs.

Hardy, J., Eldring, L. and Schulten, T. (2012) Trade union responses to migrant workers from the new Europe: A three sector comparison in the UK, Norway and Germany, *European Journal of Industrial Relations*, 18. pp347–363.

Helgadóttir, R. (2006) *The Influence of American Theories on Judicial Review in Nordic Constitutional Law*. Dordrecht: Martinus Nijhoff.

Hemerijck, A. (2000) Prospects for Basic Income in an Age of Inactivity? In Van der Veen, R. and Groot, L. (eds), *Basic Income on the Agenda: Policy Objectives and Political Changes*. Amsterdam: Amsterdam University Press.

Hirschl, R. (2011) The Nordic Counternarrative: Democracy, Human Development, and Judicial Review, *International Journal of Constitutional Law*, 9. pp449–469.

Holmøyvik, E. and Michalsen D. (2015) Lærebok i forfatningshistorie. Oslo: Pax Forlag.

Humlen, A. and Myhre, J. (2015) *Advokatforeningens aksjon og prosedyregruppe i utlendingsrett 2007–2014*. Oslo: Advokatforeningen.

Huntingdon, S. P. (1981) American Politics: The Promise of Disharmony. Cambridge MA: Belknap Press.

Kagan, R. A. (2001) *Adversarial Legalism: The American Way of Law*. Cambridge MA: Harvard University Press.

Kennedy, D. (2006) Three Globalizations of Law and Legal Thought. In Trubek, D. and Santos, A. (eds), *The New Law and Economic Development*. Cambridge: Cambridge University Press.

Khan, S. (2016) *Ingen rettigheter i Norge? Om rettssikkerhet og fattigdom*, MSc thesis. Oslo: Faculty of Law, University of Oslo.

King, J. A. (2012) *Judging Social Rights*. Cambridge: Cambridge University Press.

King, J. A. (2016) The Future of Social Rights: Social Rights as Capstone, Future of Economic and Social Rights Conference,Boston,19–20 April.

Knutsen, O. (1998) Expert judgments of the left-right location of political parties: A comparative longitudinal study, *West European Politics*, 21. pp63–94.

Kowalski, P., Büge, M., Sztajerowska, M. and Egeland, M. (2013) State-Owned Enterprises: Trade Effects and Policy Implications, *OECD Trade Policy Papers*, No. 147, OECD Publishing.

Kulne, S. (2000) The Scandinavian welfare state in the 1990s: Challenged but viable, *West European Politics*, 23. pp209–228.

Langford, M. (2014) Why Judicial Review?, *Oslo Law Review*, 1.

Langford, M. and Nilsen, J. (2011) Å leve er også å bo: Norske boutgifter – i overensstemmelse med retten til bolig, *Kritisk Juss*. pp92–119.

Langford, M. and Schaffer, J. K. (2015) The Nordic Human Rights Paradox, *SSRN Working Paper*.

Larsen, E. (2013) Chapter 2. In Danielsen, H., Larsen, E. and Owesen, I. W. (eds) *Norsk likestillingshistorie 1814–2013*. Bergen: Fagbokforlaget.

Lødrup, P. (2009) Paal Berg. In *Norsk biografisk leksikon*. Available from:https://nbl.snl.no/Paal_Berg [Accessed: 13 September 2016].

Madsen, M. R. (2015) Between the Law-State and the Welfare State: The Danish Case, The Nordic Legal Complex and Political Liberalism Workshop, Berkeley, October.

Marshall, T. H. (1964) Citizenship and Social Class. In Marshall, T. H. (ed.), *Class, Citizenship and Social Development*. Westport: Greenwood Press.

Menneskerettighetersutvalget (2011) *Rapport til Stortingets presidenskap fra Menneskerettighetersutvalget om menneskerettigheter i Grunnloven* (Dokument 16 2011–2012: Oslo).

Mestad, O. (2008) Næringsfridom i 1814 – grunnlova. In *Forfatningsteori møter 1814*. Oslo: Akademisk Publisering.

Mestad, O. (2014) Amerikansk inspirasjon i den norske grunnlova. Frihetstreet i Nord-Amerikas jord. In Forr, G. (ed.), *Rødt, hvitt og blått. Norsk grunnlov, amerikansk inspirasjon*. Drammen: ART PRO Forlag.

Michalsen, D. (2015) The Many Textual Identities of Constitutions. In Gammelgaard, K. and Holmoyvik, E. (eds) *Writing Democracy: The Norwegian Constitution 1814–2014*. Oslo: Berghahn Books.

Myhre, J. E. (2008) Academics as the Ruling Elite in 19th Century Norway, *Historical Social Research*, 33. pp21–41.

NCHR (Norwegian National Institution for Human Rights) (2015) *Criminalisation of Homelessness in Oslo: An Investigation*. Oslo: NCHR.

Neumann, I. (2010) State and Nation in the Nineteenth Century: Recent Research on the Norwegian Case, *Scandinavian Journal of History*, 25. pp239–260.

Nilssen, E. (2014) Activation Policies and Proceduralization of Law in Britain, Denmark and Norway. In Sinding Aasen, H., Gloppen, S., Magnussen, A. and Nilssen, E. (eds), *Juridification and Social Citizenship in the Welfare State*. Cheltenham: Edward Elgar.

Nonet, P. and Selznick, P. (1978) *Law and Society in Transition: Towards Responsive Law*. New Brunswick: Transaction Publishers.

Normann, T. M. (2010) Utgifter til bolig i Norge og Europa: Inntekter og boligutgifter vokser i takt, *Samfunnsspeilet*, 3.

Normann, T. M., Rønning, E. and Nørgaard, E. (2009) *Utfordringer for den nordiske velferdsstaten – sammenlignbare indikatorer*. Oslo: Nordisk Socialstatistisk Komité (NOSOSKO).

OECD (Organisation for Economic Co-operation and Development) (1981) *The Welfare State in Crisis*. Paris: OECD.

OECD (2015) Employment in the public sector. In *Government at a Glance 2015*. Paris: OECD Publishing.

Østvedt, E. (1940) *Bernhard Dunker : juristen, politikeren og kulturmennesket*. Oslo: Gyldendal.

Powell, M. (2002) The Hidden History of Social Citizenship, *Citizenship Studies*, 6. pp229–244.

Redhead, S. (2005) Toward a Theory of Critical Modernity: The Post-Architecture of Claude Parent and Paul Virilio, *Topia: Canadian Journal of Cultural Studies*, 14. pp37–56.

Rothstein, B. (1998) *Just Institutions Matter: The Moral and Political Logic of the Universal Welfare State*. Cambridge: Cambridge University Press.

Schaffer, J. K. (2015) The legal complex in struggles political liberalism in Sweden, The Nordic Legal Complex and Political Liberalism Workshop, Berkeley, October.

Schaffer, J. K. (2016) Exporting the Swedish Model of Democracy: The Narrative and the Historical Reality, Nordic Branding Workshop, Oslo, 19–20 May.

Seip, J. A. (1974) *Utsikt over Norges historie*. Oslo.

Seip, J. (2002) *Utsikt over Norges historie: Tidsrommet 1814–ca. 1860*. Oslo: Gyldendal.

Slagstad, R. (1995) The Breakthrough of Judicial Review in the Norwegian System. In Smith, E. (ed.) *Constitutional Justice under Old Constitutions*. The Hague: Kluwer Law International.

Slagstad, R. (1998) *De Nasjonale Strateger*. Oslo: Pax Forlag.

Smith, E. (2009) *Konstitusjonelt demokrati*. Bergen: Fagbokforlaget.

Smith, E. (2010) Constitutional Courts as Positive Legislators – Norway, *International Academy of Comparative Law, XVIII International Congress of Comparative Law*, Washington, 25–31 July.

Stamsø, M.-A. (2009) Housing and the Welfare State in Norway, *Scandinavian Political Studies*, 32. pp195–220.

Teubner, G. (1983) Substantive and Reflexive Elements in Modern Law, *Law & Society Review*, 17. pp239–286.

Torgersen, U. (1987) Housing: the Wobbly Pillar under the Welfare State. In Turner, B., Kemeny, J. and Lundqvist, L. (eds) *Between State and Market: Housing in the Post-Industrial Era*. Stockholm: Almqvist & Wiksell International.

Cases cited

Case C-438/05 International Transport Workers & Or v Viking Line Judgment, 11 December 2007.

Case C-341/05 Laval v Svenska Byggnadsarbetareförbundet, Judgment, 18 December 2007.

Fellesforbundet for Sjøfolk (FFFS) v. Norway, Collective Complaint No. 74/2011, Decision on the merits, 2 July 2013.

Fellesforbundet for Sjøfolk (FFFS) v. Norway, Collective Complaint No. 74/2011, Decision on the merits, 2 July 2013.

Kløfta-case, 41 Rt. 1976 s. 1 (Supreme Court of Norway).

Marbury v. Madison, 5 U.S. 137(1803) (U.S. Supreme Court).

Wedel Jarlsberg-case, Ufl 1866 p165 (Supreme Court of Norway).

Chapter 3

Unemployment and the obligatory dimension of social rights

Kenneth Veitch

Introduction

This chapter's objective is to highlight, and think through, the role of obligation in comprehending social rights in the context of the changing nature of the welfare state. There are two reasons for this focus. The first concerns the "social" dimension of social rights. References to *social* rights often assume one of two meanings. On the one hand, the "social" denotes a series of fundamental goods that human beings need access to in order to live: a home, health care, an education, and security of income, for example. Collectively, those goods enable the construction of a social existence. On the other hand, the "social" of social rights gains its meaning via a comparison of social rights with civil and political rights. In contrast to the latter types of rights – which are often characterized as negative forms of rights, encapsulating a right of freedom from state interference – social rights are identified as pointing to claims against the state; they demand state intervention in order to promote positive exercises of freedom. Moreover, it is often argued that social rights precede the possibility of the meaningful exercise of civil and political rights. What use are the latter forms of rights, it is suggested, if, for example, one lacks a basic education? In this second sense, then, the "social" of social rights finds its meaning by its location within a classificatory model of rights – specifically that proposed by T. H. Marshall in his essay "Citizenship and Social Class" (Marshall 1992).

This chapter's focus on obligation advances a different kind of engagement with the "social" dimension of social rights by shifting the focus towards the form of social relations that might be thought to underpin social rights at different stages in their history. To put it another way, an exploration of the types of obligations, or duties, of citizenship accompanying social rights has the potential to reveal the prevailing principles or political philosophy that guides social rights.

The second reason for this chapter's focus on obligation is to draw attention to the fact that social rights are not necessarily given – provisions that appear in, and can simply be read off, international covenants or countries' constitutions; rather, social rights are fostered or developed – they emerge as the end point of a process that, it is argued here, must be investigated if we are to understand their nature and meaning. Part of that process is the realization that (social) rights are structured by obligations; that there is a real sense in which obligations precede (social) rights. If this is so, then it is necessary to explore the precise nature of the types of obligation that structure social rights. In the context of the welfare state, this leads to a concern with the duties of citizenship, and especially with understanding their nature and how, and why, that nature might have shifted over time. What, for instance, are the political, economic, and social factors and exigencies that shape the obligations or duties of citizenship in the context of welfare? To what ends are those obligations directed? These are the kinds of questions that animate this chapter's analysis. In summary, the claim made here is that social rights can be understood fully only if the obligations that structure them are the subject of detailed analysis.

As a comprehensive treatment of how those themes play out across the various fields of welfare is impossible within one chapter, I have chosen to contextualize the discussion by reference to unemployment policy in Britain. The first section focuses upon Sir William Beveridge's 1942 report *Social Insurance and Allied Services* – considered to be the founding document of the post-World War II British welfare state – and Marshall's seminal essay, mentioned above. In relation to the report, this section considers, *inter alia*, what Beveridge meant by "right"; the nature of the duties he envisaged; and what kinds of principles underpinned his recommendation of the creation of a compulsory form of social insurance. Insofar as Marshall's essay is concerned, the discussion will look at his notion of social citizenship, and particularly at the nature of the rights and duties this entailed. The chapter then proceeds to an analysis of some recent thinking on the contemporary nature of social rights – including that of "third way" proponents and their critics. Of course, the discourse of "rights and responsibilities" has been central to "third way" ideas about how to reform the welfare state and, practically, to the formulation of social policies devised by politicians and leaders subscribing to this form of thinking. But rather than simply rehearsing this well-trodden terrain, the main aim of the chapter's second section is to identify a correlation between some of the key themes and principles in Beveridge's report and those emphasized by advocates of the "third way". After illustrating how those themes have influenced contemporary academic analysis of social rights and their underlying form of social relations, it is argued that a more convincing diagnosis of these highlights the need to adapt to the exigencies of contemporary capitalism and the labour market. Thus, key themes and objectives of contemporary social policy – including the development of human capital, the fostering of entrepreneurial activity, and the focus on individual responsibility – align with the needs and exigencies of today's labour market and markets generally, rather than being driven by a logic of protection against the vicissitudes of capitalism. The chapter's third section looks at contemporary British unemployment policy and, specifically, workfare, together with a Supreme Court case in which the claimants challenged the legality of two workfare schemes. The analysis in this section charts the shifting contours of social rights and, importantly, their underlying obligations by juxtaposing workfare with the earlier analysis of Beveridge's report and Marshall's essay. The overriding argument is that, while there may be overlapping themes and principles between the two eras, the differences are crucial and point to very different notions of obligation and visions of the social.

Beveridge and Marshall

Sir William Beveridge's report on *Social Insurance and Allied Services*, published in 1942, is generally considered to be the constitutive document of the British welfare state. The report can be viewed as having had two overriding objectives. First, and famously, its aim was to abolish what Beveridge termed Want. This referred to a phenomenon experienced by many individuals and families in British cities prior to the outbreak of WWII – namely, the lack of means necessary for subsistence. This was predominantly due to unemployment ("interruption or loss of earning power"), and Beveridge's report was largely concerned with devising a suitable way by which to tackle Want. The main mechanism proposed was a scheme of compulsory social insurance.[1] Under this scheme, individuals would make weekly contributions from their earnings to a State insurance fund and be able to draw benefits from it, up to subsistence level and irrespective of means, when, *inter alia*, unemployed, ill, in the event of becoming disabled, and upon retirement. In other words, access to the fund would be dependent on having contributed to it. The report's second objective was to streamline and simplify the existing patchwork of social insurance schemes, the different principles upon which they operated, and their administration. The existing setup had become too costly to run and also too complex to navigate for those it was meant to serve.

For present purposes, two important questions arise: first, do we encounter a discourse of social rights within the Beveridge report; and, second, what type of political philosophy underlies the report's proposals? Insofar as the former is concerned, while the discourse of "social rights" *per se* is absent from the report, Beveridge does occasionally speak of "right". This, however, only applies in the context of one's right to draw from the social insurance fund to which one has contributed. As well as unemployment benefit, this can be seen in relation to the report's proposal to move from a system of pensions based on need to one in which "pensions are paid as of right to all citizens in virtue of contribution" (Beveridge 1942, para. 16). Under the report, then, "right" is inextricably linked to having made a contribution; social rights, if we call them such for the moment, are predominantly the rights or entitlements of individuals who have been, but are now no longer, employed. Social rights are the individual rights of contributors to monetary benefits in hard times – benefits that replace missing income in order to prevent Want and the symptoms associated with this. As such, the report's proposals for a compulsory social insurance scheme are equated to individual contribution "rather than free allowances from the State".

Secondly, what can be said of the political philosophy underpinning the proposed reforms and the right to benefits associated with compulsory social insurance?

Harris's comment that the Report "was a complex mixture of traditional Edwardian liberalism and wartime collectivism" provides an accurate and useful starting point (Harris 2004, p290). On the one hand, Beveridge's desire to abolish Want was very much bound up with the ongoing war at the time and, in particular, with drawing on the perceived collectivism across the nation as the basis for the proposals for a new social security system. Although not stated as a guiding principle of the report's recommendations, it is clear from the following quotation that the notion of solidarity played a role in grounding the new system:

> The proposals of the Report mark another step forward to the development of State insurance as a new type of human institution, differing both from the former methods of preventing or alleviating distress and from voluntary insurance. The term "social insurance" to describe this institution implies both that it is compulsory and that men stand together with their fellows. The term implies a pooling of risks except so far as separation of risks serves a social purpose.
>
> (Beveridge 1942, para. 26)

For Beveridge, compulsory social insurance marked a shift from earlier forms of State insurance in Britain. Those earlier forms operated on the principle underlying voluntary insurance – namely, that of adjusting premiums to particular risks, rather than the pooling of risks, which was to be the underlying principle of the report's proposed scheme. Solidarity can also be detected, *inter alia*, in the scheme's universal nature, which was to extend beyond those currently covered – manual workers – to encompass all citizens irrespective of their level of income; in its provision of a flat rate of subsistence benefit to all those insured and the existence of a flat rate of contribution; and in the principle of sharing the cost of social security amongst the insured individual, his or her employer, and the state. Thus, social security was to be achieved through cooperation between the state and the individual – what Grady identifies as "a relationship characterized by joint responsibility" (Grady 2010, p164).

On the other hand, a liberal form of social relations can be detected within the report. Building on the principle that State social security should be granted on the basis of citizens' service and contribution, by limiting benefits to subsistence levels the report sought to encourage individuals to take steps to enhance their social security through voluntary action. State security, it was said, "should not stifle incentive, opportunity, responsibility". Part of the purpose of the new social insurance system was therefore to promote individual freedom and responsibility for one's own security; state security was not only designed to abolish Want – although, crucially, this was its main aim – but also to incentivize individuals by providing them with just enough, and no more, for them to want, and seek, to achieve a heightened level of social security through the exercise of their own initiative. Those themes resonate with other liberal principles running throughout the report and which can clearly be seen from the following quotation that appears under the heading "Planning for Peace in War":

> There are some to whom pursuit of security appears to be a wrong aim. They think of security as something inconsistent with initiative, adventure, personal responsibility. That is not a just view of social security as planned in this Report. The plan is not one for giving to everybody something for nothing and without trouble, or something that will free the recipients for ever thereafter from personal responsibilities. The plan is one to secure income for subsistence on condition of service and contribution and in order to make and keep men fit for service. It cannot be got without thought and effort. It can be carried through only by a concentrated determination of the British democracy to free itself once for all of the scandal of physical want for which there is no economic or moral justification.
>
> (Beveridge 1942, para. 455)

To the extent that one can conceptualize Beveridge's system of social insurance in a discourse of social rights, it is suggested that what underpins the right to pecuniary benefits is an idea of social relations based upon duty, individual responsibility, effort and reciprocity. The key duty is to engage in paid work, as it is this that produces the contributions that are the condition of access to the benefits of the social insurance fund. While solidarity (in the sense of a pooling of risks) is, as we saw above, an important feature of the proposed scheme, as Harris notes Beveridge's aim was "not to redistribute income between classes, but between times of earning and not earning, and between times of heavy family responsibilities and of light or no family responsibilities" (Harris 2004, p290, quoting the report). Thus, the type of solidarity involved in the context of social insurance here was not one designed to promote an equitable or fair allocation of resources or wealth across the various classes in society. The centrality of duty can also be found in the conditionality attaching to the receipt of different types of benefit. Thus, while unemployment benefit will continue throughout the duration of the period of unemployment, it will usually be conditional upon attendance at a work or training centre after a certain amount of time. Similarly, the ongoing receipt of disability benefit would be conditional upon the "imposition of special behaviour conditions".

In summary, the "social right" to access the funds of the new social insurance system posited both a collective and liberal vision of social relations. Regarding the former, social insurance involved the duty to participate in paid work and, through that, to contribute to a common fund that contributors and their families could access in hard times. And underpinning this obligation was the vision of a bond amongst one's "fellows" – a bond that, crucially, had as its objective a protective and compassionate function, namely the removal "of the scandal of physical want for which there is no economic or moral justification". Insofar as the liberal sense of social relations is concerned, through the provision of basic subsistence, the report emphasized the importance of incentive, individual initiative, individual responsibility, and voluntary action in its exhortation to individuals to enhance their, and their families', social security. And in addition to identifying the important role to be played by the State in tackling physical want and the other evils of squalor, disease, ignorance, and idleness, security against these was to be "combined with freedom and enterprise and responsibility of the individual for his own life" (Beveridge 1942, para. 456). Thus, the social protection offered was accompanied by the state's interest in shaping a particular type of subjectivity – one characterized by individual responsibility and enterprise.

In 1949, seven years after the publication of Beveridge's report, T. H. Marshall delivered "The Marshall Lectures" at Cambridge University (Marshall 1992). Unlike Beveridge, Marshall explicitly deployed the discourse of social rights in his now famous analysis of citizenship and rights (specifically, civil, political, and social rights). It is not the intention here to rehearse this analysis, but simply to identify a couple of pertinent points from Marshall's reflections on the rights he associates with the social element of citizenship. The first relates to his definition of social citizenship, which is as follows:

> By the social element I mean the whole range from the right to a modicum of economic welfare and security to the right to share to the full in the social heritage and to live the life of a civilized being according to the standards prevailing in the society. The institutions most closely connected with it are the educational system and the social services.
>
> (Marshall 1992, p8)

Marshall's concept of social citizenship, and therefore of social rights, is wide-ranging. While clearly incorporating what the Beveridge report called a right to benefits at subsistence level (Marshall's "right to a modicum of economic welfare and security"), it extends far beyond this. Or, perhaps better, it describes in the discourse of rights the latent aspirations to which Beveridge's proposals for the abolition of Want were presumably designed to give rise. Of particular note for this essay, in this regard, is Marshall's idea that social rights include the right "to live the life of a civilized being according to the standards prevailing in the society". For Marshall, this represented his idea of citizenship – namely, the claim "to be accepted as full members of the society, that is, as citizens". There is, he argued, "a kind of basic human equality associated with the concept of full membership of a community". Later, he explains that social rights "imply an absolute right to a certain standard of civilisation" and suggests that the types of changes proposed by Beveridge – including the system of compulsory social insurance – enhance the prospect of a civilized life for everyone in society and reduce the incidence of risk and insecurity for citizens.

The second observation to be made of Marshall's analysis of social citizenship and social rights is the importance he places, towards the end of his lecture, on the corresponding duties of citizenship and the need to discharge them. The more precise of these – such as the duty to pay insurance contributions – replicates the types of duty Beveridge demanded of citizens in his report. But Marshall also mentions the need for the discharge of less specific duties. Thus, the right to a certain standard of civilization is, he says, conditional on discharging "the general duties of citizenship". While "[t]hese do not require a man to sacrifice his individual liberty or to submit without question to every demand made by government … they do require that his acts should be inspired by a lively sense of responsibility towards the welfare of the community" (Marshall 1992, p41). It is "the general obligation to live the life of a good citizen" that constitutes the substance of those wider duties, and to the extent that Marshall lends a more particular meaning to such duties, he says the duty to work is of key importance in this respect. This duty of social citizenship does not merely envisage individuals finding a job and retaining it; rather, the essence of the duty is "to put one's heart into one's job and work hard". And it is by engaging in this activity – equivalent to a kind of service to the community and the nation (although Marshall acknowledges that there are problems with this) – that citizens will discharge their general duty and responsibility towards the welfare of the community.

What emerges from the foregoing analysis is how, for Beveridge and Marshall, social rights are structured by obligations or duties. The right to access basic levels of money or, more expansively, to live the life of a civilized being are conditional upon discharging a number of obligations – including, significantly, undertaking paid work. And those obligations, in their readings, are underpinned by a form of social relations based upon a sense of solidarity that had as its object the eradication of Want and the right to live the life of a civilized being. Simultaneously, one detects the importance of a liberal form of social relations that stresses principles of individual effort, self-responsibility, and enterprise. Bearing the foregoing analysis in mind, let us now turn to consider some of the principles that ground contemporary understandings of social rights and social policy.

Social rights and responsibilities: "Third Way" thinking and neoliberalism

> The promotion of social justice was sometimes confused with the imposition of equality of outcome. The result was a neglect of the importance of rewarding effort and responsibility, and the association of social democracy with conformity and mediocrity, rather than the celebration of creativity, diversity and excellence.
>
> Too often rights were elevated above responsibilities, but the responsibility of the individual to his or her family, neighbourhood and society cannot be offloaded on to the state. If the concept of mutual obligation is forgotten, this results in a decline in community spirit, lack of responsibility towards neighbours, rising crime and vandalism, and a legal system that cannot cope.
>
> Modern social democrats want to transform the safety net of entitlements into a springboard to personal responsibility.
>
> (Blair and Schroeder 1998, cited in Dardot and Laval 2013)

What is remarkable about those statements, which appear in Tony Blair and Gerhard Schroeder's *Europe: The Third Way/Die Neue Mitte*, is the degree to which they reflect many of the principles and themes underlying the Beveridge report and Marshall's discussion of social citizenship and social rights. It is remarkable in the sense that Beveridge's report is often held out as exemplary of a golden era of the welfare state founded on principles that can be contrasted with those underlying "third way" social policies. As I will demonstrate later, this is not to say that there are no important – indeed, fundamental – differences between the two or that Beveridge and Marshall would have approved of today's social policies; nevertheless, there are common themes, including the following: the need for a balance to be struck between rights and responsibilities; the importance of individual responsibility; the enabling state (basic state benefits should facilitate mechanisms of self-help); and the emphasis on individual initiative and creativity. The concerns and issues that led to Blair and Schroeder's statements above are many and cannot be discussed adequately in this chapter. In what follows, I will, first, briefly outline one argument concerning the impact of this philosophy upon the contemporary nature of social rights. Secondly, I will suggest that this philosophy is more adequately explained as deriving from neoliberalism and a neoliberal rationality. Finally, with reference to current unemployment policy in the UK and a recent legal case, I will analyse how obligations or duties structure social rights today and relate this back to the earlier discussion of Beveridge and Marshall.

French academic Pierre Rosanvallon has argued that, owing to the decline of traditional principles of social solidarity and the emergence of long-term unemployment and exclusion as core contemporary problems, the traditional form of social rights within the welfare state – that is, rights to compensatory benefits – is no longer fit for purpose (Rosanvallon 2000, p88). In light of those problems, he proposes re-conceptualizing contemporary social rights as rights to "social usefulness" – that is, as means of ensuring the re-inclusion of individuals in society such that they do not simply have a right to live (the right Rosanvallon equates to the social right to benefits of the classical welfare state) but "a right to live in society". Social rights are therefore bound up with social participation and the realization of citizenship. They have as their objective the construction of a new type of social bond – the re-establishment of the social relation for those currently excluded – and the right to this bond. Beyond the right to pecuniary subsistence, today's social rights incorporate "a moral imperative" too – the right to be a socially useful member of society. Rosanvallon equates the former right to passivity, and the latter to activity and the notion of active citizenship. In his view, this type of citizenship, and its corresponding right to social usefulness, form the basis of a new type of contemporary solidarity. It results in the excluded (re-)engaging or participating in society and converts the welfare recipients of the traditional system of collective insurance into citizens.

This vision of social rights in the "inclusive society" places individuals, rather than groups or classes, at its core and envisages an important role for obligation. Thus, if social rights are to be about re-inclusion in society, not only do we need to focus on the individual and his or her particular needs, circumstances and behaviour (including its constant supervision); individuals must become active, responsible citizens making and discharging a series of commitments too. In this context, the notion of contract becomes an important technique in this reformulation of social rights in that "social rights are reinterpreted as a contract articulating rights and obligations". Rosanvallon argues that these contracts, with their mutual set of responsibilities (on the individual and the state), point to a notion of the individual as "an autonomous, responsible person, capable of making commitments and honouring them". And it is through the recognition of this type of person and the obligations he or she commits to undertake that the individual is re-socialized and, as a result, society is constructed and reaffirmed. Individual responsibility is therefore an important theme of this philosophy; by accepting this responsibility, individuals are deemed to be empowered as they take ownership of, for example, their unemployment by actively adopting measures to (re-)integrate themselves into the labour market and thus society. Rosanvallon's notion of social rights posits "a contractual individualism combining respect for the individual with the reconstruction of the social bond" (Rosanvallon 2000, p92).

Rosanvallon's work presents an interesting rethinking of social rights and the form that solidarity might take in the context of contemporary welfare and social policy. Its underlying philosophy clearly maps on to the type of "third way" thinking of Blair and Schroeder set out above, and resonates with some of the themes appearing in the Beveridge report and Marshall's analysis of social rights and social citizenship. The focus on individual responsibility, reciprocity, and, what might be taken to be especially relevant here, Marshall's idea of social citizenship as a right not merely to a modicum of economic welfare but extending to include a right to live the life of a civilized being – all feature prominently in Rosanvallon's analysis. It is suggested, however, that his is a limited and sanguine account of the transformations in the welfare state and social rights that have spread across a number of Western countries in recent decades and of the type of rationality that has underpinned them. If we are to understand the structure of social rights today – especially the kinds of obligations that ground them – it is necessary to undertake a more critical and concrete analysis.

It could be argued that the problem "third way" thinkers and politicians had with Beveridge's and Marshall's reflections lay not so much in their underlying principles but in the fact that the strong link they envisaged between rights and duties failed to materialize in practice. As is clear from the quotations above, the allegation was that, while the welfare state that developed after WWII ensured social rights by providing access to a variety of protective measures, it failed to demand anything of welfare recipients in return. Along with highlighting the issue of the increasing costs of welfare as a reason for rising scepticism about the welfare state, Pierre Dardot and Christian Laval note that critiques of the welfare state beginning in the 1980s began to represent this as a vehicle of demoralization (Dardot and Laval 2013). The bureaucratic welfare state, the argument went, and still goes today, "destroys the virtues of civil society – honesty, the sense of a job well done, personal effort, civility and patriotism" (Dardot and Laval 2013, p164). The welfare state was viewed as being too generous and, because of that, accused of creating welfare dependency and inertia on the part of welfare recipients. The incentive to, and passion for, work that Marshall identified as one of the general duties of citizenship, was nullified and welfare beneficiaries, for that reason amongst others, came to be represented as morally irresponsible. In other words, state benefits may have provided the protection against the physical want, insecurity and risk that Beveridge identified as dangers; but that desired outcome had, it was argued, dulled the very initiative and individual responsibility that Beveridge believed his system would produce. Moreover, the "demoralization" thesis could not be understood simply as a moral denunciation of welfare recipients or in terms of the symbolic effects this produced; additionally, and crucially, it concerned the erosion of the types of principles upon which the prevailing economic system depended. As Dardot and Laval conclude with regard to such critiques: "In a word, social protection was destructive of the values without which capitalism could no longer function" (Dardot and Laval 2013, p165; reference omitted).

Nowhere has this critique of the welfare state been more influential and pronounced than in the creation of "welfare to work" programmes. Such programmes can be viewed as having a dual function: first, by seeking to return the unemployed to work, they aim to reduce costs and promote flexible labour markets, thereby enabling states to remain economically competitive in an increasingly global marketplace (Jessop 2002); secondly, through onerous sanctions for failing to participate in such programmes, they discipline the unemployed, thereby making them assume the individual responsibility that the welfare state had allegedly destroyed through its inculcation of passivity. "Jobseekers" were to become enterprises in themselves – entrepreneurs who take responsibility for their own development, and work on cultivating their human capital with a view to returning to the labour market as soon as possible. Social rights as such – here, in the form of the Jobseeker's Allowance (JSA) – did not disappear, but access to them was now strictly conditional upon satisfying various commitments and obligations set out in the type of contract mentioned by Rosanvallon. For authors such as Dardot and Laval though, the essence of a social policy like workfare cannot be grasped within the framework of Rosanvallon's analysis – as a qualitative shift in the nature of social rights and solidarity that promoted the integration of the excluded into society, thereby reaffirming social citizenship and social bonds. Rather, for them, it represented a rupture in the nature of society, the social bond, the individual, and the governing rationality. For the architects of New Labour and the third way, social justice and the social bond were to be re-structured around competition, individual responsibility, equality of opportunity, and the fostering of human capital, rather than around "greater solidarity and objectives of real equality". *Homo economicus* was no longer merely the creature of the market, but of social policy too; and the state's objective was no longer driven by a principle of protection, but, through "social investment" in individuals, by the desire to ensure their adaptation to markets and a market-based society. As Jacques

Donzelot summarizes: "[S]ocial policy is no longer a means for countering the economic, but a means for sustaining the logic of competition". (Donzelot 2008, p124) In short, the social policy of the third way had been defined by what Dardot and Laval call a neoliberal rationality and form of social relations, the key feature of which "is the generalization of competition as a behavioural norm and of the enterprise as a model of subjectivation" (Dardot and Laval 2013, p4). By actively embedding this norm and model both materially and symbolically, the state establishes the conditions necessary for a market-based society.

Let us now turn to consider the implications of such developments for our contemporary understanding of social rights and obligation by considering more closely the social policy of workfare as it operates in Britain and relating this back to the rights and obligations identified by Beveridge and Marshall.

Workfare in Britain: transforming social rights and obligations

As we saw earlier, the right to access monetary benefits under Beveridge's social insurance system was structured by an obligation to undertake paid work. It was by virtue of the contribution made from one's salary each week that one was entitled to access State benefits. The importance of work for Beveridge, however, extended beyond the need to have already been employed as a condition of accessing benefits. As the report noted: "The correlative of the State's undertaking to ensure adequate benefit for unavoidable interruption of earnings, however long, is enforcement of the citizen's obligation to seek and accept all reasonable opportunities of work" (Beveridge 1942, para. 130). Moreover, it was proposed that benefits for the long-term unemployed would normally be conditional on attending a work or training centre. This early form of active citizenship, however, was not novel – the requirement that the unemployed should bear and discharge obligations in return for receiving pecuniary support from the state having existed for some time already.[2] But what can be said of this obligation today? The contemporary manifestation of this requirement – the welfare-to-work or workfare scheme – is both more onerous in the demands it makes of the unemployed (not only being available for, and actively seeking, work; but in some cases, actually working) (Freedland et al 2007, p196) and more punitive in the sanctions flowing from a failure to discharge those obligations.[3] In what follows, it will be argued that, despite the similarity in certain themes and principles to be found in Beveridge's report and "third way" thinking – including reciprocity and individual responsibility – the nature of the obligations demanded of the unemployed in return for JSA is not in keeping with other core principles underpinning Beveridge's and Marshall's visions for the welfare system. Thus, while the duty to work remains alive and well in the sphere of unemployment policy today, the nature of this duty sheds a different light on the purpose and structure of contemporary social rights. Consideration of a legal case in England will help to illuminate this argument.

In *R. (on the application of Reilly and Wilson) v. The Secretary of State for Work and Pensions* (hereinafter referred to as *Reilly & Wilson*), the claimants – Caitlin Reilly and Jamieson Wilson – challenged the validity of the Jobseeker's Allowance (Employment and Enterprise) Regulations 2011 ("the Regulations") and two workfare schemes or programmes known as "the sbwa scheme" (the sector-based work academy scheme) and "the CAP" (the Community Action Programme). The sbwa scheme, which was the object of Reilly's challenge, is a voluntary scheme designed to help those able to perform work-related activity and who do not have any serious barriers to finding work to obtain short-term work-focused training and work experience linked to a genuine job vacancy. Her basic contention was that she had been incorrectly, and therefore unlawfully, required to participate in the sbwa scheme on pain of possibly losing her JSA entitlement or having her payments reduced. As she could not afford to lose her only source of income, she felt she had no alternative but to participate. Moreover, rather than simply the one week's "training" she was told she would undergo, she ended up having to work for nothing for two weeks (five hours a day, five days a week) for a budget retail outlet called Poundland. The CAP, the object of Wilson's claim, is a programme for the long-term unemployed, which individuals, selected by "random allocation", must attend if they wish to continue receiving JSA. It involves undertaking up to six months' unpaid work experience for up to 30 hours per week and "weekly job search support requirements". Wilson refused to participate in the CAP, claiming it, and his required participation, were unlawful.[4]

The claimants' actions, which went all the way to the Supreme Court, were successful because the regulations were found to have failed to describe the relevant schemes or the circumstances in which individuals can be compelled to participate in them (as was required by the enabling Act (s.17A, Jobseekers Act 1995)). As a result, the regulations were declared unlawful and quashed. For present purposes, the interest of the case revolves around the claimants' identification of what they argued was the compulsory nature of the relevant law. This was most obvious in their final ground of challenge – namely, that the schemes violated Article 4 of the European Convention on Human Rights as they required the performance of "forced or compulsory labour" (Article 4(2)). In light of the nature of the CAP (described above) Wilson argued that it imposed "very onerous obligations on individuals", requiring them to work for nothing if they wished to continue receiving JSA. For those with no savings of their own, the threat of withdrawal of the means to live effectively amounted to a compulsion to participate in the scheme. Wilson objected to working for free, particularly for such a long time and thought this was unfair. Reilly argued that the violation of Article 4 lay in not being given "the option to participate in a scheme that involved unpaid work for a private company and that the work she undertook was under the threat of a penalty" (*Reilly & Wilson* [2012] EWHC 2292 (Admin), para. 171, per Foskett J.).

None of the courts that heard the case found that the schemes violated Article 4. Agreeing with Foskett J. in the High Court, the Supreme Court stressed that the historical roots of Article 4 lay in the need to prevent exploitation of labour in the colonies. While forced labour could take different forms, its underlying essence was exploitation, and a conditional state benefit such as JSA "comes nowhere close to the type of exploitative conduct at which article 4 is aimed" (*Reilly & Wilson* [2013] UKSC 68, para. 83). The article would only be violated if, first, the work undertaken was compulsory or involuntary, and, second, the obligation to work, or its performance, was "unjust", "oppressive", "an avoidable hardship", "needlessly distressing" or "somewhat harassing" (*Reilly & Wilson* [2013] UKSC 68, para. 89). In other words, the work or its performance needed to be exploitative. The reason advanced for the Supreme Court's conclusion on this ground of challenge revolved around the inextricable link drawn by the justices between the state benefit and the condition to be met in order to receive this benefit: as JSA is designed for individuals seeking work, the purpose of the benefit – to enable a person to seek work – is furthered by the condition of working or engaging in work-related activity. As such, the condition cannot amount to exploitation. Neither were the schemes compulsory or involuntary as the claimants were free to refuse to participate in them if they so wished. Furthermore, that the work undertaken was unlikely, in fact, to improve an individual's employment prospects was irrelevant in ascertaining whether the imposition of labour as a condition of obtaining JSA amounted to forced labour under Article 4.

What can this case tell us about contemporary social rights in the context of unemployment? And how do these compare to the rights and duties of social citizenship discussed by Beveridge and Marshall? First, if, as we saw earlier, the right envisaged by Beveridge was a right to draw from the social insurance fund to which one had contributed – a right of contributors to monetary benefits during periods of interruption of earnings – as the Supreme Court noted in *Reilly & Wilson*, the JSA is an allowance designed for people who seek work, rather than for those who have simply made financial contributions to the fund. In other words, the social right to the monetary benefit cannot be divorced from the obligation actively to seek work and, where demanded, to undertake work as part of the process of trying to secure a paid job in the labour market. Of course, in return for state benefits, Beveridge spoke of the citizen's correlative obligation to seek, and accept, all reasonable opportunities for work. But the work he referred to was *paid employment within the labour market* – something very different to an obligation to undertake the type of unpaid work demanded by the CAP. The nature of the obligation underlying the social right associated with periods of unemployment has therefore shifted decisively in the direction of work – not in the sense of having engaged in paid work and contributed to the social insurance fund (although this is still important[5]); but in the sense of actively seeking work, engaging in training activities designed to ready people for employment, and working for nothing while unemployed.

Secondly, the main objective of Beveridge's report was to tackle the scourge of Want – namely, the absence of the means required for individuals to live. His scheme of social insurance was designed to address the insecurity and risk flowing from this social reality. There are signs that a similar objective does not necessarily underpin the social right synonymous with the current workfare system. For this right – to JSA – is, at least partially, built on the constant threat to *remove* the means of subsistence. If, for example, jobseekers do not undertake the obligations set out in what is now called their "claimant commitment", or fail to turn up for an appointment at the job centre, or turn down a job or training course, or do not apply for any jobs they are informed about, the sanctions regime will come into operation, progressively reducing the amount of JSA until, ultimately, it disappears completely. What the claimants in *Reilly & Wilson* called the "draconian power to take away the right to what is, in many respects, a subsistence-level payment" demonstrates that the power to *produce*, rather than to free individuals from, Want lies at the core of contemporary unemployment policy – something that has potentially negative social consequences (see, for example, Great Britain: Scottish Government 2013; Great Britain: House of Commons 2015). The social right associated with the workfare system is structured in such a way as to be inherently insecure – that is, always liable to be taken away.

Thirdly, while important, our comprehension of social rights in the context of the workfare system remains limited insofar as it is conceptualized solely at the monetary level. Here, we can return to Marshall's broader, non-pecuniary, understandings of social citizenship and social rights – and in particular, to his idea of social citizenship incorporating the right "to live the life of a civilized being according to the standards prevailing in the society", and to his contention that social rights "imply an absolute right to a certain standard of civilisation". To what extent does today's workfare system reflect those definitions of social citizenship and social rights? One might anticipate Reilly's and Wilson's answers to this question being: "very little". This was implicit in their claims that what the obligations they were being asked to discharge amounted to was forced labour and, therefore, exploitation. For them, there was something "unjust", "oppressive", "needlessly distressing", and that amounted to "an avoidable hardship" in being obliged to undertake long periods of unpaid work for organizations, including a private company.

Relatedly, when measured against Marshall's general duties of citizenship that he identified as accompanying social rights, workfare would seem to fare no better. It will be recalled that, for Marshall, those general duties were the flipside of the right to a certain standard of civilization. But in light of some of the obligations to be undertaken by individuals in return for JSA, it is difficult to comprehend how they would "be inspired by a lively sense of responsibility towards the welfare of the community" or be willing to assume "the general obligation to live the life of a good citizen". More directly, it is also questionable whether Marshall's understanding of the citizen's duty to work holds any relevance in the present context. For not only do the obligations of workfare suggest that the essence of his idea of the duty to work – putting one's heart into one's job and working hard – is unlikely to be assumed and discharged by unemployed individuals like Reilly and Wilson;[6] achieving what Marshall considered to be the other, easily dischargeable components of this duty (in light of the context of full employment in which he was writing) – to find a job and retain it – looks increasingly dubious for many involved in workfare.[7]

Finally, where does the foregoing discussion leave us? Most immediately, it directs us to the possible relevance today of the limits Marshall placed on the need to discharge the "general duties of citizenship", including the duty to work. For these, he said, "do not require a man to sacrifice his individual liberty or to submit without question to every demand made by government". While the courts in *Reilly & Wilson* denied the claimants' contention that the workfare schemes amounted to forced labour, it was clear that one of Reilly's and Wilson's core reasons for so arguing was that the threat of removal of JSA effectively denied them the freedom to choose not to undertake unpaid work. In other words, they argued that, in order to continue receiving subsistence level benefits, they had no practical alternative but to submit to the demands made by the government. The possible relevance of Marshall's qualification to the obligation to discharge the general duties of citizenship suggests a tipping point may have been reached in the duties placed upon the unemployed today.

Conclusions

This last point leads to a few conclusions. First, the nature of the relationship between social rights and obligations in the context of unemployment policy has shifted in recent decades. As noted earlier, Beveridge's idea of a social right involved a right to draw a benefit from a social insurance fund based on the contributions one had made to this through paid work. The obligation upon which this right rests is therefore the obligation to engage in paid work. The benefit was to be set at subsistence level in order to promote individual efforts to develop one's own sources, and heighten one's own level, of security. But now it is this – proving one's initiative, enterprise, and creativity, including one's susceptibility to undertaking unpaid work – rather than engagement in paid work, that has become the obligation that grounds the right to JSA. Crucially, Beveridge's objective in recommending a system of compulsory social insurance was to free the population from Want. Today's workfare system represents a shift in the settlement between social rights and obligations in the sense that access to JSA is premised on a set of obligations that are, at least to a degree, at odds with the types of obligation associated with Beveridge's social insurance system. *Reilly and Wilson* illustrates this well in that, rather than access being based on paid work, the allegation was that exploitation in the form of forced labour founds one's right to JSA, and that refusing to be exploited will lead to a sanction that will result in Want and the insecurity and poverty that are its symptoms. Such obligations and outcomes are diametrically opposed to the principles upon which Beveridge's report rested, including not only freedom from Want but the sense of solidarity implied by the institution of social insurance – namely, that "men stand together with their fellows".

Secondly, this suggests that the workfare system is not primarily driven by a protective logic, but, as Dardot and Laval argue in respect of the neoliberal state, by an adaptive one. Indeed, here, one can witness the development of a more fluid relationship between right and obligation. For the right to JSA is not equivalent to a social benefit designed to modify the vagaries, risks, and insecurities endemic in the economic system – the operating logic of the classical welfare state; indeed, quite the opposite. Through the obligations demanded of participants, the right to JSA is inextricably bound up with readying unemployed individuals for what they can expect to encounter in the contemporary flexible and competitive labour market – including temporary, insecure, low-paid, or unpaid work. The UK government's explanation of the rationale behind the workfare scheme known as Mandatory Work Activity captures this well: "MWA is intended to help claimants move closer to the labour market, enabling them to establish the discipline and habits of working life" (Great Britain: DWP 2015). The workfare system trains and disciplines individuals in order to habitualize them to the reality of contemporary labour, and exposes and reconciles them not necessarily to the old virtues of social security and freedom from Want that structured the classical welfare state, but to the "virtues" and characteristics around which the neoliberal rationality that guides the current political settlement revolves – including insecurity, risk-taking, and competition. This suggests a deeper sense of obligation at play here, deriving from the idea, inherent in the etymological root of the word, of a bond or being bound.[8] On the one hand, the jobseeker is trained to be bound to the practices and forms of labour – temporary contracts and unpaid internships, for instance – typical of what some authors have termed "the new capitalism" (Sennett 2006; Boltanski and Chiapello 2005). On the other hand, he or she is bound – subjected even – to a transformation at the level of subjectivity, to become the enterprising, self-responsible, risk-taker ready to learn new skills in order to be able to adapt to, and compete within, the dynamic contemporary labour market. What is involved here is a shift in the mode of being; as Dardot and Laval note: "at stake in neo-liberalism is nothing more, or less, than the *form of our existence* – the way in which we are led to conduct ourselves, to relate to others and to ourselves" (Dardot and Laval 2013, p3; original emphasis). It is at this deep level of the form of "relat[ion] to others" that workfare is most revealing. For it illustrates that this no longer takes the form of Beveridge's notion of men standing together with their fellows, but of the lone individual working upon his or her self with a view to competing with other, unencumbered individuals engaged in exactly the same activity. This, it is suggested here, captures the underlying sense of Blair and Schroeder's understanding of the desire of modern social democrats "to transform the safety net of entitlements into a springboard to personal responsibility".

Finally, in light of the discussion in this chapter, an urgent question presents itself: to what extent is it even relevant to deploy the discourse of "social rights" as a means of comprehending current unemployment policy in the UK? As we saw earlier, Rosanvallon argued that the old idea of social rights as a right to live associated with access to compensatory benefits needed updating in what he described as an era of long-term unemployment and exclusion. Social rights should, instead, now be conceptualized as a right to live *in society* – a right to social usefulness. The analysis in this chapter suggests that the type of contractual

Notes

1 Beveridge's subsidiary methods for tackling Want were national assistance and voluntary insurance. The conditions of social insurance's success included the establishment of a comprehensive health care system (to keep the nation healthy and, thus, able to work) and the state's maintenance of employment. In other words, creating the conditions to facilitate work was one of the report's core objectives.
2 Freedland et al (2007, Ch. 6) trace this reciprocal element of what they call active labour market policies to the 1920s.
3 The current sanction regime can be found in sections 26 and 27 of the *Welfare Reform Act 2012*.
4 Unless otherwise indicated, the sbwa scheme and the CAP will be referred to here as "the schemes".
5 Contribution-based JSA is linked to the amount of National Insurance contributions an individual has paid in the last two tax years. Importantly, however, access to this benefit also depends on undertaking the work-related measures stipulated in the individual's claimant commitment. In other words, receipt of contribution-based JSA is not solely based on having made the requisite amount of national insurance contributions.
6 In addition to claiming that the obligation to participate in the CAP violated Article 4, Wilson explained that the work he had been given to do bore no resemblance to his specific needs and to what was preventing him from entering the job market. Similar comments by others undertaking workfare schemes can be found in a recent report commissioned by the UK Government's Department of Work and Pensions (DWP 2014).
7 For evidence of the unstable, low-paid, poor-quality jobs that workfare participants tend to up in, see for example, Carpenter et al (2007) and Griggs and Evans (2010).
8 In Roman law, the term *obligatio* denoted a tie or bond between two parties – the creditor and the debtor – "by which one party was bound, and the other entitled, to some act or forbearance" (Nicholas 1962, p158).

References

BEVERIDGE, W. (1942) *Social Insurance and Allied Services*. London: HMSO (Cm. 6404).
BLAIR, T. and SCHROEDER, G. (1998) *Europe: The Third Way/Die Neue Mitte*. London/Berlin: Labour Party/SPD.
BOLTANSKI, L. and CHIAPELLO, E. (2005) *The New Spirit of Capitalism*. London: Verso.
CARPENTER, M., FREDA, B. and SPEEDEN, S. (eds) (2007) *Beyond the Workfare State: Labour Markets, Equality and Human Rights*. Bristol: Polity Press.
DARDOT, P. and LAVAL, C. (2013) *The New Way of the World: On Neoliberal Society*. London: Verso.
DONZELOT, J. (2008) Michel Foucault and Liberal Intelligence. *Economy and Society*. 37(1). pp115–134.
FREEDLAND, M. et al (2007) *Public Employment Services and European Law*. Oxford: Oxford University Press.

GRADY, J. (2010) From Beveridge to Turner: Laissez-faire to neoliberalism. *Capital & Class*. 34(2). pp163–180.

GREAT BRITAIN: DEPARTMENT FOR WORK AND PENSIONS (DWP) (2014) *Evaluation of the Day One Support for Young People Trailblazer*. London: DWP.

GREAT BRITAIN: DEPARTMENT FOR WORK AND PENSIONS (DWP) (2015) *Mandatory Work Activity Provider Guidance*. London: DWP.

GREAT BRITAIN: HOUSE OF COMMMONS (2015) *Benefit Sanctions Policy beyond the Oakley Review*. London: The Stationery Office.

GREAT BRITAIN: SCOTTISH GOVERNMENT (2013) *The Potential Impacts of Benefit Sanctions on Individuals and Households*. Edinburgh: Welfare Analysis.

GRIGGS, J. and EVANS, M. (2010) *Sanctions within Conditional Benefit Systems: A Review of Evidence*. Oxford: Joseph Rowntree Foundation.

HARRIS, B. (2004) *The Origins of the British Welfare State: Social Welfare in England and Wales, 1800–1945*. Basingstoke: Palgrave Macmillan.

JESSOP, B. (2002) *The Future of the Capitalist State*. Cambridge: Polity Press.

MARSHALL, T. H. (1992) Citizenship and Social Class. In MARSHALL, T. H. and BOTTOMORE, T. *Citizenship and Social Class*. London: Pluto.

NICHOLAS, B. (1962) *An Introduction to Roman Law*. Oxford: Clarendon Press.

ROSANVALLON, P. (2000) *The New Social Question: Rethinking the Welfare State*. Princeton, NJ: Princeton University Press.

SENNETT, R. (2006) *The Culture of the New Capitalism*. New Haven & London: Yale University Press.

Case cited

R. (on the application of Reilly and Wilson) v. The Secretary of State for Work and Pensions [2012] EWHC 2292 (Admin); [2013] EWCA Civ 66; [2013] UKSC 68.

Part II

Social rights, equalities, and inclusions

Chapter 4

Social rights and equality
From universal formalism to individualized conditionality

Maija Aalto-Heinilä

Introduction

One of the main functions of social rights or, more generally, of the modern welfare state, has always been the advancement of *equality* between citizens. For example, according to T. H. Marshall "[e]verybody would agree that the evolution of modern society has been deeply influenced in various ways by egalitarian ideas and conscious effort to put them into practice" (Marshall 1964, p63). His follower at the London School of Economics, R. M. Titmuss, reminded us that "[t]o grow in affluence [...] does not mean that we should abandon the quest for equality" (Titmuss 1987, p34). The views of these early (which here means post-war) welfare state theorists are echoed by modern scholars: according to G. Esping-Andersen, "it should be evident to all that we cannot afford *not* to be egalitarians in the advanced economies of the twenty-first century" (Esping-Andersen 2002, p3); and F. Vandenbroucke talks of "the equality principle" as being "the very cornerstone of social democracy" (Vandenbroucke 2002, pxiv).

But in what sense should the welfare state make us equal, and what kinds of social rights are needed for this task? In this chapter I try to answer these questions by looking at the conceptions of equality at play in the writings of some well-known welfare state scholars and by making more explicit the philosophical underpinnings of these conceptions. My aim is not to criticize these more practice-oriented writers for neglecting philosophical theorizing, nor to argue for a certain conception of equality, but rather to see whether any changes are detectable in the conceptions of equality and social rights between the post-war and contemporary welfare state eras, and also to show how complex and difficult the idea of equality is.

The chapter is divided into two parts. In the first part I discuss T. H. Marshall's famous analysis of social rights in post-war welfare states. The conception of equality that emerges from this analysis is equality of *welfare* (which is to be attained through benefits that guarantee a minimum income and through formal equal opportunities); although, as will be seen, the route to this conception is rather complex and involves a discussion of justified inequalities as well. In the second part I look at the kind of egalitarianism that underpins the contemporary "social investment state". I claim that the main difference between the conceptions of post-war (mainly Marshall) and contemporary theorists (Esping-Andersen, Giddens and Rosanvallon) is that the latter are more concerned with a person's *actual* opportunities or capabilities, rather than with mere *formal* equal opportunities. The strengthening of equal opportunities is a common reaction against the problem of social *exclusion* that plagues modern societies. However, some differences exist in the way contemporary theorists understand the idea of equal opportunities (and social rights). Roughly, these differences turn on the question of what role we should assign to individual merit and responsibility *vis-à-vis* obligations of reciprocity.

Marshall and equality in the early (post-war) welfare state

In his classic essay "Citizenship and Social Class" Marshall connects "the modern drive towards social equality" with the evolution of citizenship, and shows how this evolution has, on the one hand, abolished old class distinctions and increased equality, but on the other hand has enabled and justified new forms of social inequality (Marshall 1950, p10). The central question of the essay is whether the basic equality that is embodied in "the formal rights of citizenship" (Marshall 1950, p9) is consistent with inequalities of social class; and, as we shall see, Marshall answers this question in the affirmative (both in this early essay and in his later writings).

Marshall famously divides the evolutionary process of citizenship in England into three elements or historical phases. The first phase consists of the acquisition of civil rights in the 18th century – that is, "the rights necessary for individual freedom – liberty of the person, freedom of speech, thought and faith, the right to own property and to conclude valid contracts and the right to justice" (Marshall 1950, p10). The second element of citizenship is political, by which Marshall refers to the acquisition of political rights (mainly in the 19th century) – that is, rights "to participate in the exercise of political power" (Marshall 1950, p11). The expansion of political rights made it possible, through collective action, to enlarge the concept of citizenship in the 20th century so that it included a social element as well. By this element Marshall means:

> ... the whole range from the right to a modicum of economic welfare and security to the right to share to the full in the social heritage and to live the life of a civilized being according to the standards prevailing in the society.
>
> (Marshall 1950, p11)

Thus, Marshall sees citizenship as a developing institution; it is a "status bestowed on those who are full members of a community" (Marshall 1950, p28), and the direction of the development of this status has been "towards a fuller measure of equality, an enrichment of the stuff of which the status is made and an increase in the number of those on whom the status is bestowed" (Marshall 1950, p29).

In the early stages of this development the equality of citizens consisted, as we saw, only of equal civil rights. These kinds of negative, freedom-protecting, rights were indispensable to the developing competitive market economy:

> They gave to each man, as part of his individual status, the power to engage as an independent unit in the economic struggle and made it possible to deny to him social protection on the ground that he was equipped with the means to protect himself.
>
> (Marshall 1950, pp33–4)

However, obviously not everyone was equally well equipped to protect himself in the markets, and thus equality in terms of civil (and political) rights is consistent with great social and economic inequalities. As Marshall puts it, it is no solace to a pauper if you explain to him "that his property rights are the same as those of a millionaire", and similarly the rights to freedom of speech and to political participation have "little substance if, from lack of education, you have nothing to say that is worth saying, and no means of making yourself heard if you say it" (Marshall 1950, p35). What are needed to correct this situation are social rights: "These blatant inequalities are not due to defects in civil rights, but to lack of social rights" (Marshall 1950, p35). But exactly what kind of equality is the aim of social rights?

Equality as sufficientarism

In the passage already quoted in which Marshall defines the social element of citizenship, he talks of the right to "a modicum of economic welfare and security" and the right "to live the life of a civilized being according to the standards prevailing in the society" (Marshall 1950, p11) Thus, one aspect in the equality that social rights try to advance is *economic* equality. By this Marshall does not mean absolute equality of income, but nor is the aim of the welfare state mere abatement of destitution. (Marshall 1950, p47) Rather, the aim is to offer to all the economic resources to live like "a civilized being" (i.e., to attain the standards of decent life that prevail in the society). Expressed in the jargon of egalitarian theories, the underlying ideal of (economic) social rights seems to be a version of *sufficientarism*. This can be defined as a doctrine according to which:

> ... it is morally valuable that as many as possible [...] should enjoy conditions of life that place them above the threshold that marks the minimum required for a decent (good enough) quality of life. Sufficiency can rationalize egalitarian transfers of resources from better to worse off persons when such transfers would increase the total number of people who ever achieve sufficiency.
>
> (Arneson 2013, Ch. 6.1)

Of course, what is a "sufficient" level of income is difficult to define in a non-arbitrary way. However, Marshall's understanding of the function of social rights gives us some guidelines for determining the threshold. For, as we saw, he refers to the "standards prevailing in the society". This suggests that what is sufficient to live a decent life is to a large extent relative to the society in which one lives. That is, the criterion of sufficiency is not mere physical survival but, rather, to use Adam Smith's famous words, that everyone is able "to appear in public" without shame (Smith 2009, p676). Equality, in general, is a *relational* concept that requires inter-personal comparisons (see Gosepath 2007, Ch. 1). And, it can be argued, one can truly compare one's life with someone else's, and come to have expectations about it, only if that life is *shared* with other people – if the parties to the comparison partake of the same culture, share a common history, and live in relative proximity to one another – in short, if they interact with one another.[1] Indeed, Marshall tells us how the pressure to equalize men's living conditions was connected with the development of the mass media and mass production of goods which helped to bring "the components of a civilized and cultured life [...] within the reach of the many" (Marshall 1950, p47). In other words, because a certain way of living became concretely visible and conceivable to more and more people within a society, it became natural to think of it as something everyone had a right to.

So what if a sufficient minimum income – or, more generally, material level of well-being – cannot be given an absolute definition that applies across nations; it is always relative to the standards that prevail in the society and concerns people who interact in certain ways. And, of course, within a single society the standards are continually changing. In Adam Smith's Europe, a linen shirt and leather shoes were items without which even "the poorest creditable person" could not appear in public unashamed (Smith 2009, p676); when Marshall was writing, the sufficient minimum included things like radio or television sets and the possibility to take a day off to watch a football match (Marshall 1950, p82); while nowadays, for example, mobile phones and fast internet connections are necessary for full social citizenship.

It is important to notice that the idea of social rights as guaranteeing a sufficient income for everyone can be seen as *opposed* to egalitarianism, if by egalitarianism one means that equality is valuable *per se*, something that always trumps other values. The idea in sufficientarism is to raise the level of income or material well-being of those who are below the sufficiency threshold. As Marshall describes it, the earliest aim of social rights was "to raise the floor-level in the basement of the social edifice, leaving the superstructure as it was" (Marshall 1950, p47). To put the point more generally, "[w]hen we envisage a more equal world, we tend to think of changes that make some people better off" (Arneson 2013, Ch. 6). But if equality of citizens is thought to be the ultimate aim of the welfare state, why not reduce inequalities by diminishing the incomes (or material well-being) of those who are better-off? To use Marshall's metaphor, why not destroy the skyscraper and force everyone to live in bungalows (Marshall 1950, p47)? This is the famous "levelling-down" objection that is taken to show that advocates of equality in fact think that equality is at most instrumentally valuable, but not valuable for its own sake. Here is Arneson's vivid description of the levelling down objection:

Perhaps the better off person has a nice house, and we can burn down the house costlessly, making him worse off, but without improving the condition of anyone else. This is leveling down. [...] The objection simply is that it is counterintuitive to claim that in any respect increasing equality by making someone worse off and no one else better off is improving the situation. Leveling down is pointless or worse.

(Arneson 2013, Ch. 6)

In other words, if equality was the most important value, it would not matter *in what sense* people were equal with one another: they might as well be all equally poor, or all equally unfree, or equally homeless, as long as there were no differences between them. Clearly the aim of social rights is not equality-no-matter-what, but equality that at the same time respects the rights of those who are better off.

Equal opportunities and the social right to education

Marshall, too, notices the possible untoward consequences of the equalizing process and asks whether there are some "natural limits to the contemporary drive towards greater social and economic equality" (Marshall 1950, p48) – that is, whether some competing values or principles inhibit the destruction of all stratified social edifices and make some inequalities morally acceptable. Interestingly, it is possible to block the levelling down objection and justify the existence of social inequalities by appealing to equal social rights. In this case the rights are those that guarantee equal opportunities (rather than concrete material benefits), especially the right to education. The right to education is a generator of social inequalities because of the close link between education and occupation. To qualify for a job, one needs certificates, degrees and diplomas (today no less than when Marshall was writing); and everyone has an equal right, not to get top jobs, but to climb up the educational ladder as far as one's abilities allow, and (through a process of testing and selecting) to acquire the degrees and diplomas attached to the different rungs of the ladder. This gives those from lower social classes the chance to be equal or better than their upper-class friends, thereby changing the old structure of social inequalities. Marshall describes the social right to education (and its connection to both equality and inequality) in the following way:

The right of the citizen in this process of selection and mobility is the right to equality of opportunity. Its aim is to eliminate hereditary privilege. In essence it is the equal right to display and develop differences, or inequalities; the equal right to be recognized as unequal. In the early stages of the establishment of such a system the major effect is, of course, to reveal hidden equalities – to enable the poor boy to show that he is as good as the rich boy. But the final outcome is a structure of unequal status fairly apportioned to unequal abilities.

(Marshall 1950, pp65–6)

The underlying moral intuition here is that those who do well at school or work *deserve* to be better off than those who do not do so well. So *deserts* is one value that competes with equality and sets a "natural limit" to the drive towards greater social and economic equality. The basic idea of the "deserts principle" is that "it is desirable that each person should gain good fortune corresponding to her virtue (deservingness)" (Arneson 2013, Ch. 6.3). This principle permeates our thinking about distributive justice, whether we are distributing positive goods (such as money or rewards) or negative ones (such as punishments). Indeed, that each should get what they deserve is so widely accepted and natural a way of thinking about justice that it usually needs no further justification; the burden of proof is on those who want to challenge this principle. We shall later see that it can be challenged, and that therefore we may be justified in setting at least a limit to the inequalities that the deserts principle enables. But at the moment it suffices to note that principles other than "the equality principle" are clearly at work in the normative foundations of the welfare state and social rights, a matter of which Marshall was well aware.

A hyphenated society

Placing a high value on individual deserts belongs intimately to the ethos of the competitive market economy. Thus, Marshall's adoption of the deserts principle is connected with his reluctance to renounce the market economy (which is what some more radical egalitarians were willing to do).[2] An ideal society, for Marshall, was a combination of three elements or sectors: democracy, welfare and capitalism (just as citizenship consists of civil, political and social elements). Marshall calls this a "hyphenated" society, where the three different elements (which are connected with a hyphen) are on the one hand in open confrontation with one another (as in the combination "bitter-sweet"), but in which, on the other hand, "the differences [between the elements] strengthen the structure because they are complementary rather than divisive" (Marshall 1981, pp124–5). So Marshall suggests that we should view Western post-war societies as combinations of three different sectors or realms, each of which has its own guiding principles, but which together make up the best possible social system that respects all the values which we hold dear.

The guiding principle in capitalism, of course, is free competition in the markets, while in democracy it is majority rule. The "welfare principle" is independent of both economic value ("it is a fundamental principle of the welfare state that the market value of an individual cannot be the measure of his right to welfare"; Marshall 1972, p107), nor can the welfare principle be derived from majority rule: "[welfare's] duty is to provide not what the majority want but what the minorities need [...] welfare stresses the right to receive; democracy the duty to participate" (Marshall 1981, p126).

In an ideal society all three elements co-exist and a balance is struck between them that prevents any one of them gaining too much power over the others.

Democracy is, of course, the cornerstone of modern societies. But, as J. S. Mill warned us, democracy can be a tyrannical power against minorities (Mill 1856, Ch. 1), whose well-being has to be secured by social rights and the welfare sector. Likewise, if the capitalist market economy is not in any way regulated by the state and supplemented by welfare services, inequalities between people become intolerable. But – and this is one of Marshall's main points – modern welfare societies cannot completely renounce the market economy. If we take the first and most urgent task of the welfare state to be the banishment of poverty, this task:

> ... must be undertaken jointly by welfare and capitalism; there is no other way. Not only is there no evidence in history or in contemporary affairs to suggest that conflict between these two components must frustrate any effort at a joint solution but, on the contrary, it is clear that our particular type of [hyphenated] social system has got nearer to achieving this objective than any that has gone before or now exists.
>
> (Marshall 1972, pp117–18)

An obvious alternative to welfare-capitalism is some version of socialism or communism. But Marshall does not want to go in that direction – not only because, as we saw above, he thinks that there is no empirical evidence of the superiority of socialism in promoting welfare, but above all because all alternatives to welfare-capitalism would have to be "something more totalitarian and bureaucratic" (Marshall 1972, p121); in other words, they would diminish our freedom too much. In general, all welfare policy decisions contain something "intrinsically authoritarian" and "paternalistic" (Marshall 1972, p109). The welfare state tries to educate people, "not only in schools and colleges, but in its health service and welfare centres"; in doing so, it is "creating and, quite frankly, inculcating concepts and standards of welfare which are not universally accepted". (Marshall 1972, pp109–10). So Marshall seems to be saying that without the counter-balancing forces of the market economy, with its values of freedom and individualism, the welfare state would end up forcing or brainwashing us to live according to its conception of the good life; but paradoxically, by suffocating citizens' freedom it could not succeed in its task of producing welfare, since freedom and the possibility to make choices is an essential part of the concept of welfare.

Equality of welfare

Thus, Marshall's final position seems to be that although, on the one hand, the welfare state is only one sector in modern democratic-welfare-capitalist societies, yet on the other hand welfare is the ultimate aim of the whole three-partite structure. So Marshall's final answer to my original question – what kind of equality is the aim of social rights and the welfare state? – is equality of *welfare*. But, as should be evident by now, Marshall sees welfare as a complex concept; it needs to be analysed before we can see what kind of equality is in question here.

In his 1964 lecture "Welfare in the Context of Social Development" Marshall characterizes welfare as being "precariously perched" on the "slippery slope from the sublime to the ridiculous" (Marshall 1964, p53). This means that welfare is neither an abstract and objective thing, connected with "human character and destiny", nor a subjective concept, connected with material things such as "baths and refectories" (Marshall 1964, p53). It is located somewhere between pure objectivism and mere subjectivism. But although it is not identical with material wealth, it is nevertheless a very close neighbour of it; wealth and welfare are "intermittently entangled" with one another:

> For it is obvious that welfare, in the broadest sense, is achieved largely by the consumption of goods and services that money can buy, and money is wealth. And it is also true that welfare, or social, services have been mainly concerned, during the greater part of their history, with supplying goods and services to those too poor to buy them for themselves; welfare in this sense was a substitute for money, or wealth.
>
> (Marshall 1964, p54)

However, money cannot be used to measure commodities such as "sympathy, courage, hope, and even perhaps happiness" (Marshall 1964, p54); and clearly at least one of these – happiness – is as intimately connected with the concept of welfare as wealth. But although very closely related to it, welfare is not identical to happiness; for happiness is a concept that is "too subjective, too unaccountable, too intimate", and cannot serve as the direct object of social policy. Instead of welfare being reducible to wealth and happiness, the latter are, according to Marshall, "the poles of the axis along which welfare moves" (Marshall 1964, pp54–5).

Another axis or dimension along which the concept of welfare moves is formed by the two poles of "the individual and the society". Welfare is an individual matter in the sense that "it is only individuals who can have wants and be conscious of their satisfaction". But, on the other hand, "the circumstances which affect the welfare of individuals very often operate in and on groups as wholes" – for example, "a *family* is poverty-stricken, or a *neighborhood* is unhealthy" (Marshall 1964, p55; emphasis in the original). Another sense in which welfare can be understood to be moving between the individual and the society is that both freedom to make our own independent choices (and live with their consequences), as well as being part of a wider group or community, are indispensable parts of human welfare, indeed ingredients out of which our identities and self-respect are made (we return to this issue in the second section). Marshall's abhorrence of totalitarian regimes shows that he clearly regarded individual freedom as an essential constituent of welfare.

What this analysis reveals is that welfare is to a large extent a *qualitative* concept: it contains elements which cannot be straightforwardly measured with money. Because welfare contains these qualitative aspects – happiness, freedom, being an equal member of a group – a society which allows some differences in the quantitative elements of welfare (i.e., inequality of incomes) is not thereby an anti-welfarist society. In other words, qualitative equality of welfare is consistent with quantitative inequality of income:

> [Welfare] operates on the assumption that equality of persons is compatible with inequality of incomes provided the inequality is not too great. It does not require that all work should be equally rewarded, but it does insist that doctors should regard all their patients, and school teachers all their pupils, as deserving to be treated with the same care, and that all dwellings, however different in size, should be equally convertible by the families that occupy them into homes. And that is as near as I can get to a demonstration of what I mean when I speak of a qualitative equality of welfare that can co-exist with a quantitative inequality of income.
>
> (Marshall 1964, pp65–6)

So in the end the most important sense in which the welfare state tries to make us more equal is equality of welfare. Social rights, which on the one hand secure that everyone's basic material needs are satisfied, and on the other hand give everyone equal opportunities (through the right to education), go some way towards achieving this aim. But social rights and, more generally, the welfare state, can only go so far; what is needed to attain real equality of welfare is as much a matter of individuals' *attitudes* as of social legislation. As we have seen from this study of Marshall, a society can never attain dead-level equality, nor is it a desirable aim if we want to live in free democracies. Therefore it is important to properly understand the principles which justify and explain certain unavoidable inequalities; for lack of understanding of these principles causes envy and jealousy, which in turn are feelings that undermine social solidarity (a necessary ingredient of the welfare state) and certainly do not increase anyone's well-being.[3]

Equality and social rights in the "social investment state"

Social rights in Marshall's post-war Europe were more or less standardized benefits or services that were applicable to clearly identifiable *groups* (such as the unemployed). However, as many writers have pointed out, in today's post-industrial societies welfare recipients do not form homogeneous groups (see e.g. Rosanvallon 2013, p97, and van Kersbergen and Vis 2014, pp156–7). In other words, the ways in which an *individual* can be excluded from society are many and different. "Social exclusion" is a term that is meant to draw attention to the fact that being poor is not the only way of being disadvantaged: deprivation can take many different forms in present-day societies (see Diamond and Giddens 2005, p110). This is because many new social *risks* have arisen due to changes in the economic and social structures of modern societies.

These changes are well known: the economic order has become global and extremely complex; most European countries are struggling with economic recession or slow growth-rates; technological advances have made many old, secure, well-paid production jobs disappear, quite new skills are needed in the labour markets and, in general, job security has diminished and forms of employment become more precarious; the population is aging; transformations have occurred in household and family structures, due to a changed conception of women's role in society; and family arrangements are not as stable as in post-war societies, with single-parent households very much on the rise.[4]

The problem of social exclusion, which is linked to these new social risks, is of fundamental importance to contemporary welfare state theorists. According to Giddens, a "focus on social exclusion" is one of the "key elements" of the so-called third way (or new social democratic) approach to welfare reform (Giddens 2000, p104); likewise, Esping-Andersen asserts that "[t]he foremost challenge we face is to avert that social ills become permanent, that citizens become entrapped in exclusion or inferior opportunities in such a way that their entire life chances are affected" (Esping-Andersen 2002, p6). But what is the best way to tackle the problem of exclusion – what kinds of social rights (and corresponding theories of equality) are needed? I will look at three slightly different answers to these questions.

Esping-Andersen: fair equality of opportunity and the social right to childcare

According to Esping-Andersen, the best guarantee against social exclusion is to strengthen equal opportunities – that is, to furnish all citizens with the skills and capabilities needed to survive in the changed circumstances (see e.g. Esping-Andersen 2005). Although equalizing opportunities was also one of the aims of the post-war welfare state, it did not succeed in its attempt to abolish the importance of class in competitive markets. Class divisions may not be so visible any more, but they are perhaps even more decisive nowadays:

> In knowledge-intensive economies, life chances will depend on one's learning abilities and one's accumulation of human capital. As is well established, the impact of social inheritance is as strong today as in the past – in particular with regard to cognitive development and educational attainment.
>
> (Esping-Andersen 2002, p3)

So if we want to advance equality and get rid of the impact of social inheritance in modern "knowledge-intensive" economies, we need to pay more attention to the distribution of "human capital". Human capital here means, above all, skills that enable quick learning of new things and smooth adaptation to changed circumstances; these qualities are essential for succeeding in present-day societies. What is noteworthy is that an equal distribution of these kinds of skills requires more than the social right to education – that is, a state-funded school system. This is because the abilities in question (e.g. cognitive and non-cognitive skills, motivation to learn, health) are already developed in early childhood, so that "the seeds of inequality are sown prior to school age" (Esping-Andersen 2007, p23). Thus, a true equalizing of opportunities requires paying attention to social origins and family conditions, because the earliest years of children's lives are decisive for their subsequent success at school and in working life (Esping-Andersen 2007, p25). In practice, this means that the welfare state should provide affordable, high-quality childcare for families (for obviously it cannot be expected that all families will be able themselves to organize their homes into stimulating learning environments, even if they had the required knowledge and intentions). So the social right to childcare becomes crucial in the fight against social exclusion; as Esping-Andersen puts it, "very early child investment matters most" (Esping-Andersen 2007, p25). Moreover, this right should be universal and unconditional (rather than targeted) (Esping-Andersen 2007, p27). Esping-Andersen seems, in general, to be suspicious of individualized, targeted benefits: "if equality remains a priority, targeted welfare performs poorly" (Esping-Andersen 2002, p15).

Translated into the language of egalitarian theories, the aim here is *fair* equality of opportunity. This is a term used by John Rawls (and, unsurprisingly, Esping-Andersen refers to Rawls's theory of justice as underpinning the idea of social inclusion; see Esping-Andersen 2002, p9). Fair equality of opportunity is not guaranteed if all have merely the same legal rights to pursue advantaged social positions. Even if it is only diligence and talent (and not e.g. wealth) that determines success in education and in the labour markets, it can lead to injustice if one does not take into account the fact that the distribution of "natural assets" (natural talents and abilities; or human capital) is a matter of sheer luck, as is also the fact whether those talents are favoured or disfavoured by society (Rawls 1971, p72). As Rawls reminds us, everyone's starting points in life are a matter of arbitrary chance; no one *deserves* their good or bad starting point; therefore society should equalize the outcomes of the "natural and social lottery" and provide everyone with real equal opportunities. So the principle of fair equality of opportunity means that "positions are to be not only open in a formal sense, but that all should have a fair chance to attain them" – that is, "[t]he expectations of those with the same abilities and aspirations should not be affected by their social class" (Rawls 1971, p73).

The chances are fair only if the social system somehow eliminates the influence of social and natural contingencies. These can to an extent be eliminated by a free and universal schooling system and, as Esping-Andersen argues, with universal early childhood care. But it should be noted that if we wanted to implement the principle of fair equality of opportunity fully into practice, we would have to go much further than this. For example, "all efforts by parents to give their children a comparative advantage in competition for desirable positions [should be] entirely offset" (Arneson 2013, Ch. 2). This would require massive interference with parental freedom; or maybe even abolishing the institution of family altogether, as in Plato's utopia.

Rawls himself seems to think that fair equality of opportunity is secured as long as the basic institutions of society are just: if the principles that guide the distribution of *primary goods* (e.g., rights, liberties, wealth and opportunities) are just. And the principles are just if they are formulated behind the famous "veil of ignorance", which forces us to think what it would be like to be in the shoes of the worst-off member of the society. This thought-experiment leads us to choose principles of justice which give the best possible outcome for the worst-off group – that is, principles according to which part of the wealth of those who were lucky in the natural lottery (who, for example, are talented and hard-working) is redistributed to compensate for those who were not so lucky. This is Rawls's "difference principle" or "maximin principle", which allows for social and economic inequalities only if they are arranged so that they are both "to the greatest benefit of the least advantaged [and] attached to offices and positions open to all under conditions of fair equality of opportunity" (Rawls 1971, p302). The difference principle thus sets a limit on the deserts principle that we discussed in the first part of this chapter. And it makes sense, according to Esping-Andersen, to endorse this principle in present-day societies, where no one will know whether they will personally fall victim to the new social risks (Esping-Andersen 2002, p9).

Giddens and "the new egalitarianism"

Anthony Giddens, just like Esping-Andersen, highlights the importance of strengthening equal opportunities in today's post-industrial societies: "The priority is to invest in human and cognitive capacities that promote individual opportunity, rather than in reparation after the event" (Diamond and Giddens 2005, p105). However, some differences exist between Esping-Andersen's and Giddens's ways of understanding what equality of opportunity means and what kind of social rights it requires. Although Giddens has also talked of the importance of paying attention to children ("[t]he future of the European social model is bound up with successful investment in children"; Giddens 2007, p95), the main tenets of his "new egalitarianism" are an emphasis on economic dynamism and tying social rights with responsibilities. Thus, in contrast to the old egalitarianism of the British left, the new egalitarianism asserts that a dynamic and flexible economy is "the necessary precondition for future distribution" (Diamond and Giddens 2005, p106); it wants to equalize life chances across generations by levelling up rather than levelling down – that is, it does not want to "penalize success" (Diamond and Giddens 2005, pp106, 112); and, most importantly, "[n]ew egalitarianism ties rights to corresponding responsibilities [...]. Benefits depend not only on a person's means but also on his or her behavior" (Diamond and Giddens 2005, p107). In other words, "[t]hose who profit from social goods should both use them responsibly, and give something back to the wider social community in return" (Giddens 2000, p52). For example, the New Deal for Young People in the United Kingdom gave the following four options to the unemployed:

> ... subsidized employment in the private sector; subsidized and temporary work in the voluntary or environmental sectors; full-time education; or

training. There is, however, no "fifth option" of passively living on benefits, and failure to comply with the rules can lead to a loss of benefits and eventual suspension.

(van Kersbergen and Hemerijck 2012, p484)

In terms of social rights, this kind of egalitarianism requires "individually tailored measures that carefully identify target groups and objectives [...]. Active welfare replaces the 'one size fits all' postwar welfare state" (Diamond and Giddens 2005, p113). Thus, rather than being universal and unconditional, the new social rights are, to use Pierre Rosanvallon's phrase, "individualized" (Rosanvallon 2000, p83), and often based on a contract between the state and benefit recipient (e.g. a behavioral contract between a tenant and social housing authorities (see Diamond and Giddens 2005, p114)).

The underlying philosophical theory of equality in Giddens's "new egalitarianism" is, on the one hand, the capabilities approach (to which Giddens explicitly refers; see Giddens 2000, pp86–7); but, on the other hand, it closely resembles Dworkin's "luck-egalitarianism" (or "responsibility-sensitive" egalitarianism). Amartya Sen has argued that instead of considering the distribution of resources, a theory of justice should look at the distribution of *capabilities*. Capabilities refer to certain basic things that a person is able to do and to be; for example, to move about, to meet one's nutritional requirements, to be adequately clothed and sheltered, and to have the power to participate in the social life of the community (Sen 1997, p484). To secure the same basic capabilities for everyone – that is, to give everyone the same *actual* opportunities, or the same *substantive* freedom – may require an unequal distribution of resources. This is because the ability to convert goods into capabilities varies from person to person. For example, a cripple needs more material resources and support in order to enjoy the same real opportunity for movement as a non-cripple (Sen 1997, p484) or a pregnant woman needs more nutritious food than a non-pregnant one in order to attain the same level of health (Nussbaum 2011, p57). This kind of approach fits well with the idea of individually tailored social rights: since the same resource means different things to different people, its fair distribution is not quantitatively equal, but adjusted to each person's specific situation.

However, in another sense the capability approach does not fit well into the normative foundations of the modern welfare state. This is the theory's insistence on the distinction between capabilities and functionings. Capabilities enable the achieving of functionings – that is, the doings and beings that a person values. For example, the capability of political participation enables a person to be politically active if they so choose (Nussbaum 2011, pp24–5). But in the capability approach, it is not essential that a person actually avails herself of real opportunities: "[t]he focus of the capability approach is [...] not just on what a person actually ends up doing, but also on what she is in fact able to do, whether or not she chooses to make use of that opportunity" (Sen 2010, p235). This means that if a person, for example, does not want to get a proper education or to participate in the social life of the community, then that is her choice and it must be respected. So in this theory, the freedom to choose is more important than the achievement of functionings. This ill suits the ideology of the active welfare state, which presupposes that capabilities (which social rights and the welfare state help to attain) *are* used, i.e. that people are active and cultivate their talents and participate in civil society. If they do not, they are not only morally blameworthy,[5] but may actually be deprived of their capability-ensuring social benefits.

Luck-egalitarianism is a theory that pays more attention to individual responsibility (which, as we saw, is a key feature of Giddens's "new egalitarianism"). The basic idea of luck-egalitarianism is that we should be responsible for those things or events that we freely choose (to do); but not for events or circumstances that we did not freely choose, that are a matter of brute luck. Thus, distributions of social goods should be sensitive to individuals' free decisions, but not to the results of brute luck.[6]

The most important proponent of luck-egalitarianism is Ronald Dworkin. One way in which Dworkin formulates his complicated theory is by distinguishing between a person's *personality* (which includes the person's character, convictions, preferences, motives, tastes and ambitions), and *personal resources* (e.g., health, strength, talent) (Dworkin 2000, p286). A just political community should, according to Dworkin, aim at erasing or mitigating differences between people's personal resources (i.e., should try to improve the position of, e.g., physically disabled people), but should not aim to mitigate differences that result from different personalities (Dworkin 2000). So if, for example, someone's tastes are expensive, society should not be required to assume the costs of satisfying them.

Luck-egalitarianism is obviously a very close relative to Rawls's theory of justice – it is based on Rawls's idea of the social and natural lottery – but it is also a criticism of Rawls's maximin principle. Dworkin thinks that Rawls is not sensitive enough to personal ambition and responsibility. According to Dworkin, "there is nothing to be said for a world in which those who choose leisure, though they could work, are rewarded with the produce of the industrious" (Dworkin 2000, p2). And it is a violation of the principle of *equality* if we do not take personal ambition into account:

> ... we must, on pain of violating equality, allow the distribution of resources at any particular moment to be (as we might say) ambition-sensitive [...] for example, those who choose to invest rather than consume, [...] or to work in more rather than less profitable ways must be permitted to retain the gains that flow from these decisions.
>
> (Dworkin 2000, p89)

So Dworkin, like Giddens, thinks that success should not be penalized. This means that responsibility-sensitive egalitarianism can tolerate vast economic inequalities (if they are based on personal merit and ambition). This is clearly different from Esping-Andersen's Rawlsian, more redistributive ethos.

Rosanvallon's "society of equals"

As can be seen, views differ as to what kinds of social rights and what conception of equality we should adopt in present-day welfare states. Should social rights be universal or individualized, and should we favour a heavily redistributive state or reward ambition and risk-taking (as a result of which inequalities can grow)? To conclude this section, I will look at Pierre Rosanvallon's sketch of a "society of equals", which can be seen as an attempt to reconcile these conflicting ideas about social rights and equality.

Rosanvallon, like Giddens, thinks that the traditional (universal, unconditional) conception of social rights "can no longer respond to the new challenges of exclusion"; we need to consider individuals "in their own specific situations" (Rosanvallon 2000, p96). This is, as we saw, because the excluded do not form a homogeneous class: there is, for example, no typical long-term unemployed person or a stereotypical bad debtor (Rosanvallon 2000, p97). Rosanvallon is, however, aware of the risks that individualized, custom-tailored social rights bring in their wake. One danger is that the welfare state transforms into "the management and supervision of behaviors" (Rosanvallon 2000, p102). Furthermore, the risk exists of unequal treatment and arbitrariness in decision-making if social workers can no longer apply standardized measures but instead "must help a million different persons [and] deal with their personal situation" (Rosanvallon 2000, p102).

In order to avoid these risks, without giving up the demand for individualized treatment, we need, according to Rosanvallon, to conceive of social rights as *procedural* rights. This means that we have an equal right to *equivalent*, but not *identical*, treatment (Rosanvallon 2000, p105); or, as he puts it in his recent book, "[t]he norm [...] becomes *fairness of treatment* (where 'fair' means that everyone has an equal right to equivalent treatment), so that the needs of the singular individual can be taken into account" (Rosanvallon 2013, pp267–8). As I understand it, Rosanvallon is saying that because people's situations are different, the specific *content* of social rights cannot be identical for everyone; but the procedures must be the same for everyone. And an important part of these procedures is the possibility to appeal (so as to reduce the likelihood of arbitrary treatment): "Individuals must be able to challenge decisions easily" (Rosanvallon 2013, p269).

Rosanvallon suggests that this conception of social rights means that we must also rethink the relationship between the individual and society:

> The development of a procedural right is also a novel relationship between the individual and society. The objective of the classical subjective rights [...] was to construct the individual, constitute his autonomy. [...] But this traditional approach to rights is no longer adequate when its object becomes the social relation itself, which is at stake in inclusion. The object of the right is not an allowance, but a social relationship that can be encompassed only by a procedural right.
>
> (Rosanvallon 2000, pp105–6)

The idea that the object of social rights is the social relation itself becomes understandable, I think, if we look (again) at Rawls and his idea of the social basis of self-respect. As we have seen, Rawls talks of social or primary goods whose distribution the principles of justice should regulate. Primary goods include rights, liberties, wealth, and opportunities, but the most important primary good in human life is *self-respect*. The underlying Kantian thought here is that we all deserve equal respect in so far as we are human beings (i.e., beings who are rational and free and capable of having a conception of our own good, and capable of having a sense of justice) (see Rawls 1971, p505). The government can recognize this equal human worth by publicly affirming the status of equal citizenship for all. But in addition to this formal recognition, self-respect requires that there should be "for each person at least one community of shared interests to which he belongs and where he finds his endeavours confirmed by his associates" (Rawls 1971, p442). In other words, self-respect has a social basis: it requires interaction with other people, and more particularly, with people who have similar interests and who see one's endeavours as worth pursuing. Vandenbroucke has argued that the active welfare state should aim for equal distribution of opportunities to participate in such groups and communities: that is the most important sense in which we should be equal. This goes beyond mere participation in labour markets; it can also include other activities that build respect and self-respect, such as "caring for a friend or a family member, voluntary social or cultural work or education" (Vandenbroucke 2000, pxii). This is, I think, another way of saying that the object of social rights is the social relation itself.

This conception of social rights requires a similar conception of equality. Rosanvallon argues that the dominant way of understanding equality of opportunity justifies huge differences in wealth because it looks at *individual* situations alone: if some people work hard, then why should they not become "filthy rich" (Rosanvallon 2013, p256)? This meritocratic, individualist conception of equality (that is not very remote from Giddens's "new egalitarianism") forgets that "inequality also has a societal dimension [...] [w]ell-being depends on the quality of personal relationships, individual recognition, and feelings of usefulness" (Rosanvallon 2013, p256). Thus, equality must be seen as a *relation*. More specifically, it has, according to Rosanvallon, three dimensions: *singularity, reciprocity* and *commonality*.

By singularity Rosanvallon means every person's uniqueness and difference from others. This is not quite the same thing as the individualism that underlies classic subjective rights; rather, into the idea of singularity is built the idea of reciprocity and being a member of a society:

> If the meaning of a person's life lies in his difference from others, then he must coexist with them [...] singularity is defined by a *relational* variable; it is not a state. The difference that defines singularity binds a person to others; it does not set him apart.
>
> (Rosanvallon 2013, p260)

Singularity is not a sign of withdrawal from society (individualism as retreat or separation). Rather, it signals an expectation of reciprocity, of mutual recognition.

(Rosanvallon 2013, p261)

So singularity as a *concept* requires other people from whom one differentiates oneself. But it also requires reciprocal social relations because the policies that enable everyone to achieve singularity are expensive: social rights that are tailored to everyone's unique situation obviously require more resources than traditional "one size fits all" social benefits. This means that "[i]f taxpayers are to pay for such [individualized social rights], the expense must be seen as socially legitimate" (Rosanvallon 2013, p267); therefore "the implementation of an active singularity policy cannot be separated from the development of policies of reciprocity and commonality" (Rosanvallon 2013).

Rosanvallon thinks that reciprocity "is an essential part of [our] makeup" (Rosanvallon 2013, p270) – that is, we are not, by nature, purely self-interested egoists. But there are tendencies in modern societies that tend to weaken feelings and obligations of reciprocity – for example, free-riding (such as tax evasion) and social separatism (i.e., the tendency of people with similar backgrounds, jobs and hobbies to form separate groups) (see Rosanvallon 2013, pp273–80). In order to prevent a total crisis of democracy (to which these tendencies can lead), we need to strengthen reciprocity and what Rosanvallon calls "commonality" by, for example, encouraging everyone's active participation in social events and meetings, upholding good public services, and providing enough public, shared spaces where one can concretely experience "living alongside others" (see Rosanvallon 2013, pp281–8).

In short, Rosanvallon proposes that we should try to build a "society of equals" where equality is, through the dimensions of singularity, reciprocity and commonality, understood as a relation (rather than a matter of individual situations). Redistributive policies are acceptable only if they do not undermine the ideal of equality as relation; but on the other hand, this ideal is required to justify redistribution: "If the meaning of taxation is to be restored in order to enable ambitious programs of redistribution, we must first build up equality as relation and make it the centerpiece of political action" (Rosanvallon 2013, p297).

Conclusion

My initial general question was in what sense the welfare state and social rights should make us equal. Even this brief survey of only a few theorists' work suggests that no simple answer to this question is available. The equality that is the aim of the welfare state can mean a more equal division of income and material resources; formal equality of opportunities; equality of welfare; fair equality of opportunity; equal capabilities; or equal rights to participate in society (i.e., a "society of equals").

Despite this multiplicity of different egalitarian ideals, some generalizations can be made. Both early and contemporary welfare state theorists talk of equal opportunities, but whereas Marshall linked this with the right to education, present-day scholars highlight the importance of paying attention to early childhood: the capabilities needed to avoid social exclusion in later life are developed mostly before school age. So a shift has been taking place from the ideal of *formal* equality of opportunity to *fair* equal opportunities, or equal *capabilities*.

Child-focused policies can be regarded as social *investments* rather than social spending; thus, contemporary welfare states are often called "social investment states" (which Giddens defines as "state-provided or regulated investments in human or social capital" (Giddens 2007, pxiii). But the term "investment" reveals that something is expected in return: namely, that in later life children will become good, productive, responsible adults who will look after themselves. In general, the prevailing attitude towards the welfare state and social rights seems to be that "you don't get something for nothing" – so much so that instead of a "social investment state", some writers have started referring to the "conditional welfare state" (see e.g. Dwyer 2008).

Notes

1 According to Arneson (2013, Ch. 5), "[m]any philosophers hold that the requirements of social justice including requirements of egalitarianism are triggered by social interaction. When people interact in certain ways, then and only then do egalitarian justice requirements apply and become binding on them".
2 Marshall mentions Evan Durbin's book *The Politics of Democratic Socialism* (London: Routledge, 1940) as an example. See Marshall (1972, p104).
3 This is my understanding of the points Marshall makes in pp118–19 in "The Value Problems of Welfare-Capitalism" (Marshall 1972).
4 New social risks are described, e.g., in Esping-Andersen (2002, pp2–3); Vandenbroucke (2002, ppix–x); van Kersbergen and Hemerijck (2012, pp475–81); van Kersbergen and Vis (2015, pp137–59); Giddens (2000, p103).
5 As de Graaf and Maier in their recent article point out, the new welfare arrangements (such as the New Deal) lead inevitably to moral condemnation of the "losers": "under the new discourse and practice the so-called losers are not just losers – they could have been winners if they had only assumed their personal responsibility. This is what they failed to do, and so they have only themselves to blame" (de Graaf and Maier 2015, p13).
6 For different versions of luck-egalitarianism, and the relation between justice and luck in general, see Lippert-Rasmussen (2014).

References

ARNESON, R. (2013) Egalitarianism [Online]. In *Stanford Encyclopedia of Philosophy*. Available from: http://plato.stanford.edu/entries/egalitarianism/ [Accessed: 22 February 2016].
DIAMOND, P. and GIDDENS, A. (2005) The new egalitarianism. In Giddens, A. and Diamond. P. (eds) *The New Egalitarianism*. Cambridge: Polity Press, pp101–119.
DWORKIN, R. (2000) *Sovereign Virtue*. Cambridge, MA: Harvard University Press.

DWYER, P. (2008) The conditional welfare state. In Powell, M. (ed.), *Modernising the Welfare State*. Bristol: The Policy Press, pp199–218.

ESPING-ANDERSEN, G. (2002) Towards the Good Society, Once Again?, In Esping-Andersen, G. and Hemerijck, A. (eds) *Why We Need a New Welfare State*. Oxford: Oxford University Press, pp1–25.

ESPING-ANDERSEN, G. (2005) Inequality of incomes and opportunities. In Giddens, A. and Diamond, P. (eds). *The New Egalitarianism*. Cambridge: Polity Press, pp8–38.

ESPING-ANDERSEN, G. (2007) Equal Opportunities and the Welfare State, *Contexts*, 6 (3). pp23–27.

GIDDENS, A. (2000) *The Third Way and Its Critics*. Cambridge: Polity Press.

GIDDENS, A. (2007) *Europe in the Global Age*. Cambridge: Polity Press.

GOSEPATH, S. (2007) Equality. [Online]. In *Stanford Encyclopedia of Philosophy*. Available from: http://plato.stanford.edu/entries/equality/ [Accessed: 22 February 2016].

de GRAAF, W. and MAIER, R. (2015) The Welfare State and the Life Course: Examining the Interrelationship between Welfare Arrangements and Inequality Dynamics [Online]. In *Social Policy & Administration*. Available from: http://onlinelibrary.wiley.com/doi/10.1111/spol.12153/full [Accessed: 22 February 2016].

van KERSBERGEN, K. and HEMERIJCK, A. (2012) Two Decades of Change in Europe: The Emergence of the Social Investment State. *Journal of Social Policy*, 41 (3), pp475–492.

van KERSBERGEN, K. and VIS, B. (2014) *Comparative Welfare State Politics: Development, Opportunities, Reform*. Cambridge: Cambridge University Press.

LIPPERT-RASMUSSEN, K. (2014). Justice and Bad Luck [Online]. In *Stanford Encyclopedia of Philosophy*. Available from: http://plato.stanford.edu/entries/justice-bad-luck/ [Accessed: 12 March 2016].

MARSHALL, T. H. (1950) *Citizenship and Social Class*. Cambridge: Cambridge University Press.

MARSHALL, T. H. (1964) Welfare in the Context of Social Development. In Marshall, T. H. (ed) *The Right to Welfare and Other Essays*. London: Heinemann Educational Books, 1981, pp53–66.

MARSHALL, T. H. (1972) Value Problems of Welfare-Capitalism. In Marshall, T. H. (ed) *The Right to Welfare and Other Essays*. London: Heinemann Educational Books, 1981, pp104–122.

MARSHALL, T. H. (1981) *The Right to Welfare and Other Essays*. London: Heinemann Educational Books.

MILL, J. S. (1856) *On Liberty* [Online]. The Project Gutenberg EBook. Available from: www.gutenberg.org/files/34901/34901-h/34901-h.htm [Accessed: 22 February 2016].

NUSSBAUM, M. (2011) *Creating Capabilities*. Cambridge, MA: The Belknap Press of Harvard University Press.

RAWLS, J. (1971) *A Theory of Justice*. Cambridge, MA: The Belknap Press of Harvard University Press.

ROSANVALLON, P. (2000) *The New Social Question. Rethinking the Welfare State*. Translated by Harshav, B. Princeton, NJ: Princeton University Press.

ROSANVALLON, P. (2013) *Society of Equals*. Translated by Goldhammer, A. Cambridge, MA: Harvard University Press.

SEN, A. (1997) Equality of What?, In Goodin, R. E. and Pettit, P. (eds), *Contemporary Political Philosophy – an Anthology*. Oxford: Blackwell, pp476–485.

SEN, A. (2010) *The Idea of Justice*. London: Penguin Books.

SMITH, A. (2009) *An Inquiry into the Nature and Causes of the Wealth of Nations*. Ed. by Soares, S. M. Amsterdam: MetaLibri (Published originally in 1775–1776).

TITMUSS, R. M. (1987) The Irresponsible Society. In Titmuss, R. (ed) *The Philosophy of Welfare. Selected writings of Richard M. Titmuss*. London: Allen & Unwin, pp60–86.

VANDENBROUCKE, F. (2002) Foreword. In Esping-Andersen, G. and Hemerijck, A. (eds) *Why We Need a New Welfare State*. Oxford: Oxford University Press, ppviii–xxiv.

Chapter 5

New social risks and new social rights in the French welfare system

Philippe Martin

Introduction

Since the creation of the National Social Security system in 1945, the core of French social rights – meaning the rights of individuals to particular benefits, allowances and services in cases of need – has been guaranteed through contributory social security schemes. The French social security programme was designed as a "general regime" aiming to cover the population through a system of social insurances. As this chapter will demonstrate, this system of social insurances has been theoretically anchored in the notion or paradigm of *social risks*, which assumes that the legislation defines those risks or, at least, names them by recognizing different *branches* of the Social Security system, according to the model of the International Labour Organisation's Social Security (minimum standards) Convention no 102, (ILO 1952).

Ideally speaking, the Social Security system was expected to create a new social order in which people – and not only workers – would be entitled to solid rights and thus become truly emancipated. In this vision, social assistance schemes and means-tested rights would only play a residual part. This was the view of the founders of the 1945 social security plan. Unfortunately, this ideal goal was never totally achieved. The social security schemes based on "socio-professional" solidarities and organized in the sphere of employment failed to cover the whole population, meaning that the ancient social assistance techniques had to be redesigned and modernized in order to cover the "interstitial population". Moreover, with deindustrialization and some other societal factors such as ageing, new kinds of social risks appeared: especially social exclusion and loss of autonomy in elderly people. Those new social risks are heavily challenging the traditional French welfare system.

Obviously, the challenge is a financial one and the political debate about social exclusion and ageing in our society mainly reflects this aspect: how can the French economy sustain the burden of the "new poverty" and of long-term care policies for an ageing population? But what is also challenged is the French path of social rights: how far, and with which concepts and techniques, can the French welfare system extend itself to encompass those "new social risks", and what kind of "new" social rights are supposed to be recognized and implemented?

This chapter aims to describe the current evolutions of the French welfare system and analyse its ability to create or extend social rights in response to new social risks. First, a brief description of the French path to welfare will be offered. The limitations of the traditional French approach to social risks will be noted. In particular, it will be shown how the underlying design of social rights, based as they are on socio-professional solidarities, has functioned to limit the scope of social protection. Second, the chapter will identify some of the so-called "new social risks", note how these are related to post-industrial society, and describe the emergence of new social policies in France that have sought to address those new social risks. The chapter then analyses the common features of the new social rights that accompany the new social risks. These rights are underpinned by a corpus of concepts and values which express a genuine axiological dimension: social action and social work must not only protect vulnerable individuals, but also promote their autonomy, dignity, participation rights and citizenship. The legal materials suggest that the new policies are, or should be, "person oriented", which is a substantial change compared to the classical approach, which considers the "recipient" as an abstract category. This change has consequences for the technical structure of the relevant social rights which appear to be more *procedural*: involving such things as assessment procedures, coaching, personalization and individual agreements. Finally, the chapter discusses the extent to which the French welfare system has been transformed by those new social policies and rights. It is observed that they have only resulted in a *partial* revolution, since the social protection system remains rather segmented and bureaucratic.

The French path to welfare

The French welfare system is basically a Bismarckian one that integrated Beveridgian views. Palier and Bonoli (1995) observe that "the French social security system, as created in 1945, aimed to fulfill Beveridge's goals with bismarckian means". This has posed some problems, chief amongst which is how to cover the whole population against social risks by means of social insurances deeply rooted in occupational solidarities. This is the French dilemma about the personal scope of application of the social security system. The French "social risks approach" to welfare led to two categories of social rights: strongly guaranteed social security rights, on the one hand, and weak or "poor" social assistance rights on the other. Therein lie the limits of the system.

The nature and scope of the National Social Security system

As Palier and Bonoli (1995) observe, the 1945 National Social Security system and the social security law were designed as a response to classical "industrial" social risks, through the institution of social insurance. The French legal vocabulary still refers to the notion of risk, stating that the Social Security system "guarantees workers and their families against all kinds of risks that may reduce or annihilate their earning capacities" (Art. L. 111–1 of the Social Security Code).

The French social security goals may appear rather ambiguous: from the beginning, social security has technically been focused on workers (and their families) while, simultaneously, expressing the will to protect the whole population. In his famous speech given in March 1945 at the *Ecole Nationale d'Organisation Economique et Sociale*, Pierre Laroque, a founder of the French Social Security system said: "Therefore, if this guarantee, in order to be really complete, must apply to all families, it must nevertheless be admitted that Social Security is first and foremost the security of workers, the security of the families that earn their living from the work of one or several of its members". Obviously, the system designed in 1945 assumed that every citizen should be directly or indirectly linked to employment. In addition, it should be noted that the idea of Laroque was to achieve a "social democracy", which meant that the system should not be managed by a bureaucratic (state) administration, but by the workers' (and employers') representatives themselves.

This looks like the typical "corporatist model", and according to the dominant interpretation, these social insurances can be considered as labour market institutions. As analysed by Esping-Andersen (1990), they are a form of welfare capitalism particularly suited to Fordism. In this system, social rights are employment-related and, from this point of view, one can consider this kind of welfare as producing a rather weak or partial de-commodification:[1] the social insurance system mainly provides workers and their families with monetary benefits, which compensate for loss of salary (social risks) and aim to maintain their level of income. As they are "earnings-related", they tend to reproduce social positions and labour market structures and inequalities.[2] This kind of analysis, however, needs to be qualified. The French social insurance system was not only designed to support people (workers) in cases of loss of salary due to the occurrence of a social risk such as sickness, maternity, occupational accident, unemployment, invalidity or old age; it was also intended to ensure access to medical care for (almost) the whole population and to provide generous benefits for those responsible for maintaining children.[3] As noted, the founders of the French Social Security system had the idea that social rights should be linked to employment, which supposes forms of solidarity based on transfers between the members of the (wide) community of the affiliated: all employees and the self-employed must necessarily be affiliated to a social security regime, which implies the payment of social contributions; students also have a duty of affiliation; the unemployed and pensioners are also affiliated under special conditions.

From a sociological perspective, Robert Castel talked about the "salary-based society" (*la société salariale*), describing the French path for welfare and social protection. He meant that, during the 20th century, or, at least until the 1980s, political, economic and social actors shared a common purpose which was to integrate the main part of society into the employment relationship so that social rights and forms of solidarity mainly derive from this legal and social form of relationship. Those social rights are considered by Castel (1995) as *social property*. Castel shows that the social rights granted to the workers by social legislation since the end of the 19th century have been a way to overcome the ancient opposition between (unprotected) labour and property (capital). He wrote: "social security arises from a kind of *transfer of property* through the mediation of labor and under the aegis of the State" (Castel 2003, p274; original emphasis). Another French sociologist, Bernard Friot (1998), however, disagrees with the dominant view about "welfare capitalism" and considers the French salary system – the "socialized salary" – as an anti-capitalistic project. According to Friot, under the Social Security system, employees are granted rights and guarantees which are not related to property, finance or inheritance, or to public aid, assistance or charity. In a rather paradoxical way, he states that some categories of people who do not belong to the labour market (civil servants, retired persons, carers, parents, and unemployed people) are nevertheless salaried as they participate in national production. To Friot, those categories of people are not inactive since they produce some economic value by paying social security contributions.

The dominant view in the French literature is that the current Social Security system is the result of a historical "social compromise", made after World War II, between labour market forces and actors – trade unions, employers' associations and, of course, the state – regarding the (rationalized) organization of economic production, which implied a strong degree of social solidarity. In this sense, the organization of French social protection can be analysed as a kind of neo-corporatism: the state provides the legal framework and makes mandatory the coverage by social insurances that are administered by the relevant social partners.[4] The social rights guaranteed in this way are "mediated" by the institutions of the labour market. Residually, the state and the local authorities directly cover the situations of need uncovered by the social security schemes (the social insurances): poverty, social exclusion, disabilities and so on.

Historically, the French social welfare model was built under the influence of the doctrine of *solidarism* developed at the end of the 19th century by Léon Bourgeois (1896). According to this doctrine, all human beings are linked to one another by mutual responsibility, so that everyone and, by extension, the society (the *Republic*, in Bourgeois's conception) has a duty to help and assist those in need or suffering misfortune. This doctrine helped to establish a legal basis for public social assistance and, later, underpinned a system of compulsory social insurance. This system, and the solidarity underpinning it, was organized through communities of affiliation, the main one being the community of workers. The French path to social solidarity – that is, solidarity faced with social risks – including social rights was therefore largely based on employment.

In reality, however, two circles of social solidarity have coexisted in France. At the core of the system are social security rights, which basically aim to provide people with monetary support (organizing an *economic security*) legitimated by their affiliation to socio-professional schemes. Those are contributory benefits "earned" by the worker's participation in the labour market and they aim to compensate for loss of salary or income. The mechanisms of Social Security are a mix of commutative and distributive justice, since benefits are generally earnings-based but are paid according to the recipients' needs. At the periphery of the system are social assistance rights based on "national solidarity": the duty of the nation to help "every human being who, as a consequence of old age or his physical or mental state, or of the economic situation, is unable to work", as stated by the Preamble to the French Constitution of 1946. It can be noted that this constitutional duty is reminiscent of the ancient idea of society's "sacred debt" towards "unfortunate citizens" unable to work, recognized by the Preamble to the Constitution of 1793. Social assistance rights are based on distributive solidarity rather than on social security contributions. Social assistance programmes provide people with means-tested benefits which are tax funded.

It is important to note that social assistance rights based on this extended notion of national solidarity – where the community of affiliation is the whole nation – were supposed to remain subsidiary ones. At the end of the 19th century, they were meant only to substitute for family duties under the civil law. After World War II, their purpose has become to repair some sorts of social maladjustment. The system organizes a dichotomy between people considered as *able* (to go to school, to work, to engage in family life) and those deemed to be *unable* (disabled persons, the elderly, problem children). Social assistance programmes play a subsidiary role for those who are not entitled to social security benefits and develop some specific social policies outside of the range of social risks covered by the social insurance system. Social assistance law grew and developed in this period (1950s–1970s) and was heavily structured by a vertical and categorical approach to beneficiaries: for each category of *unable* persons, there was a set of special rights, conditions, institutions and social services.

The limits of the system

This "social risks approach" led to a non-universal welfare system: only workers were directly entitled to social security rights, while their families were indirectly covered. French social security was conceived as an occupational social protection system, and its improvement was sought through an extension of the categories of potential beneficiaries entitled to indirect rights, rather than via a real universalization which would have been based on the recognition of citizenship rights. The ancient social assistance law, which continued to exist alongside the social security schemes, was modernized by the 1953 Act.[5] Social assistance and (local) social services are designed to respond to social needs – or wants in Beveridge's vocabulary – which are legally distinguished from social risks: means-tested rights and (tax-funded) benefits *versus* contributory social rights. Social assistance rights were supposed to play a subsidiary and residual role.

This system, as designed in 1945, has nevertheless had to cope with the significant economic and social transformations that have appeared in recent decades: high unemployment rates plus fundamental changes in family models seriously challenged the French welfare system which had to confront different forms of social exclusion. In fact, the social insurance system – and especially the sickness insurance scheme – failed to cover social categories such as the long-term unemployed, divorcees and lone parents. Socio-professional solidarities were not designed to deal with this growing "interstitial population". Before new forms of coverage were implemented (for instance, the Universal Health Coverage programme under the 1999 Act), those who were excluded from social security were only entitled to some form of "poor services", in reference to Titmuss's expression (1968) that "services for the poor end up being poor services" – adapted by Imbert (1989), who described the French contemporary "poor laws" (that is, social assistance law) as a system of "poor rights", meaning weak forms of protection.

Identifying and dealing with the "new social risks"

The use of the terminology of "social risks" and the reference to "new social risks" requires some explanation. First, it should be observed that the notion of social risk is more common in countries which have built their welfare system on the basis of social insurance, as shown by Ewald (1986) in his historical study of the French welfare state. Secondly, one should note that the notion of social risk – and *a fortiori* of new social risks – is not well defined from a legal point of view. In sociology, however, a rather abundant literature has tackled this theme, showing from a theoretical and historical point of view how welfare states have responded to social issues in industrial and post-industrial societies. Empirical studies highlight the policies implemented at national level which aim to cope with new social risks, especially arising from deindustrialization and as a result of ageing. In the case of France, I will illustrate how the political and legal framework adapts itself to the issues of poverty/social exclusion and long-term care.

New social risks and post-industrial societies

According to the sociological or socio-legal literature – we specifically refer here to Esping-Andersen et al (2002), Taylor-Gooby (2004) and Bonoli (2005, 2006) – the new social risks are those which appear in the context of deindustrialization, especially precarious employment, long-term unemployment, the working poor, and lone parents. Actually, the concept of new social risks is closely linked to the notion and theory of social exclusion. However, some authors such as Bonoli (2005) and Morel (2003) also consider long-term care (LTC) and social services for the elderly as "policies for the new social risks". It is clear that the risk of becoming functionally dependent in old age and to need help in the activities of daily living (ADL) is not related to ability/inability to work or to one's employment situation. LTC is not a typical industrial risk, such as occupational accident, sickness, maternity, unemployment or even old age (though it has to do with ageing). The need for LTC can be conceived as the risk of finding oneself in a situation of social and economic insecurity due to a loss of autonomy.

Theoretically, this "risk" could be covered by social security plans and some countries such as Germany, Austria, Luxembourg and Japan have included LTC in their system of social insurance. We can state that, if a social security response needs to be found for the elderly who lose their functional autonomy, it is because in such a situation, the economic load on the individual can quickly become unsustainable and the possibilities of family care (for free) in society are currently limited.

From a general point of view, the notion of new social risks raises the question of the peculiar vulnerability of some social groups or categories. Unlike the legal classification of the "classical" social risks covered by social security schemes, the features of the new social risks are not precisely determined; as Pollak (2011) notes, the notion refers to rather heterogeneous situations. Actually, it is not or not yet a legal notion; much more a *critical concept* used by researchers to describe the limits and crisis of the welfare state. From that perspective, the new social risks are all kinds of social situations that challenge the capacities of the Welfare state in terms of coverage. Basically, it concerns addressing the rise of inequalities and social exclusion, as well as the long-term needs of some categories of the population. As noted by Rosanvallon (1995), the classic social insurance system, based on non-predictable risks for individuals, is no longer valid. So, according to him, the point is to recognize new social rights that entitle citizens to a "right to inclusion", in which people participate in society and not only receive money and benefits. This assumption is nowadays widely shared by many academics, legal scholars included, such as Vielle who writes: "Nowadays, social risk is conceived in terms of 'poverty risk factors' and the State is expected to intervene upstream, through preventive and individualized measures, in order to limit the social risk occurrence" (Vielle 2014, p6).

New social policies in France: reforming the ancient social assistance approach

The two main social policies that illustrate this new framework for social action are the policy against poverty and social exclusion and the policies dealing with disabilities and long-term care. Local authorities are now in charge of vulnerable or frail populations: persons in precarious situations, the disabled and the dependent elderly. Though they are distinctive measures, those policies generally aim to help people recover autonomy. Indeed, it can be assumed that they both wish to tackle situations of deprivation that affect not only the material or functional autonomy of the individuals concerned, but also their social citizenship.[6] In those cases, people need a kind of *compensation*, not only in the form of monetary allowances, but also in the sense of personal support services that aim to facilitate access to fundamental social rights, freedoms, goods and services (for instance, the right to work, the right to healthcare, the right to education and culture, freedom of movement, the right to housing, to food and food security, and so on).

Poverty/social exclusion (RMI and RSA measures)

The French approach to poverty and social exclusion, with the RMI (revenu minimum d'insertion, 1988 Act) substituted by the RSA (revenu de solidarité active, 2009 Act), was a serious step toward renewal of the traditional French social model. Those new measures focused on individual situations and the provision of a range of adequate social services – meaning personalized services "packaged" through an assessment of individual needs and abilities rather than delivering "top down" monetary benefits to people legally entitled as elements of some abstract legal category (e.g., employed/unemployed; able to work/disabled).

The 1988 Act states that "every person who, because of age, mental or physical state, or the economic and labour market situation, finds him or herself unable to work, has a right to obtain from society suitable living conditions". This not only means that people in those situations have a right to receive a minimum allowance; the law creates a subjective right to "social inclusion", especially as far as employment, education, vocational training, health and housing are concerned. So the right takes the form of a mix of cash benefits (a differential minimum allowance) and personal guidance and support services. The main idea is that people must not be treated or considered as *assisted*, but as actors of their proper inclusion in society. This is the reason why, under the 1988 Act, the beneficiaries of the minimum income were supposed to sign an individual *contract for inclusion* that formalizes the mutual commitments of the recipient on the one hand, and the public authority on the other.

Even if the political discourse has more recently tended to emphasize the "rights and duties" dimension, and despite some inflexions of the legislation,[7] the French approach to poverty and social inclusion has nothing to do with *workfare*. It means that the poor do not have to deserve the financial aid they are granted and that society cannot force them to accept any kind of job in return for this aid. The legislation defines what a *reasonable job offer* must be in this case. The minimum income has been conceived as the economic condition required from national solidarity in order to help people remain included in society.

However, this measure has evolved from the former RMI to the current RSA. The management and funding of the minimum income and of the inclusion actions have been entirely transferred to local authorities (in 2003). Moreover, as the RMI, in practice, was more oriented toward *social* rather than *professional* inclusion, it appeared that it did not fit well with the European guidelines and strategies on employment and social inclusion. Indeed, when the Open Method of Coordination (OMC) for social inclusion was launched, after the Lisbon Summit in 2000, the main consensus among the European member states was that employment is not only a way to solve the problem of poverty and exclusion, but also a form of preventing these. The social inclusion OMC was designed to complement the European Employment Strategy so that the stress was put on "promoting labour market participation". This undoubtedly had an impact on the French approach to social inclusion. The 2003 Reform created an incentive for employers to employ beneficiaries of the RMI through a special contract of employment through which the employer was granted a portion of the allowance (RMI) due to the beneficiary. This measure was called "RMA", meaning *minimum income for activity*. So, the French model for inclusion adapted itself to the European requirements for active policies. This evolution was continued by the 2009 Reform which replaced the RMI by the RSA (active solidarity income). With this new measure, the government aimed to achieve two goals: orienting more people toward professional inclusion by strengthening the duty to search for a job, and supporting the *working poor* by making it possible to combine the allowance with a certain amount (62 per cent) of income from work. Despite the fact that this new policy did not fully achieve its goals – as a result of the economic crisis, a large proportion of RSA recipients remain unemployed – it is clear that it transformed the law. Individuals are now entitled to a right to personalized supports.

These new policies can be characterized as a third phase in the evolution of social assistance law. The old social security system – based on social insurance and socio-professional solidarity – was no longer able to function as a mechanism of inclusion and social cohesion, thereby potentially resulting in what Castel (1995) described as "social disaffiliation". Hence, a new paradigm had to be invented: social integration. The RMI is therefore not only a measure that provides indigent people with a minimum income; in order to maintain individuals' citizenship, it combines this with a process of social inclusion. It is a novel form of social intervention. Furthermore, when the issues of old age and long-term care appeared on the political agenda in the 1990s, there was much debate around whether to solve these problems by creating a novel form of a social security scheme (a specific form of social insurance) or not. Eventually, it was decided that the best solution would be a new tax-funded scheme created within the field of social assistance.

Disabilities and long-term care (APA and PCH)

Traditionally, French social assistance law was organized on the basis of categorical policies and sets of measures aimed at supporting specific populations (e.g., abandoned or "endangered" children; the elderly; the disabled). As far as the elderly and disabled people are concerned, until the end of the 1990s, social action was mainly aimed at providing minimum financial resources in order to protect these groups from poverty. Those benefits – the minimum old age allowance and the disability allowance for adults – were, and still are, managed and paid by national social security bodies, but belong to the sphere of social aid as they are means-tested and non-contributory. Thus, there was not much room for local social action and it was up to the local authorities to implement voluntary programmes and social services, such as home care.

A significant change occurred in 2001 with the creation of a new social allowance, known as the APA (Allocation Personnalisée d'Autonomie). People of 60 or more, needing help with daily living activities, can receive an allowance the amount of which is directly related to the degree of "dependence" (i.e., loss of the person's functional autonomy). This allowance is supposed to cover, fully or partially, the personal plan for autonomy, which is designed and proposed by the medico-social services and must be accepted voluntarily by the individual. This is a national, non-means-tested allowance managed by local authorities. In the same vein, the 11 February 2005 Act concerning the *equal rights and opportunities, participation and citizenship of disabled persons* creates a disability compensation benefit (*Prestation de Compensation du Handicap* (PCH)) which is more or less designed like the APA: it is a national allowance whose purpose is to financially support disabled people (under 60 years' old) who need personal and/or technical help with daily living activities. Assessment criteria, co-payment rules and maximum amounts of PCH are, however, distinct from those applicable to the APA. Disabled persons are cared for by local entities called *Maison départementale des personnes handicapées* (departmental centre for disabled persons) – public establishments acting under the control of the local authority (*Conseil départemental*).

The features of those new national allowances (APA and PCH) illustrate the evolution of French social action policies and law. They are national allowances conforming to the principle of equality, but they are locally managed (proximity = efficiency); however, they are not shaped as classical social assistance rights since they are not means-tested and not supposed to be recoverable by public authorities from the beneficiary's estate after his or her death. They are hybrid rights, in between social security benefits and traditional social assistance programmes. Both allowances aim to compensate for a loss of autonomy, and can be considered as a fundamental element of French long-term care policy. However, those measures remain segmented by the current legislation that has not yet unified the rules applicable to each category and the institutions in charge of personal support. One explanation is that, in France, long-term care policies have traditionally been structured on the basis of gerontology, so that the stress was placed on old age and on the concept of dependence due to ageing. A comparative overview (Martin 2014) shows that in most countries, the loss of autonomy is linked to the generic concept of disability and has nothing to do, legally, with age. However, in France, the right to the APA and, consequently, the right to the PCH are conditioned by the age of the beneficiary: the artificial threshold being 60. Though the 2005 Act had opened up the possibility of the convergence of both rights – some authors such as Elbaum (2008) speculating on the constitution of the so-called "fifth risk" – things have remained the same and the recent reform of the APA passed in December 2015 has not moved things forward. The reason is, sadly, a financial one: the maximum amount of PCH is higher than that of the APA, and the elderly in receipt of the APA are much more numerous than the disabled receiving the PCH, so that levelling both allowances upwards would be financially unsustainable.

In summary, the new framework for social and medico-social action was epitomized in the 2002 *Reform of Social Assistance and Medico-social Action Act.* Theoretically, social and medico-social action is no longer based on the distinction between the able and the unable. Even if the act speaks of categories such as vulnerable persons, the poor, the disabled, and the elderly, it is supposed to be based on "a continual assessment of the needs and expectations of the members of all social groups". This approach is also supposed to be more *horizontal*. Social and medico-social action involves state services, local authority services, social security bodies, associations and medico-social institutions (such as nursing homes). Besides, the beneficiaries are expected to play an active role in those measures, collectively (participation rights *via* the role of committees) and individually (personal plans and individual agreements). Technically, the benefits can be granted to people having a regular and permanent residence in France. Thus, in a way, those rights could be analysed as citizenship rights, though their founding principle is not that clear; as they are still influenced by social assistance concepts and techniques, they continue to be viewed as a legal response to particular states of need. Nevertheless, if one considers the goal of those measures, which is to help people recover a form of autonomy in society, the so-called "new rights" can be seen as the expression of social solidarity towards a new risk – namely, the loss of individual autonomy, which requires specific forms of social intervention and protection.

The features of the new social rights

The new social and medico-social action policies are underpinned by a corpus of concepts and values that express what is here called a genuine axiological dimension. Traditionally, social assistance aimed at protecting vulnerable people, such that social intervention was mainly designed as a form of tutorship (the "tutelary approach") and social rights were granted under social control. In contrast, the recent legislation places emphasis on dignity, autonomy, personalization and other principles, which ought to transform the framework and practices of social work. Those principles and values also have some technical implications for social rights in that the new rights tend to be *procedural* ones. This, however, has not resulted in a wholesale transformation of the bureaucratic system, or meant a total absence of social control.

Axiological principles and values embodied in the legislation

Some interesting axiological principles are to be found in the developments of the French legislation, especially the 2002 *Reform of Social Assistance and Medico-social Action Act*, and the 2005 *Equal Rights and Opportunities, Participation and Citizenship of Disabled Persons Act*. Those legal provisions contain and/or express concepts such as autonomy, dignity, empowerment, participation and citizenship, which are meant to guide social action – that is, not only local decisions and regulations but also the practices of social workers. Those principles are universal and are to be applied to all categories within the scope of social and socio-medical action (the unemployed entitled to the RSA, beneficiaries of the APA, of the PCH, etc.).

The 2002 Act (Art. 1) defines the goals of social and socio-medical action and states that the measures in favour of vulnerable persons must aim to promote and develop "autonomy and protection", "citizenship" and "social cohesion". It also states (Art. 2) that "medico-social action is based on the principle of equal respect for the dignity of all human beings and aims to respond adequately to the needs of each of them and to guarantee equal access across the whole (French) territory". Article 7 protects the individual rights and liberties of the person under the care of all kinds of medico-social institution, and especially respect for the following: dignity, private life, intimacy, personal security; freedom of choice (between the various tailored solutions that are proposed and offered to the individual); the right to participate, directly or indirectly, in the elaboration and implementation of the individual plan that is drawn up.

The 2005 Act specifically deals with representation of the disabled and participation in decision-making; the right to obtain solidarity from the nation; and equal access to fundamental rights and the full right to citizenship. Article 11 of the 2005 Act contains some provisions about the right to disability compensation. It states that: "The compensation requirements are expressed in an individual plan which is concerned with the needs and the wishes of the disabled person as they are expressed in his/her life project".

One may doubt the effectiveness of those fundamental rights in practice. Sociological and empirical studies tend to show that it will take time to achieve a total transformation of the traditional medico-social institutions (especially nursing homes). Placing the individual beneficiary of social benefits and services at the centre of social intervention involves a major change in the professional culture and practices of managers, professional carers, social workers, and so on. However, some changes can be noticed, partially due to the action of administrative bodies, which control and assess the activity of those institutions.[8]

The sense of the new principles of social action

Those legal provisions suggest that the new policies are, or should be, "person oriented", which is a substantial change compared to the classical approach, which considered the "recipient" as an abstract category. Social action is being transformed, but the sense of the transformation is still rather unclear for the actors (local authorities, social workers), so that analysis of the concepts of personalization, dignity and autonomy seems necessary.

Personalization is a rather ambiguous concept. In one sense, it can mean individualization of the social measures, services and benefits provided to vulnerable persons. And, effectively, the legislation has created a "tool box" for that purpose: assessment procedures in order to establish the individual's abilities, disabilities and needs; individual plans and personalized projects defining the actions, services and benefits that shall be provided to the beneficiary (or the actions expected of him/her, in the case of the RSA). Those plans require an agreement and this leads to a form of "contractualization" of the situation of the recipient, which is completely novel in French social law. But personalization can also be understood as "empowerment", which happens to be a fundamental concept in the new social policies regarding vulnerable or frail persons. This means that the law must protect the dignity, the autonomy, and the fundamental rights of those receiving social services and benefits. This implies freedom of choice – especially in the case of placement in nursing homes and other institutions – and participation rights: the right to be involved in the decision-making process which affects the individual. In practice, it will appear somewhat difficult to obtain clear consent – for instance, in the decision to admit a dependent elderly person into a nursing home – and it supposes a certain revolution in the way social agents and workers deal with those situations.

Dignity is a key concept in the contemporary development of fundamental rights at the international level. Basically, it means that people's physical and moral integrity have to be respected and protected. In the sphere of social and socio-medical action, it implies that recipients of benefits and services must be treated decently. One area where the issue of abuse or ill-treatment has come to prominence recently is the case of dependent elderlies placed in nursing homes. Recommendations and guidelines have been adopted and their purpose is to improve the quality of the services provided by the socio-medical institutions, especially the institutional nursing homes for dependent elderlies. It makes clear that the concept of dignity challenges the classic "tutelary approach" in the field of social assistance. Social workers and other professionals who provide help and services to dependent persons are not only supposed to protect them as vulnerable persons, but to respect their will and their personal choices, and finally, to treat them as citizens and equals.

Autonomy is consubstantial with dignity. Philosophically speaking, the individual is supposed to be autonomous, meaning that everyone is their own lawmaker. In practice, social workers have to cope with the issue of persons who may suffer mental disease or disorder, especially in the case of Alzheimer's. In these cases, the law tends to strike a balance between protection (legal forms of protection of incapable adults) and autonomy, so that freedom of choice and individual consent are always required as far as possible. But autonomy is also a goal: personal care is supposed to compensate for loss of functional autonomy, while simultaneously professional caregivers are asked to let the individual do what he/she can by him/herself. The role of the social worker is to stimulate the individual so that he/she can recover some kind of social autonomy.

The procedural character of the new social rights

As already noted, the new rights are universal ones, tax funded, set out under national legal rules and managed at the local level (decentralized policies) for better efficiency. But the major change, as compared with the *classical* system of social rights – that is, rights to social security benefits – is that the new social rights are designed through a process of proceduralization of the law.[9] First, the policies about social inclusion, disabilities and long-term care are "defined, conducted and evaluated through processes that ensure an effective participation of beneficiaries". Second, individual social rights – the rights to the RSA allowance and to the PCH and APA benefits – are supposed to be *produced* by a set of procedures and tools as an output of a formalized process in which contractualization plays an important role. The beneficiaries of the RSA must sign a "mutual commitment agreement" and disabled persons entitled to a "compensation plan" related to the PCH or APA benefits are supposed to express their will and their own life project. The current legislation emphasizes assessment procedures, coaching, personalization and individual agreements. In the new vocabulary of social policies and rights, we find expressions such as "healthcare circuit", "(social) care pathway", "pathway to integration", "individualized plan" and "agreements". This change has to do with the axiological frame of reference.

The new emerging social model obviously favours the subject and subjectivity. What is important is not being integrated into the collective norm as a worker or, failing that, being entitled to a form of monetary compensation. Rather, what is important is empowerment and personal capabilities, in the sense that the beneficiaries of the new social rights are theoretically actors in the construction of an individual *project* (of social integration with the RSA measure; of a life project with respect to the APA and PCH) suited to their abilities and – to a certain extent – to their will. Indeed, those procedures are meant to adapt and optimize the social and legal response to each individual case. The recipient – the user of social services – is placed at the centre of the system.

In practice, however, procedures also tend to be seen as a new form of social control, another kind of bureaucracy as defined by Weber (2013) and Crozier (1963), even if this assumption can be slightly qualified in the sense that some differences exist between inclusion policies through the RSA, and LTC policies for disabled and elderly people. In France, Robert Lafore (2004) described and analysed the effects of the transfer of responsibilities from the State to local authorities (*départements*) as regards social and socio-medical action. He wrote that the two faces of the *département* (i.e. as a regulator and manager of social services to individuals, and as the "mastermind of the inclusion policies") could possibly converge towards a control of individuals and excluded groups because of the current strong financial constraints. According to him, though the new social policies – focused on the user's rights and the quality of services – seek to dispense with the ancient tutelary forms of management (of poverty, exclusion, etc.), the traditional administrative habits could gradually return. As far as the RSA measure is concerned (social and professional inclusion and minimum income), the logic of activation implies new forms of control of the unemployed;[10] as regards LTC policies, empirical studies (INSERM, 2011) tend to show that individual plans are not truly contractual ones and that the individual is seldom "at the centre of the service"; they also show a low user participation rates. More recently, Lafore (2013) analysed French "local welfare" and noted that, rather than implementing universal policies and actions, the legislation had added "new segments" which implied new specialized administrative sectors, so that the traditional sectorial and vertical model is still significant. Finally, despite the trend

New social risks and new social rights   113

to make access to social rights more procedural and participative, what can be observed is resistance to change of the administrative structure which manages the so-called new social policies.

Conclusions: how far has French welfare been transformed?

This chapter has shown that new social rights have emerged in the French welfare system. The system's centre of gravity, which previously concentrated on social insurance, has partially shifted to the field of new social action policies dealing with social exclusion and loss of autonomy. Those new policies and rights have interesting characteristics: they are more procedural and based on universal benefits. In a way, one could imagine a global transformation towards a more flexible and democratic system of social rights, based on a collective identification of the social needs of the population (addressed by various actors such as the State, local authorities, social security bodies and citizens' associations), an individual assessment and a personalized assistance plan including monetary benefits and social services. This model seeks to dispense with the ancient division between social risks and social needs that has traditionally structured the French system: (national) social security rights, on the one hand, and (local) social assistance rights, on the other.

However, one can observe that the French social protection system remains rather segmented. As far as poverty and long-term unemployment are concerned, they continue to have different legal statuses, constructed in the classical "vertical way": the unemployed entitled to unemployment benefits scheme (UBS); the long-term unemployed no longer entitled to the UBS but covered, instead, by a substitutive tax-funded scheme; beneficiaries of the minimum income entitled to social inclusion programmes; and beneficiaries of the minimum income entitled to professional support programmes. This segmentation is partially due to the coexistence of contributory and non-contributory schemes; but it is also the result of assessment procedures that are supposed to individualize social and legal treatment.[11] In theory, the system should be flexible, so that people can easily move from one category to another; but in practice, this does not seem to happen, as shown by empirical studies (DARES, 2013). In addition, it has to be said that the system is very complex and remains rather bureaucratic, which explains the phenomenon of non-use or renunciation of social rights, especially the RSA, noted by the ODENORE (Observatory on Non-Take Up of Social Rights and Public Services) and Warin (2007). As far as LTC is concerned, French social policies remain segmented by the age criteria: two different legal statuses, one for the disabled and another for dependent elderlies aged 60 and above. The government is perfectly aware of this situation, but the current reform seems to fall short of the goal of unification.

Moreover, theoretically, the new social rights system contains a promise of democratization of public action through the dynamics of the proceduralization of law. This new approach could replace the former model of social democracy imagined by Pierre Laroque and embodied in the social security organization but

Notes

that has progressively succumbed to statism and bureaucracy (as described by Martin 2013). However, it is not clear whether the management of the so-called "reformed social assistance" policies and measures achieves the goals provided by the new legal framework. Nevertheless, and despite the difficulties of radically transforming the former Bismarckian system, the new rights, because they embody core values such as personal autonomy, dignity, participation, and citizenship, are certainly a vehicle for transforming social work. Finally, really significant change could be driven by a "bottom-up" movement, combined with a progressive reform of the system's legal and institutional structures.

Notes

1　De-commodification is defined by Esping-Andersen as the degree to which welfare states weaken the "cash nexus" by granting entitlements independent of market participation.
2　The author of "The three worlds" considers that the continental European welfare systems, qualified as corporatist and statist, are modestly de-commodifying.
3　French family benefits have mainly been funded by a social contribution exclusively paid by employers. This means that social security benefits are not necessarily to be seen as a *counterpart* of the contributions paid by employees. They are, instead, a "socialised salary".
4　Neo-corporatism can be defined as a form of tripartism made up of triangular relationships between the state, the employers' organizations and the trade unions. In this model, the state plays a prominent role as it must create the relevant "neo-corporatist arrangements". On neo-corporatism in the French social security organization, see Jabbari (2012).
5　The 1953 Act (*Décret* of 29 November 1953) changes the vocabulary: the term "social assistance" is substituted by the notion of *social aid*, considered as more in keeping with human dignity. It codifies the former legislation and organizes more systematically the social goals of public authorities on the basis of four "pillars": protection of the children "in danger" (*childhood protection*); aids and services for the elderly; aids and services for the disabled; and social action for families.
6　The notion of social citizenship was first highlighted by Marshall (1950). Here, it is referred to in the sense of full participation in society.
7　The "RSA and inclusion policies Reform" Act 2008 has hardened the process and those who refuse to sign the contract for social inclusion or the individualized plan for professional inclusion can, after a certain period, have the payment of the allowance suspended.
8　Some of these actions can be coercive (the local health agencies monitor the activities of nursing homes); some are more educational (a national agency is in charge of drawing up recommendations, codes and guides for good practice).
9　Proceduralization of the law is a rather controversial concept in the theory of law. We mainly refer, here, to Habermas's works. See Habermas (1984, 1996).
10　With "Active Solidarity Income" (RSA), national solidarity towards the socially excluded is "activated" in the sense that social services aim to help those people to return to the labour market. However, according to the legislation, the recipient of benefits and services also has a duty to be *active* and must prove that he or she is taking steps to find a job or, at least, to improve his or her capacity for social (re)integration.
11　The recipients of the RSA are supposed to be assessed through an individual interview. Depending upon the outcome of this, they will either fall under the Employment

Public Service or be managed by social workers (social inclusion guidance). In the latter case, social guidance should only be temporary and lead to professional inclusion measures.

References

BONOLI, G. (2005) The politics of new social policies: coverage against new social risks in mature welfare states, *Policy and Politics*, 33 (3). pp431–449.

BONOLI, G. (2006) New Social Risks and the Politics of Postindustrial Social Policies. In ARMINGEON, K. and BONOLI, G. (eds). *The politics of postindustrial welfare states.* London: Routledge.

BORGETTO, M. and LAFORE, R. (2000) *La République sociale. Contribution à l'étude de la question démocratique en France.* Paris: PUF.

BOURGEOIS, L. (1896) *Solidarité.* Paris: Armand Colin.

CASTEL, R. (1995) *Les métamorphoses de la question sociale, une chronique du salariat.* Paris: Fayard.

CASTEL, R. (2003) *From Manual Workers to Wage Laborers: Transformation of the Social Question.* New Brunswick, NJ and London: Transaction Publishers.

CROZIER, M. (1963) *Le phénomène bureaucratique.* Paris: Le Seuil.

DARES (2013) *L'accompagnement des bénéficiaires du RSA.* Analyses, DARES (Ministère de l'Emploi), No. 008.

ELBAUM, M. (2008) Les réformes en matière de handicap et de dépendance: peut-on parler de cinquième risque? *Droit social*, 11. pp1091–1102.

ESPING-ANDERSEN, G. (1990) *The three worlds of welfare capitalism.* Cambridge: Polity Press.

ESPING-ANDERSEN, G. (1999) *The Social Foundations of Postindustrial Economies.* Oxford: Oxford University Press.

ESPING-ANDERSEN, G., GALLIE, D., HEMERIJCK, A. and MYLES, J. (2002) *Why we need a new Welfare State.* Oxford: Oxford University Press.

EWALD, F. (1986) *L'Etat providence.* Paris: Grasset.

FRIOT, B. (1998) *Puissances du salariat. Emploi et protection sociale à la française.* Paris: La dispute.

GUILLEMARD, A.-M. (2010) *Les défis du vieillissement. Age, emploi, retraite, perspectives internationales.* Paris: Armand Colin.

HABERMAS, J. (1984) *Theory of communicative action.* Boston, MA: Beacon Press.

HABERMAS, J. (1996) *Between facts and norms.* Cambridge, MA: MIT Press.

ILO (International Labour Organisation) (1952) *Convention Concerning Minimum Standards of Social Security*, No. 102.

IMBERT, P.-H. (1989) Droits des pauvres, pauvres droits? Réflexions sur les droits économiques, sociaux et culturels, *Revue de droit public et de science politique*, 3. pp739–766.

INSERM (2011) *Qualité de mise en œuvre de l'APA à domicile.* Final Report, MiRE/Ministère des Affaires Sociales.

JABBARI, E. (2012) *Pierre Laroque and the welfare state in postwar France.* Oxford: Oxford University Press.

LAFORE, R. (2004) La décentralisation de l'action sociale. L'irrésistible ascension du département providence, *Revue Française des Affaires Sociales*, 4. pp17–34.

LAGRAVE, M. (2008) Hommage à Pierre Laroque à l'occasion du centenaire de sa naissance, *Revue française des affaires sociales*, 1. pp151–163.

LAFORE, R. (2013) Où en est-on du département providence? *Informations sociales*, CAF, 5. pp12–27.

MARSHALL, T. H. (1950) Citizenship and Social Class and Other Essays. Cambridge: Cambridge University Press.

MARTIN, P. (2013) The Role of Non Public Actors in French Social Security: The New Features of Solidarity. In PENNINGS, F., ERHAG, T. and STENDAHL, S. (eds). *Non Public Actors in Social Security Administration. A Comparative Study*. Alphen aan den Rijn: Wolters Kluwer.

MARTIN, P. (2014) La dépendance comme risque social. Un éclairage par les comparaisons internationales. In Martin, P. (ed) *La dépendance des personnes âgées, un défi pour l'Etat social*. Bordeaux: PUB.

MOREL, N. (2003) Providing coverage against new social risks in Bismarckian welfare states: the case of long term care, ESPAnet inaugural Conference Changing European Societies – The Role for Social Policy, Copenhagen, 13–15 November 2003, Danish National Institute of Social Research.

PALIER, B. (2002) *Gouverner la sécurité sociale. Les réformes du système français de protection sociale depuis 1945*. Paris: PUF.

PALIER, B. and BONOLI, G. (1995) Entre Bismarck et Beveridge "Crises" de la sécurité sociale et politique(s), *Revue française de science politique*, 4. pp668–699.

POLLAK, C. (2011) Essai d'approche positive des nouveaux risques sociaux, *Travail et Emploi*, 125. pp67–77.

ROSANVALLON, P. (1995) *La nouvelle question sociale. Repenser l'Etat-providence*. Paris: Éditions de Seuil.

TAYLOR-GOOBY, P. (2004) *New risks, New Welfare: The Transformation of European Welfare State*. Oxford: Oxford University Press.

TITMUSS, R. (1968) *Commitment to welfare*. London: George Allen and Unwin Ltd.

VIELLE, P. (2014) *Sustainable work: the role of social systems with regard to men and women's careers, including cover for risks over their life course*. Report for EUROFOUND.

WARIN, P. (2007) *L'accès aux droits sociaux*. Grenoble: Presses Universitaires de Grenoble.

WEBER, M. (2013) *Economy and society*. Berkeley, CA: University of California Press.

Chapter 6

Asylum seekers, social rights and the rise of new nationalism
From an inclusive to exclusive British welfare state?

Katie Bales

Introduction

Over the last two decades the social entitlements of those seeking refuge within the United Kingdom (UK) have been dramatically altered to reflect a growing political consensus that citizens' rights should be prioritized over the rights of the asylum seeking community (Bales 2013). As a result, asylum seekers' access to work is now severely restricted and they are supported through a separate welfare benefits system that grants weekly cash payments at approximately half the level afforded to national citizens. Despite a wealth of non-governmental organization (NGO) data documenting the serious negative effects of the asylum support system including poverty, malnutrition and depression (Refugee Action 2010; Teather et al 2013; Carnet et al 2014), the UK government continues to implement restrictive policies upon the asylum-seeking community, most recently evidenced by the government's reduction in support rates for children via the Asylum Support (Amendment No 3) Regulations 2015, SI 2015/1501 and the complete withdrawal of support from failed asylum-seeking families who refuse to return under Part 5 of the Immigration Act 2016. The overarching justification for these restrictions is that "people that have not established the right to be in the UK should not have access to welfare provisions on the same basis as those whose citizenship or status gives them an entitlement" (Home Office 1998, para. 8.18). Immigration status as opposed to need is thus the key factor in determining access to means tested benefits within the UK. This chapter's objective is to make sense of this discrepancy between the social rights of citizens and those of asylum seekers using the conceptual lens of nationalism. Though social exclusion on the basis of national origin and citizenship is often explored within academia (Benhabib 2004; Morris 2003, 2009; Anderson 2013), this chapter seeks to advance the literature by building upon the idea that social provisions serve as a marker of national identity. As a result, changes to welfare state policies can lead to different conceptions of "nation" which serve to reinforce social exclusion and the othering of specific groups such as asylum seekers.

Through examining the role of nationalism within the contemporary and post-World War II British welfare state, this chapter will argue that our concept of "nation" has radically altered over the last century. This is partly due to the dismantling of the welfare state, which constitutes both a product, and a source, of national solidarity. The changing nature of both welfare and our construct of "nation" is thus claimed to have contributed to the marginalization of the asylum seeking community, who have been categorized as "exploitative, criminal and bogus ... seeking only to abuse ... soft-touch Britain" (Schuster and Bloch 2002, p397). Though the chapter acknowledges that exclusion has always been a pervasive feature of welfare provision, it argues that the realignment of welfare politics from communal to individualistic policies has intensified social divisions amongst communities. Accordingly, Delanty (1996) believes that increasing individualism has led to an "exclusive" form of nationalism which focuses upon the internal problems of the state and the withdrawal of social rights from "undeserving" groups such as immigrants. Delanty notes, however, that this construct of nationalism is very different from our understanding of nationalism after WWII, which is credited within much of the literature as solidifying our concept of the British nation and generating a sense of solidarity amongst previously disparate classes, including non-citizen groups. It is these notions of the "inclusive" post-WWII nation and the "exclusive" contemporary nation which the chapter explores in an attempt to understand why the social rights of asylum seekers have regressed over the last two decades and how these changes relate to the shifting political ideologies of the collective and neo-liberal welfare state.

As there is no single definition of nationalism, the chapter will begin by examining relevant literature on the concept of "nation". Drawing on authors such as Gellner (1983), Miller (1995, 2008), Béland (2005), Béland and Lecours (2008), the chapter will suggest that the idea of nation is defined by a combination of subjective and objective factors. Objective criteria such as shared culture, race or institutional features of the state are not, therefore, automatic triggers of identity or nationalist sentiment as shared characteristics must also exist alongside subjective and mutual recognition (Miller 1995, p22). The nation is therefore an "imagined community" (Anderson 2006) which is created and sustained by active thought processes and engagement. Applying this broad definition of nationalism, the chapter will then discuss the differences between our understanding of "nation" and "citizenship" which, quite simply, acts as a link between the territorial and institutional structures of the state and the nation residing within it. The second and third sections of this chapter will contrast the meaning of nationalism within the post-WWII and contemporary welfare state with a view to assessing how different constructs of nation can contribute to inclusive and exclusive welfare policies. The final section of the chapter will offer some conclusions regarding the significance of nationalism within welfare provision and whether our changing understanding of nation is partly responsible for the increasing restrictions placed upon the social rights of asylum seekers. Throughout the chapter the term "asylum seeker" will refer to anyone seeking protection in the form of refugee status or humanitarian protection who has not received a final determination of their claim, as defined by section 94(1) of the Immigration and Asylum Act 1999.

Social rights and the nexus of nation, state and citizenship

Nationalism is an ambiguous concept. Although currently within the UK, the concept of nationalism appears to be synonymous with anti-immigration policy, Nigel Farage and the UK Independence Party (UKIP), the theory of nationalism goes beyond the popular misgivings of the far right and is rooted in our understanding of "nation", community and social solidarity. Indeed a number of authors write that nationalism is intrinsic to the establishment and maintenance of social institutions such as the welfare state (Tamir 1993; Miller 1995; Keating 1996; Taylor 1996; Miller 2008; Johnston et al 2010) which, in turn, enabled the state to win the loyalty of its people (Halfmann 2000; McEwen 2002). Before fully examining the numerous features of nationalism, it is important to distinguish between a number of distinct but interlinked terms, those being: nation, state and citizenship. This relationship is important as numerous legal entitlements flow from the status of citizenship, though, by definition, these entitlements do not extend to non-citizens such as asylum seekers. Accordingly, the nexus between nation, state and citizenship is important when analysing the ways in which the concept of "nation" serves to exclude disparate groups from accessing social benefits.

The term "state", in its most simplistic construction, refers to an institutional body that claims legitimate force over a specific geographical area, such as the UK. When one refers to the "nation state", the emphasis is upon an alliance between the nation residing within a specific territory and the legal and political institutions of the state, a link that is becoming increasingly tenuous within the UK following the 2015 General Election and the rise of the Scottish National Party. Where national and state boundaries coincide an institutional scheme of democratic and political co-operation is imposed upon the nation. In order to enjoy uninhibited rights of entry to the state and abode within it, alongside a number of other civil, political and social rights, an individual must either possess or acquire the status of citizen. "Citizenship" is therefore a legal and formal status afforded to persons either automatically by descent or birth within the UK, or through the means of registration or naturalization as per section 1 of the British Nationality Act 1981. Aside from the legal definition, citizenship is also regarded within social theory as a status bestowing rights in exchange for civic responsibilities and obligations (Marshall 1950) – a theory that will be explored later in the chapter.

Consequently, formal citizenship differs from the concept of "nation", which is not legally defined but rather an identity delineated on the basis of common objective and subjective criteria recognizing that a nation is "animated not only by a sense of togetherness but also by a belief in a common destiny supported by an overarching identity" (Béland and Lecours 2008, pp15–16). Nation, however, remains linked to the concept of citizenship as citizenship status acts as a formal link between the institutions of the state and the nation. Of course not all citizens would classify themselves as nationals of the state (and vice versa) due to the different ways in which citizenship can be attained, but this does not undermine the institutional link as most citizens will also be nationals, or from nations residing within, the state. As mentioned earlier, in defining a "nation", both objective criteria and the subjective opinions of a community are central. This is elaborated upon by Gellner who claims that "nations maketh a man", asserting that shared characteristics alone are meaningless in the absence of shared recognition (1983, p7). Similarly, Miller (1995) claims that nations are "imagined communities" which rely upon collective acts of imagination and belief that can be expressed through different media such as newspapers, books, songs and television. Consequently, when individuals identify themselves as belonging to a particular nation, they imply that those who are included as co-nationals share that belief and reciprocate the commitment.

The common objective characteristics of a nation are often linked to the following: a shared history amongst peoples; ethnicity; a defined homeland; and/or a common language or religion. Common feeling may also arise from a consensus on political or constitutional principles such as belief in democracy, individual liberty and the rule of law (principles that the current Conservative Government have equated with "British values") (HM Government 2015, p2), or from social institutions such as the welfare state. Accordingly, Béland and Lecours (2008, p24) contend that social provisions are now an established identity marker for national identity, recognizing that social policy:

> ... can serve to establish identity distinctiveness in a different manner from, but parallel to, culture and/or history. Like culture, social policy can be treated and articulated by national leaders as symbols of wider sets of values, social priorities, and political culture.

The creation of social policy is regarded as a process of "nation-building" as it fosters an alliance between nation and state (Béland and Lecours 2008, p22). This is also acknowledged by Bommes and Geddes who note that the sovereignty of nation states over a given population was, and still is, based on the exchange of the political provision of welfare in return for the internal loyalty of its citizens (2000, p1). As such, the prevailing understanding of welfare provision in the relevant literature is that it arises as a product of national solidarity whilst mutually re-enforcing our concept of "nation". The significance of this conclusion is that as the political ideology of the welfare state mutates, so too will our construction of national identity.

Consequently, Delanty cites the erosion of the collective welfare state alongside changes to family life, work, and Europeanization as the primary factors shaping the creation of a new form of nationalism (2008, p686). A reduction in state interventionist welfare policies and a move towards individualism is therefore considered to be responsible for greater levels of social discontent, as although neo-liberal reforms have given more autonomy to workers, they have also generated greater feelings of insecurity as the possibility of downward mobility is ever present. Delanty contends that this new form of nationalism manifests itself in identity politics and the rhetoric of "everyday racism" which shifts from prejudice regarding race or colour to prejudice based on protecting jobs and concerns over welfare benefits and cultural difference (2008, p677). From this perspective, the increasing exclusion of immigrants from social programmes can be attributed to the forces of new nationalism which pursues strategies of exclusion, as distinguished from post-WWII nationalism which Delanty regards as "inclusive" (1996, para. 2.1). Institutionally within the UK, the retraction of social rights from asylum seekers over the last three decades appears to support this theory as the group has moved from a position of equality with national citizens (receiving income support at 90 per cent of the rate afforded to national citizens under regulation 21 of the Income Support (General) Regulations 1987, SI 1987/1967) to a separate "asylum" support system that grants support at approximately 50 per cent of the rate afforded to national citizens, as per the Asylum Support (Amendment No 3) Regulations 2015, SI 2015/1501.

Yet, although Delanty's theory rests upon the idea that the British nation is becoming increasingly "exclusive" and unwilling to accommodate social rights claims from outsiders, exclusion as a prerequisite of social solidarity is a well-recognized phenomenon. Indeed, De Beer and Koster (2010, p22) point out that if solidarity were extended to the global population it may not constitute solidarity at all as "an often neglected consequence of solidarity is that the inclusion of those people who belong to the circle of solidarity inevitably means the exclusion of others who fall outside this circle". Similarly, Miller believes that once a national community is established, special obligations arise between fellow co-nationals which are exclusive of the obligations owed to wider humanity (1995, p49). The "special obligations" arising from a shared nationality are then institutionalized and translated into the rights and obligations that attach to citizenship status (Miller 1995, p71). Though Miller acknowledges that citizens may not always be nationals of the state, he notes that the majority of citizens would recognize their common obligations as arising from a common nationality which is extended to non-nationals through their assimilation (1995, pp71–4). Hence, Miller argues that the practice of citizenship would be very different if it were not tempered by the bonds of nationality which creates a social solidarity amongst citizens. Were the bonds of nationality to be removed from this scenario, Miller believes that solidarity would rest upon a strict relationship of reciprocity alone, providing strong ethical reasons for co-ordinating the boundaries of citizenship and nationality so that co-operation and redistribution are afforded on the basis of more than just rational self-interest (1995, p73). In agreement, Taylor writes that in order to prevent inequality, states must be able to create redistributive policies requiring a high degree of mutual commitment amongst members demanding "much greater solidarity towards compatriots than toward humanity in general" (1996, p120). Much literature therefore indicates that exclusion on the basis of nationality is a necessary condition of successful redistributive policies. Such a notion confirms that our concept of nation is mutually reinforced by welfare state policies whilst also constituting a foundation upon which welfare state policies are built. In order to better understand the role of nationalism in forming inclusive or exclusive social policies, the remainder of this chapter will explore how our construct of nation has developed over the last century. Beginning with an examination of early 20th-century welfare provisions and then the post-WWII welfare state, the chapter will consider the significance of these periods in shaping our sense of nation and the national willingness to extend social rights to non-citizens. Discussion will then move to the impact of Margaret Thatcher's election in 1979 and the imposition of neo-liberal welfare reforms which, as numerous authors suggest (Hall 1983; Jessop et al 1988; Marquand 1988; Delanty 1996, 2008; McEwen 2002), resulted in the retrenchment of the post-WWII welfare state and the transformation of the British "nation". Charting the development of the British nation in this way, the chapter will analyse whether we have moved from an inclusive to exclusive form of nationalism to the detriment of the asylum seeking community, who face increasing restrictions upon their social rights.

Inclusion, exclusion and the development of the post-WWII "nation"

Pre-WWII mechanisms of exclusion

Although this chapter contends that neo-liberal reforms to the post-WWII welfare state have contributed to a new and exclusive form of nationalism, reflection upon early redistributive arrangements within Britain shows that exclusion on the basis of nationality or residency was commonplace. Exclusive social legislation can be traced back to the Poor Relief Act of 1662 which introduced settlement regulations as a form of protection against the costs of the wandering poor. Under this Act individual parishes were responsible for the payment of poor law relief but only to their "own" population which meant that strangers could be removed within 40 days of their arrival, aimed at appeasing local rate payers who were anxious to keep poor law costs down (Fraser 2009, p41). The immigration controls of the early 20th century, implemented via the Aliens Act of 1905, also rested upon the notion that social rights should not be extended to foreign nationals, who were categorized as "undesirable" if they were unable to support themselves or if they were likely to become a charge upon the state. Reflecting the political rhetoric of the period, Conservative MP William Evans Gordon stated in 1902:

> Not a day passes but English families are ruthlessly turned out to make room for foreign invaders. [...] It is only a matter of time before the population becomes entirely foreign. [...] The working classes know that new buildings are erected not for them but for strangers from abroad.
>
> (Cohen 2003, p81)

Accordingly, when the Liberal Government (1905–1915) introduced the first two major pieces of modern social legislation – the Old Age Pensions Act of 1908 and the National Insurance Act of 1911 – immigrants were prevented from accessing pensions and health insurance due to residency and nationality requirements. These policies primarily affected Jewish refugees and are regarded by Cohen as "particularly vicious" given that national insurance was contribution based (1985, p74). Cohen thereby contends that the early social legislation of the 1905 Liberal government "legitimised welfare as a nationalistic and racist concept" (2003, p90).

The idea that social rights should be an exclusive privilege of citizenship was also carried into the post-WWII period by theorists such as Marshall who considered "social rights" to be the final endowment of citizenship status, following the granting of civil and political rights. For Marshall, social rights embodied "the right to a modicum of economic welfare and security" enabling one "to live the life of a civilized being according to the standards prevailing in society", which could be realized through access to the welfare state (1950, p11). Accordingly, Marshall interpreted the state's redistributive obligations as being tantamount to the realization of the structural implications of citizenship which acted as "an empowering project forthe disadvantaged and excluded classes" (Bommes and Geddes 2000, p2). Within Marshall's work, however, no reference is made to non-citizens and although the reasons behind this remain unclear, his failure to acknowledge their status means that his vision of citizenship is "ill prepared for the question of how to include aliens in the community" (Halfmann 2000, p42). Yet despite the creation of exclusionary social policies such as the Old Age Pensions Act 1908, and Marshall's influential theories of citizenship, the institutional arrangements of the post-WWII welfare state did not distinguish between citizen and non-citizen claimants. As a result, Delanty considers the post-WWII nation to be one that was "inclusive" and based on a strong sense of national identity. Though strong nationalism may appear antithetical to an inclusive national community, the literature surrounding the post-war period suggests that this form of nationalism was built upon collectivism and shared responsibility which contributed to a more receptive, inclusive nation.

The post-WWII "nation"

Miller writes that often nationality plays a fairly peripheral role in life and may only be evoked or displayed in the wake of an exceptional event such as armed conflict or natural disaster. In such instances even those that profess their indifference to nationality in normal circumstances are likely to discover their sense of national identity, as their well-being is closely bound to that of the community (1995, p15). This assertion is supported by many post-WWII writers such as Titmuss (1950), who records that WWII triggered a collectivist feeling of British solidarity leading to the creation of the post-war welfare state. Similarly, Sullivan asserts that this post-war solidarity was fostered through a high degree of equality and shared misery caused by the conflict and wartime policies such as the rationing of food and clothing, which were applied to all within the UK regardless of class (1996, p32). During this period economic levelling was also taking place via a high tax on personal income, a reduction in levels of inflation, and the fact that the war had significantly reduced unemployment as the previously unemployed became service men and women, producing weapons and other necessary equipment (Sullivan 1996, p33). As the hazards of war carried little social discrimination, government assistance for the rebuilding of homes and other services was offered to all as a means of rebuilding the community. In addition to economic factors, the war also led to the mixing of different social classes as individuals from different backgrounds were brought together for protection in air raid shelters or via the comradery of the armed forces. Accordingly, "the mood of the people changed and, in sympathetic response, values changed as well. If dangers were to be shared, then resources should also be shared" (Titmuss 1950, p56). The result was the election of the Clement Attlee Labour Government (1945–1951) and the creation of the British welfare state which embodied three elements of Esping Andersen's (1990) ideal-type: work related social insurance combined with both conditional (means tested) and universal benefits which sought to relieve the conditions of poverty experienced by previous generations, thereby operating as "an attack upon Want" (Beveridge 1942, p6). Consequently, collectivist feeling amongst the British public was utilized by policy-makers in establishing new systems of social security, the redistributive nature of which was depicted as a profound national tie and a substantive bond between citizens (Keating 1996, p20; Béland and Lecours 2008). It is perhaps then no accident that the three primary pieces of welfare legislation following the election of the post-war Labour Government – the National Insurance Act 1946, the National Health Service Act 1946 and the National Assistance Act 1948 – contained the word "national" in their titles (McEwen 2002). Contrasting the post-WWII welfare state with the reforms made under Margaret Thatcher's government, Jessop et al build upon the idea of a distinctly inclusive national welfare state where "no fundamental antagonism between the different classes was implied. All were actual or potential members of one nation" (1988, p88). Soysal substantiates this position by claiming that whilst attempting to correct the social inequalities caused by a capitalist market, the post-WWII welfare state "evolved as an empowering project for the disadvantaged and excluded classes" (2012, p2). With regards to the post-WWII period, the notion that state welfare fostered a collective and "inclusive" sense of nation (Delanty 1996) also extends beyond academic commentary as reflected in the eligibility requirements for accessing social provisions and, thereby, social rights. Accordingly, under the National Assistance Act 1948 and the National Health Service Act 1946, mere presence within the state was sufficient for qualification meaning that asylum seekers and refugees were able to access benefits and services on the same terms as national citizens. In this way, the post-war welfare state broke away from the previous nationalist restrictions imposed upon Jewish refugees under the Old Age Pensions Act 1908 and the National Insurance Act 1911. Discrimination on the basis of nationality, however, remained pervasive, even during the "glory years" of the Keynesian welfare state. This is because although access to social rights appeared universal, the entry of foreign applicants remained restricted by the immigration controls of the Alien Acts of 1905 and 1920 and the Aliens Order 1953, which permitted immigration officers to exclude individuals if they were considered "undesirable" due to their likely charge upon the state. Though this restricted foreign nationals' entry, refugees gained protection from the non-refoulement provision contained in Article 33 of the Convention Relating to the Status of Refugees 1951, which prevented the expulsion of foreigners where to do so would risk their persecution. From an internal perspective the post WWII welfare state could thus be considered inclusive as anyone within the state was eligible to receive benefits. Exclusion was prevalent however at the border of the nation state meaning that the post-WWII era was certainly not devoid of the insider/outsider binary.

The continued division of citizens and foreign nationals during the post-WWII period comes as no surprise to Cohen (1985) and Bakshi et al (1995) who regard such distinctions as an inevitable consequence of a social system built upon "nationhood" and British supremacy. Indeed, the Beveridge report, which is widely regarded as one of the founding documents of the post-WWII welfare state, acknowledges the importance of sustaining the British race, noting that "in the next thirty years housewives as mothers have vital work to do in ensuring the adequate continuance of the British Race and British Ideals in the World" (1942, p117). Such literature suggests that feelings of superiority and exclusion permeated the formal immigration arrangements of the territorial state, which sought to exclude those who were "undesirable" at the border. Having gained entry, such sentiments also existed at an informal level in the guise of public ill-feeling towards non-citizen groups within the state. Although levels of immigration were relatively low throughout the 1950s, an appeal for immigrants of "good stock" saw a rise in newcomers from Europe and the commonwealth countries, resulting in a rapid increase of the non-white immigrant population (National Archive 2015). Bakshi et al (1995) assert that this recruitment of ex-colonial labour enabled the expansion of the welfare state by keeping public sector wages to a minimum which would have been contested by the white unionized working class. In turn, this facilitated the upward movement of white labour into higher skilled and better paid employment, "reinforcing the political, cultural and economic segregation of the post-war workforce" (Bakshi et al 1995, p1546). Despite the resultant benefits from increased levels of Commonwealth migration to the UK, demands for tighter immigration controls emerged alongside increased levels of racism towards the black community, based upon the white population's perceived threat "to their own rising patterns of social and private consumption" (Bakshi et al 1995, p1547). Consequently, the Commonwealth Immigration Act 1962 was introduced. This sought to curb immigration from Commonwealth countries by introducing a limited number of work vouchers for prospective immigrants.

Though this policy and the existence of the Aliens Acts contradicts the notion of the "inclusive" post-WWII nation, the literature surrounding this period indicates a strong sense of British nationhood based upon a collective political ideology aiming to eliminate "want" from separate class groups. Post-war nationalism was therefore introspective in the sense that it was built upon a strong sense of British identity. Despite exclusionary border controls and the continuation of xenophobic attitudes towards Jewish refugees and black Commonwealth citizens, the social institutions of the post-WWII welfare state remained open to non-citizens, who were able to access social rights equivalent to those granted to national citizens. The exact reasons for these universal policies remains unknown but it is logical to assume that their neutrality resulted from the collective feeling of solidarity prevalent after WWII, which led to the pooling of risks amongst the national community. Indeed, Goodall claims that the primary component needed for an environment of trust to develop amongst citizens and foreigners is a sense of equality amongst the hosts which remains one of the most prolific factors in fostering good relations between citizens as hosts and immigrants as guests (2010, p6). This contention is also supported by Dorling (2011, p7) who asserts that within a society divided by wealth:

> ... those at the top more often look down on others with ever greater disdain and fear ... . Those at the bottom are also less likely to trust others and more likely to become fearful in a society that so clearly values them so little. Racism rises in just these kind of circumstances.

In summary, then, though the post-war nation was more ethnically and culturally homogenous than the British nation of today, it is argued that one of the central causes of national solidarity was the building of welfare institutions which helped to form a social glue between citizens and non-citizens. The creation of new forms of social assistance led to greater feelings of trust amongst co-nationals which in turn contributed to universal access to welfare provision, at least at an institutional level. However, McEwen writes that the concept of nationhood upon which the welfare state was founded was undermined by the New Right and the emergence of Thatcherism which threatened the "ability of multinational states such as the UK to continue to nurture a shared identity and sense of belonging to the state through recognition of social rights and the delivery of welfare services" (2002, p69) – a narrative that is broadly supported within the wider literature (Hall 1983; Jessop et al 1988; Marquand 1988; Delanty 1996, 2008). For that reason the next section will examine the ways in which the neo-liberal agenda of Margaret Thatcher, and the retrenchment of the post-WWII welfare state, impacted upon the concept of nation, and whether this change encouraged the exclusion of non-nationals from access to social rights.

Exclusionary nationalism and individual responsibility: the rise of Thatcherism

As a result of the domestic, and later global, recession of the mid 1960s and 1970s, the Callaghan Labour Government (1974–1979) was forced to implement austerity strategies as a means of managing the economic crisis. Hall (1983) writes that the governmentality of the working class by the Labour Party during this period led to the fragmentation of this class as the government was required to discipline and limit the very classes it claimed to represent. This was evident in the introduction of the social contract which allowed the state to limit wage demands, quickly turning the state into the "enemy of the people". Increasing restrictions on workers and collective bargaining led to a political backlash, the revolt of trade unions and the "winter of discontent" (1978–1979), which involved a number of public sector strikes plunging the country into disarray and damaging public confidence in the Labour Party. As Margaret Thatcher was the Conservative successor to Edward Heath, the stage was set for her to deploy the "discourses of nation" and "people" against class and "unions" (Hall 1983, p27), as Heath had already built a political narrative positing the "greedy working class" as holding the nation to ransom. Accordingly, Jessop et al claim that Thatcherism was a tale of "two nations" in the form of the "unification of a privileged nation of 'good citizens' and 'hard workers' against a contained and subordinate nation" (1988, p87), confirming the idea that British identity under Thatcherism shifted in line with corresponding changes in social policy.

Throughout the chapter, the policies of Margaret Thatcher's Conservative government have been described as "neo-liberal". This is understood here as an economic model of governance that prioritises individual liberty and posits the free market as the most effective way of allocating resources, rejecting micro-economic interventions by the state and other collective organizations. During Margaret Thatcher's reign as Conservative prime minister (1979–1992), there was a decrease in the collective rights of trade unions and a reduced role for the state in achieving full employment. Accordingly, Marquand contends that Thatcher was not neo-liberal by force majeure but by choice and conviction as she rejected Keynesian macro-economic management on the grounds that the market was the most efficient means of distributing resources (1988, pp161–4). The national traditions of Thatcherism rested upon economic liberalism and the minimal state as opposed to the active social state (Marquand 1988, p161). Claims from McEwen (2002) and Delanty (1996, 2008) that the British nation was radically altered following the rise of Thatcherism in the UK are therefore supported within the academic literature of the period which associates "being British" with competition and profitability.

Embracing the politics of the "New Right", the Thatcher government's primary aim was to cut welfare spending by promoting independence as opposed to dependence upon benefits – something which was thought to have created an "underclass". This was achieved via a sustained campaign to target and prosecute those guilty of benefit fraud which fuelled a rhetoric of "scroungerphobia", labelled by Sullivan as the "pathologising of poverty" (1996, pp233, 238). Consequently, a neo-liberal sense of "Britishness" developed as "the essence of the British people was identified with self-reliance and personal responsibility, as against the image of the over-taxed individual, enervated by welfare state 'coddling'" (Hall 1983, p29). The ideological connection between British national identity and the welfare state that emerged after 1945 was therefore weakened by Thatcher as social divisions grew, exacerbated by tax cuts for the rich, benefit cuts for 16–25 year olds and reductions in pensions (Gladstone 1999, p77). Indeed, Béland and Lecours (2008) write that the instrumentality of social programmes in nation building can be easily disrupted by the rising costs of social programmes or an ideological shift within government such as that of neo-liberalism which constrains social policy expansion: "In this context, the advantages for citizens to invest their loyalty in the nation promoted by the central state could diminish. From a broader perspective, social policy retrenchment can mean the weakening of a practical manifestation of nationhood" (pp21–2).

As the concept of nation within this chapter is understood as a process always in flux, it is argued that national identity was reformed under Margaret Thatcher's government as the social institutions which once bound the nation together were systematically undermined. As a result of decreasing social mobility, the nation became increasingly fractured, with the productive being pitted against the parasitic and heightened competition arising amongst lower status groups. According to Jessop et al, the productive sector are those members of society who produce goods and services that can be profitably marketed without the need for state subsidies, while the parasitic includes the unemployed, pensioners, the disabled and those who are unprofitable in terms of capitalist forms and accounting, such as asylum seekers who are prevented from entering the labour market (1988, p88). Such a proposition should not be regarded as radical as Gellner (1983) notes that within an industrial population (or in this case post-industrial), those that are easily recognized as being new to the nation and who are concentrated towards the bottom of the social scale, are likely to be discriminated against. Gellner uses the hypothetical example of a foreign blue population noting that non-blue groups who are also low down on the social scale will be specifically prone to anti-blue feelings through fear of being pushed downwards. Because they have "little else to be proud of", Gellner claims that this group will cling to their only distinction which is "non-blueness". Correspondingly, in a nation such as the UK with high income inequality (European Commission 2015), newcomers will be regarded with contempt by some sections of the community and perceived as a drain on resources.

An examination of the timeline relating to the withdrawal of social rights from asylum seekers further demonstrates that in conjunction with the rise of the New Right and the targeting of the underclass, the nation became more exclusionary as immigration controls became increasingly linked to welfare throughout the late 1970s and 1980s. Consequently, alongside means tests and eligibility tests, "status tests" were established to prevent "overseas visitors" from accessing welfare benefits, altering the previously universal access of the post-war welfare institutions. The Immigration Rules were therefore altered to prevent certain categories of immigrant from accessing supplementary benefits (then known as Income Support), which were "commandeered to exclude from benefit whole categories of people who had enjoyed entitlement for decades" (Storey 1984, p19). Storey credits these changes with causing institutional discrimination within the provision of social security as welfare officials, charged with the job of determining entitlement, targeted members of the growing black community on the assumption that they were visitors as opposed to permanent residents (1984, p22). In 1987 the Income Support (General) Regulations were introduced which excluded people categorized as having no right to be in the country from accessing support, however asylum seekers remained entitled to claim benefits at a reduced rate of 90 per cent on the basis that they were urgent cases under Regulation 21(3) and Schedule 7 of the 1987 Regulations. Schuster and Bloch write that this was because refugees and asylum seekers were still regarded as persons who deserved compassion because of what they had endured, meaning it was politically expedient to respond humanely to those fleeing persecution (2002, p397). However, as the asylum-seeking population grew alongside the political rhetoric of individual responsibility and the targeting of problem populations, the exclusionary boundaries of "new nationalism" were realigned and positioned firmly at the feet of the asylum-seeking community. From 1996 a series of restrictive support provisions were therefore introduced which culminated in the Immigration and Asylum Act 1999, implemented by the Blair Labour Government (1997–2007). This Act continues to exclude asylum applicants from accessing national welfare benefits such as income support or universal credit. Restrictions on employment were also introduced via Schedules 2 and 3 of the Immigration Act 1971 and paragraph 360A of the Immigration Rules.

In addition to the rise of the New Right and the shift to individualist, market-led social policies, it is suggested that the steady decline of asylum seekers' social rights implies that the concept of the post-WWII nation was altered following the election of Margaret Thatcher. Increasing restrictions upon the asylum seeking community also indicate that "new nationalism" is generally exclusive, despite the fact that a growing number of international instruments and EU laws recognize the legitimacy of social rights claims from asylum seekers (see Council Directive 2003/9/EC of 27 January 2003 laying down minimum standards for the reception of asylum seekers and the International Covenant on Economic, Social and Cultural Rights 1966). In further opposition to this theory of "exclusive nationalism" are the institutional arrangements of the European Union (EU) and the Treaty on the Functioning of the European Union which enables the movement of workers as a capital commodity and reduces institutional barriers in accessing cross-border social rights. Cosmopolitan developments within the EU therefore refute the idea that the British nation is becoming increasingly "exclusive", yet as Benhabib notes, while "throughout the EU a dissociation of the privileges of political citizenship from nationality can be observed for EU citizens, for third-country nationals, the ties between identities and institutions, between national membership and democratic citizenship rights, are reinforced" (Benhabib 2004, p156). Such a contention is particularly salient following the UK government's refusal to opt in to the Single Permit Directive (2011/98/EU), which requires common rights for EEA citizens and third country nationals working legally within the state. Consequently within the UK, the social divisions between citizens, European Economic Area (EEA) citizens and third country nationals remain firm. Though the institutional arrangements of the EU reflect a certain level of cosmopolitanism, such policies do not of course reveal the political and social unease with which the British public (NatCen Social Research 2015) or UK government regard EU membership – as confirmed by the recent Brexit referendum result.

Acknowledging the current crisis of EU legitimacy, Delanty (2008, 2014) writes that increasing demands upon the welfare state from EEA citizens is one of the primary factors fuelling anti-EU rhetoric as such demands ignore the following: the shift from democratic capitalism to neo-liberal politics; an increase in the use of state-based austerity measures; and the declining power of the middle class, which places the group in a precarious position in terms of social mobility (2014, p210). Consequently, while the nation state is retreating from the social commitments with which it had been associated following WWII, the European project is moving towards transnationalization with little regard for the internal concerns of states. This has led to the affirmation of the idea of exclusionary nationalism (Delanty 2008, p685). As a result, the decline of nation-based social solidarities and the rise of new nationalism cannot be separated from anti-European sentiment as social insecurity and increasing demands for social protectionism mutually reinforce anxieties about economic status and migration. Increased insecurity amongst European citizens thus leads to the strengthening of boundaries against third party nationals.

Conclusions: a new and exclusive nation

Exacerbated by conditions of austerity, Rex (1996) writes that "new nationalism" vehemently opposes immigration. In light of the retraction of social rights from asylum seekers over the last three decades and comprehensive research that reveals public ill-feeling towards the group (Hobson et al 2008, p20), it is argued that asylum seekers are a primary target of new nationalism. Though many commentators believe that the weakening of British identity is a result of heightened immigration (Goodhart 2013; Goodwin 2011), this chapter claims that exclusion cannot be regarded as a natural by-product of migration but rather must be seen within the context of the neo-liberal agenda and growing income inequality in the UK caused, at least in part, by the withdrawal of the welfare state. This contention is supported by a 2013 report commissioned by the Government into the impact of immigration upon British identity which found that increased ethnic diversity alone did not result in a lack of social cohesion between groups, but rather that this only occurred in combination with socio-economic deprivation (Owen 2013). Accordingly, "the new politics of nationalism is a politics of cultural contestation articulated around social issues" (Delanty 1996, p8), a nationalism of resistance against the state which seeks to deconstruct the security of the post-war welfare institutions (Delanty 1996; McEwen 2002). This is perhaps most evident in the Scottish National Party's increasingly popular call for independence as the "cutbacks and reforms to the UK's system of state welfare impacted upon the strength of support for home rule and the nature of sub state nationalist demands" (McEwen 2002, p87). Data from the 2014 British Social Attitudes Survey also revealed that 76 per cent of UKIP supporters strongly agreed that "there is one law for the rich and one law for the poor" in the UK and that "ordinary people do not get their fair share of the nation's wealth" (NatCen Social Research 2015, p28), encouraging the notion that people are turning to UKIP as a means of registering their protest against the state's existing institutional economic arrangements. Conditions of inequality thereby corrode trust between citizens and affect our ability to empathize with others (Wilkinson and Pickett 2011). New nationalism is not therefore built upon an image of the British people as an ethnically or culturally homogenous collective but rather with strong emphasis upon who the British people are not. The faces of immigrants have thus "served as ideal, identifiable flashpoints for new repertoires of belonging and othering" which serves the "otherwise alienated consumer-citizen's need for inclusion and belonging" well (Demmers and Mehendale 2010, p68).

In conclusion, the withdrawal of social rights from asylum seekers over the last century, from a position of equality with citizens after WWII, to enforced poverty today, is an indication of the changing nature of the British "nation" which posits itself in opposition to the immigrant community. Though much literature indicates that this is an inevitable consequence of increased migration, I argue that one of the most prolific factors guiding the exclusionary nature of contemporary nationalism is the neo-liberal agenda which has resulted in a culture of individualism and social insecurity as a result of the retrenchment of the welfare state. As evidenced by the post-war welfare state, nationalism does not automatically result in exclusion, but rather is shaped by the objective and subjective factors guiding our understanding of what it means to be British. Increased solidarity and trust amongst citizens, fostered by a strong sense of nation can therefore contribute to increased hospitality and the redistribution of resources amongst nationals and non-nationals such as asylum seekers. Yet, the rhetoric of the new nationalism pulls worryingly in the opposite direction, resulting in the social construction of asylum seekers as the enemy of the nation who deserve lesser living standards than those afforded to our own citizens.

References

ANDERSON, B. (2006) *Imagined Communities: reflections on the origin and spread of nationalism.* London: Verso Books.

BAKSHI, P., GOODWIN, M., PAINTER, J. and SOUTHERN, J. (1995) Gender, race and class in the local welfare state: Moving beyond regulation theory in analysing the transition from Fordism, *Environment and Planning A*, 27. pp1539–1554.

BALES, K. (2013) Universal credit: not so universal? Deconstructing the impact of the asylum support system. *Journal of Social Welfare and Family Law*, 35. pp427–443.

BÉLAND, D. (2005) Ideas and Social Policy: An Institutionalist Perspective. *Social Policy and Administration*, 39. pp1–18.

BÉLAND, D. and LECOURS, A. (2008) *Nationalism and Social Policy – The Politics of Territorial Solidarity.* Oxford: Oxford University Press.

BENHABIB, S. (2004) *The Rights of Others: Aliens, Residents and Citizens.* Cambridge: Cambridge University Press.

BEVERIDGE, W. (1942) *Social Insurance and Allied Services.* London: Macmillan.

BOMMES, M. and GEDDES, A. (eds) (2000) *Immigration and Welfare: Challenging the borders of the welfare state.* London: Routledge.

CARNET, P., BLANCHARD, C. and ELLIS, J. (2014) *The Azure Payment card: The humanitarian cost of a cashless system.* London: British Red Cross.

COHEN, S. (1985) Anti-semitism, immigration controls and the welfare state. *Critical Social Policy,* 5. pp73–92.

COHEN, S. (2003) *No one is illegal: asylum and immigration control, past and present.* Stoke-on-Trent: Trentham Books.

DE BEER, P. and KOSTER, F. (2010) *Sticking Together or Falling Apart: Solidarity in an Era of Individualization and Globalization.* Amsterdam: Amsterdam University Press.

DELANTY, G. (1996) Beyond the Nation-State: National Identity and Citizenship in a Multicultural Society. *Sociological Research Online,* 1. ppxi–xii.

DELANTY, G. (2008) Fear of Others: Social Exclusion and the European Crisis of Solidarity. *Social Policy & Administration,* 42. pp676–690.

DELANTY, G. (2014) Introduction: Perspectives on crisis and critique in Europe today. *European Journal of Social Theory,* 17(3). pp207–218.

DEMMERS, J. and MEHENDALE, S. (2010) Neoliberal Xenophobia: The Dutch Case, *Alternatives,* 35. pp53–70.

DORLING, D. (2011) *Injustice: why social inequality persists.* Cambridge: Policy Press.

ESPING ANDERSON, G. (1990) *The Three Worlds of Welfare Capitalism.* Portland, OR: Polity Press.

EUROPEAN COMMISSION (2015) *Research findings – Social Situation Monitor – Income inequality in EU countries* [Online]. Available: http://ec.europa.eu/social/main.jsp?catId= 1050&intPageId=1870&langId=en [Accessed 12 May 2015].

FRASER, D. (2009) *The Evolution of the British Welfare State.* Basingstoke: Palgrave Macmillan.

GELLNER, E. (1983) *Nations and Nationalism.* Oxford: Blackwell Publishers.

GLADSTONE, D. (1999) *The Twentieth-Century Welfare State.* London: Macmillan Press Ltd.

GOODALL, C. (2010) *The coming of the stranger: Asylum seekers, trust and hospitality in a British city.* Nairobi: UNHCR.

GOODHART, D. (2013) *The British Dream: Successes and Failures of Post-War Immigration.* London: Atlantic Books.

GOODWIN, M. (2011) *New British Fascism: The Rise of the British National Party.* London: Routledge.

HALFMANN, J. (2000) Welfare state and territory. In Bommes, M. and Geddes, A. (ed.) *Immigration and Welfare: Challenging the borders of the welfare state.* London: Routledge.

HALL, S. (1983) The Great Moving Right Show. In Hall, S. and Jacques, M. (ed.) *The Politics of Thatcherism.* London: Lawrence and Wishart.

HOBSON, C., COX, J. and SAGOVSKY, N. (2008) Saving Sanctuary: The Independent Asylum Commission's first report of conclusions and recommendations: How we restore public support for sanctuary and improve the way we decide who needs sanctuary. The Independent Asylum Commission.

HOME OFFICE (1998) *Fairer, Faster and Firmer – A Modern Approach to Immigration*. London: HMSO.

HOME OFFICE (undated) *Asylum*, Cm 4018. London: HMSO.

JESSOP, B., BONNET, K., BROMLEY, S. and LING, T. (1988) *Thatcherism: A tale of two nations*. Cambridge: Polity Press.

JOHNSTON, R., BANTING, K., KYMLICKA, W. and SOROKA, S. (2010) National Identity and Support for the Welfare State. *Canadian Journal of Political Science*, 42. pp349–377.

KEATING, M. (1996) *Nations against the State: the new politics of nationalism in Quebec, Catalonia and Scotland*. Basingstoke: Macmillan.

MARQUAND, D. (1988) *The Paradoxes of Thatcherism*. In Skidelsky, R. (ed.) *Thatcherism*. London: Chatto and Windus.

MARSHALL, T. H. (1950) *Citizenship and Social Class and Other Essays*. Cambridge: Cambridge University Press.

MCEWEN, N. (2002) State Welfare Nationalism: The Territorial Impact of Welfare State Development in Scotland. *Regional and Federal Studies*, 12. pp66–90.

MILLER, D. (1995) *On Nationality*. Oxford: Oxford University Press.

MILLER, D. (2008) Immigrants, Nations, and Citizenship. *The Journal of Political Philosophy*, 16. pp371–390.

MORRIS, L. (2003) Managing contradiction: Civic stratification and migrants' rights, *International Migration Review*, 37(1). pp74–100.

MORRIS, L. (2009) Civic stratification and the cosmopolitan ideal, *European Societies*, 11. pp603–624.

NATCEN SOCIAL RESEARCH (2015) *British Social Attitudes: The 32nd Report*. R. ORMSTON and J. CURTIS (eds). London.

OWEN, D. (2013) *Future Identities: Changing identities in the UK – the next 10 years*. London: Government Office for Science.

REFUGEE ACTION (2010) *Asylum Support Cuts*. London: Refugee Action.

REX, J. (1996) National Identity in the Democratic Multi-Cultural State. *Sociological Research Online*, 1.

SCHUSTER, L. and BLOCH, A. (2002) Asylum and welfare: Contemporary debates. *Critical Social Policy*, 22. pp393–414.

SOYSAL, Y. N. (2012) Citizenship, immigration, and the European social project: rights and obligations of individuality, *The British Journal of Sociology*, 63. pp1–21.

STOREY, H. (1984) United Kingdom Immigration Controls and the Welfare State, *Journal of Social Welfare*, 6. pp14–28.

SULLIVAN, M. (1996) *The Development of the British Welfare State*. Hertfordshire: Prentice Hall/ Harvester Wheatsheaf.

TAMIR, Y. (1993) *Liberal Nationalism*. Princeton, NJ: Princeton University Press.

TAYLOR, C. (1996) Why Democracy Needs Patriotism. In Cohen, J. (ed.) *For Love of Country: Debating the Limits of Patriotism, Martha C. Nussbaum with respondents*. Boston: Beacon Press.

TEATHER, S., CARMICHAEL, N., DAKIN, N., DINENAGE, C., SHARMA, V., AVEBURY, E.., LISTER, R., PACKER, T. R. R. J., FINCH, N., and REED, M. (2013) *Report of the Parliamentary Inquiry into Asylum Support for Children and Young People*.

THE NATIONAL ARCHIVES (2015) *Brave New World: Postwar immigration* [Online]. Available from: www.nationalarchives.gov.uk/pathways/citizenship/brave_new_world/immigration.htm [Accessed 10 May 2015].

TITMUSS, R. (1950) *Problems of Social Policy*. London: HMSO.

WILKINSON, R. G. and PICKETT, K. (2011) *The spirit level: Why greater equality makes societies stronger*. New York: Bloomsbury.

WOLFE, A. and KLAUSEN, J. (1997) Identity Politics and the Welfare State. *Social Philosophy and Policy*, 14. pp231–255.

Part III

Social rights and the market

Chapter 7

From social rights to economic incentives? The moral (re)construction of welfare capitalism

Sabine Frerichs

Introduction

The notion of "welfare capitalism" refers to a political-economic regime that integrates the functions of a capitalist market economy with the functions of a democratic welfare state. The term is commonly used by Esping-Andersen (1990) in *The Three Worlds of Welfare Capitalism*, but it is also linked to Marshall's (1950, p14) idea of three generations of rights, which all form part of modern citizenship: civil rights, political rights, and social rights. The question that this chapter seeks to address is how social rights, which Esping-Andersen and Marshall understood as the apex of the democratic welfare state, remain bound to the logic of the capitalist market economy. Employing the perspective of the economic sociology of law, it will be argued that the transformation of welfare capitalism over the last few decades has led to a reinterpretation of social rights in the light of economic incentives. To make this point, changes in the financial structure of the welfare state, both on its revenue and expenditure side, will be connected with changes in the moral discourse on citizens' rights and duties, which is increasingly informed by economic arguments.

The chapter first outlines the analytical framework that connects the language of social rights with the concept of welfare capitalism. In the perspective of the economic sociology of law, scholarship in comparative and critical political economy can be fruitfully integrated and related with the moral-economy approach, which is particularly suited to document a loss of entitlements, or accustomed social rights. The following analysis is divided into two parts. The chapter first turns to the revenue side of the welfare state and explores the moral economy of taxation, emphasising changes over time and across different welfare regimes. What we can, by and large, observe, is a move from "contribution tax" to "exchange tax", or a renegotiation between social rights and property rights. The chapter then proceeds to discuss the expenditure side of the welfare state and the moral economy of debt, again focusing on the overall patterns of development. Accordingly, we are not only witnessing a transition "from welfare to workfare" but also "from welfare to debtfare", which replaces unconditional social rights or welfare benefits with activation in the labour market and the credit market. The chapter concludes by interpreting the above developments in the light of the social contract, or social compromise, underlying welfare capitalism.

Analytical framework: the concept of welfare capitalism and the language of rights

The term "welfare capitalism", as it will be used in this chapter, refers to a political-economic regime that integrates the functions of a capitalist market economy with the functions of a democratic welfare state. Pierson (2010, p1519) speaks of a combination of "a market-based economy under (predominantly) private ownership with a system of welfare services and income transfers underwritten or delivered by the state". Garland (2014, p346) highlights the complementary but also contradictory nature of "privately-determined economic action" in the sphere of market capitalism and "publicly-determined social protection" in the sphere of the welfare state. This tension is inbuilt in the notion of welfare capitalism.

As a specific, historical concept, welfare capitalism refers to the institutional compromise between "capital" and "labour" in post-war (Western) political economies (cf. Pierson 2010, pp1518–19). The three decades after World War II are often dubbed the "golden age" of the (national) welfare state. In this sense, the twentieth century witnessed not only the formation of the "classic" welfare state but also the beginnings of its transformation. However, neither welfare capitalism nor the welfare state ceased to exist after this transformation – its "technologies of social insurance, social regulation and social provision" are still an essential part of modern government (Garland 2014, p336). As a generic concept, welfare capitalism may refer to any combination of capitalism and welfarism in the above sense, at different times and scales. This explicitly includes the Europeanized regime of welfare capitalism of today, in which national and supranational economic and social policies closely interact (Hay and Wincott 2012, pp132–3). Moreover, welfare capitalism can also be related to earlier forms of social organization that had naturally integrated the "economic" and the "social", before the industrial revolution overturned the traditional social order and the ideology of *laissez faire* capitalism took hold in the nineteenth century (Garland 2014, pp352–4; cf. Polanyi 1957 [1944]).

Thanks to *The Three Worlds of Welfare Capitalism* (Esping-Andersen 1990), welfare capitalism has become a very common term in "comparative political economy". Using this term, Esping-Andersen (1990, pp1–2) aims to point out that his interest is not only in the welfare state in a narrow sense, which would mainly consist in "income transfers and social services", but also in its broader role in the political economy, which includes "issues of employment, wages, and overall macro-economic steering". However, the ensuing research programme on the different worlds of welfare capitalism, which aims to fit national welfare regimes into typologies (Ferragina and Seeleib-Kaiser 2011), rarely revisits the original concept of welfare capitalism (Schelkle 2012), and it certainly neglects the "government of the economy" as one of its core aspects (Garland 2014, pp344–5).

If we want to learn about the transformation of welfare capitalism, the "mainstream welfare state literature" (Vis 2007, p106) has its clear limitations. Its analytical interest is in corroborating or questioning the distinction between "liberal", "corporatist" and "social-democratic" welfare-state regimes (Esping-Andersen 1990, pp26–7), as well as "familialistic" ones (Guillén and Álvarez 2001). The standard approach in comparative political economy is thus preoccupied with cross-national comparison and usually assumes divergent development paths. This is different in the neighbouring field of "critical political economy", which is more concerned with capitalist development in a historical-comparative perspective (cf. Vis 2007, p106). At its core is regulation theory, an approach that is from the outset interested in the two complementary poles of capitalist social formations, which are evident in the concept of welfare capitalism: a specific "accumulation regime" on the one hand (e.g., Fordism, Postfordism), and a respective "mode of regulation" on the other (e.g., Keynesian welfare state, Schumpeterian workfare regime) (Jessop 1993). Compared to the standard approach, the critical approach seems better suited to identify what "variegated" national welfare regimes have in common, how they complement each other, and how they cope with the challenges and crises arising from the same global context of capitalist development (cf. Brenner et al 2010).

For Esping-Andersen (1990, p21), "the core idea of a welfare state" is social citizenship, a concept originally coined by Marshall. Marshall (1972, p16) likewise engages with the notion of welfare capitalism, which he specifies as "democratic-welfare-capitalism". This concept preserves Marshall's (1950, p14) famous idea of three generations of rights, which all form part of modern citizenship: civil rights emerged in the eighteenth century, political rights in the nineteenth, and social rights in the twentieth. In democratic welfare capitalism, the three constitutive elements, or generations of rights, are expected to be in a good balance. This is assumed to be the case:

> ... when a country with a *capitalist* market economy develops *democratic* political and civil institutions and practices out of which emerge a mixed economy including both private and public capitalism [...], together with that complex of public social services, insurances and assistances which [...] all the world knows as the *welfare* state.
>
> (Marshall 1972, p18; original emphasis)

In short: this is a capitalist market economy governed by a democratic welfare state.

In this chapter, social rights will be approached from a sociological point of view, as part of collaborative efforts to advance the "economic sociology of law" (Swedberg 2003, 2006; Frerichs 2009, 2011; Ashiagbor et al 2013). The subject matter of this field of study are the interrelations between law, economy, and society, and one of its core problems is the "constitution" of modern capitalism, or the construction of the "market society" of today by means of law and economics (Frerichs 2012).

In this chapter, the focus is on the moral construction, and reconstruction, of welfare capitalism in the language of social rights. The question to be addressed is how the structural transformations of the welfare state, which have taken place in the last forty years, translate into, or are legitimated by, semantic changes concerning the "subject of rights". The different generations of rights merging in the concept of democratic welfare capitalism – "negative liberty rights" (civil rights), "positive liberty rights" (political rights), and "entitlement rights" (social rights) – are connected with different "right-bearing subjects" (McClure 1995, p168). These various subjects, or subjectivities, not only complement each other but may also conflict with each other, like the different components of welfare capitalism more generally.

Thus, there is always a trade-off between civil rights and social rights, that is, between rights to private property, personal security, and non-interference by others, "including government itself", on the one hand, and "rights to public provision, guarantee, or support, in particular in the form of claims to the public supply of specific goods, services, or income" on the other (McClure 1995, p167). Put differently, in the modern welfare state, the subject of property rights always has to compromise with the subject of social rights.

This chapter argues that the language of social rights increasingly gives way to the logic of economic incentives, which, strictly speaking, address a different subject: the market citizen. This argument will be substantiated by linking structural changes in the political economy of welfare capitalism with semantic changes in its moral economy. The moral-economy approach goes back to Thompson (1971; 1991, pp259–351), but it prefigures in Polanyi's work (1957 [1944]; cf. Hann 2010). Writing about bread riots in eighteenth century England, Thompson (1971, p136) links "the breakthrough of the new political economy of the free market" to "the breakdown of the old moral economy of provision". For him, the bread riots that broke out at the height of a food crisis were not simply "rebellions of the belly" but had to be understood in culturally more meaningful terms: as a defence of "traditional rights or customs" (Thompson 1971, pp77–8). This included the "deeply-felt conviction that prices *ought*, in times of dearth, to be regulated" (Thompson 1971, p112; original emphasis).

However, the concept of the moral economy does not have to be limited to a traditional social order that somehow balanced the "economic" with the "social" – a socially embedded economy in Polanyi's words (1957 [1944], p57); it can also be applied to the modern welfare state, which put an end to the reign of *laissez faire* capitalism:

> Much of the history of social struggle from, say, 1830 to 1950 could, in fact, be written as the attempt to create, in place of the wreckage of local moral-economies, an analogous "moral-economy state" to provide national social insurance along comparable lines – no longer seen as a matter of local reciprocity but as right of citizenship.
>
> (Scott 2005, p397)

In this chapter, the concept of the moral economy is used to refer to the semantic side of welfare capitalism, including the classic concept of social citizenship as well as its transformations, which amount to a loss of entitlements.

Who pays? The revenue side of the welfare state and the moral economy of taxation

Welfare state research following the standard paradigm is preoccupied with public social spending. Indeed, this is the biggest budget item on the expenditure side of advanced political economies today (cf. Martin et al 2009, p26). Obviously, this has not always been the case. It was only in the twentieth century that social spending became a bigger budget item than military spending and that the "transition from the warfare state to the welfare state" was made (Martin et al 2009, p11). However, as to the revenue side, both warfare and welfare state were and are premised on the tax state: the extraction of taxes from "capital" (i.e., first of all, corporate taxes; one could add property taxes and taxes on personal capital income) and "labour" (i.e., taxes on labour income, including social security contributions; one could add consumption taxes, which likewise target households). In terms of "the sheer volume of cash transferred between state and society", taxation is a much bigger item than social transfers, and it likewise has redistributive implications (Martin et al 2009, p26). Hence, in contemporary welfare regimes, the revenue side, or "Who pays?", matters as much as the expenditure side, or "Who gets what from government?" (Howard 2009, p87).

The functions of the tax state, as it developed in the 20th century, reflect the constitutive elements of democratic welfare capitalism, which are materialized in the three generations of rights. Ideal-typically, the liberal tax state of the 19th century combines a low level of taxation with a low level of intervention. The financial function of taxes is complemented by a restrictive political function. The famous slogan of "no taxation without representation" suggests that even the "minimal tax state" cannot do without public consent, that is, parliamentary control. The budgetary powers of parliament took shape in the form of the principles of "annualisation (the duration of authorization and execution is one year), unity (a single document for the whole budget), universality (no allocation or compensation between revenue and expenditure), and speciality (giving the detail of expenditure)" (Leroy 2011, pp142–3).

In contrast, the interventionist tax state of the 20th century ideal typically combines a high level of revenues with a high level of expenditure. With liberal democracies turning into welfare democracies, or "fiscal democracies" (Genschel and Schwarz 2013), the political mandate of the tax state has become much broader, and the range of tax functions has increased. The interventionist tax state is committed to macro-economic steering, income redistribution, the protection of particular social groups, the promotion of specific economic sectors, regional development and, increasingly, environmental protection (Leroy 2011, p308).

It is characteristic of the modern welfare state that solidarity is formally organized, typically on the national level, and that social obligation is translated into legal obligation, which includes, first and foremost, the obligation to pay taxes. Against this backdrop, it can be rightfully claimed that "[i]n the modern world, taxation *is* the social contract" (Martin et al 2009, p1; original emphasis). Leroy (2011, p319) speaks of a "socio-financial democratic contract" which establishes a link "between mass taxation and social rights". Since social contractarian perspectives of the state are popular across the social sciences, the question is what a sociological interpretation of the fiscal contract offers that other approaches – namely legal and economic ones – do not (Leroy 2011, pp105–7; Campbell 2009b, p258).

To illustrate, it seems useful to start from a legalistic view of taxes as a one-sided financial obligation to the state: "the obligation to contribute money or goods to the state in exchange for nothing in particular" (Martin et al 2009, p3). While legal scholarship is more concerned with the "normative validity" of the legal order, sociologists as well as economists are more interested in its "empirical validity" – that is, how it actually shapes human conduct (Weber 1978 [1922], p312). However, whereas economists usually assume self-interested behaviour, which suggests that people observe the law only if compliance is less costly than non-compliance, sociologists are more interested in norm-oriented behaviour, such as that people observe the law because they consider it legitimate (cf. Weber 1978, p36). The moral economy of taxation becomes visible in the motives of tax compliance or tax evasion.

Leroy (2011, pp271–4) distinguishes between the "sociological figures" of "obligation tax", "exchange tax" and "contribution tax", which capture different interpretations of the fiscal contract. If taxation is understood as "obligation tax" and complied with for the law's sake, the ground of legitimacy is legality, or the procedural rationality of the law. More interesting are the two other, more substantive interpretations: one is more economic, focusing on personal benefits, the other is more political, focusing on the common good. As soon as there is an expectation to get something in return – be it in the form of "personal goods" or "public goods" (Mathew 2010, p238), the interpretation of the fiscal contract is that of an "exchange tax". This is an economic concept of taxation, according to which taxes are the "[p]rice paid by the taxpayer for the benefit (services) which he receives from society" (Leroy 2011, p271). In contrast, the "contribution tax" stands for a socio-political concept of taxation, according to which taxes are a legitimate contribution to the financing of regulatory and redistributive welfare policies, which may enjoy wide support even among taxpayers who do not immediately benefit (Leroy 2011, p278). Whereas in the economic conception, the fiscal contract is mainly understood in utilitarian terms, in the socio-political conception, it is interpreted in more solidaristic terms.

Different tax regimes can be compared in terms of their revenue levels and revenue structure. Our interest here is not only in cross-national comparison but also in historical comparison: how tax regimes have developed over time, with a focus on the last four decades and the international context. In member countries of the Organisation for Economic Co-operation and Development (OECD), the average tax revenue level is about one third of the national output (OECD 2014). If we compare the US and Sweden, which can be regarded as "prototypes" of the liberal and the social-democratic welfare regime, respectively, it shows that the revenue level in the US was much lower and remained relatively stable over the whole period, whereas the revenue level in Sweden was much higher, increased until the late 1980s but decreased thereafter. At its peak, the Swedish tax revenue level was almost at fifty per cent and almost twice as high as in the US. The revenue levels of corporatist welfare regimes developed between these poles. It has been argued that the gap between the revenue levels in the US and European countries would diminish by a few percentage points if the former's "'hidden welfare state' of tax expenditures" was considered (Howard 2009, p89). However, this typically benefits higher income classes more than lower ones.

The revenue structure is determined by the combination of taxes and similar revenue sources, including personal income taxes, social security contributions, consumption taxes, corporate taxes, and property taxes. In OECD countries, the biggest revenue source is "labour", with personal income taxes and social security contributions adding up to more than 50 per cent of total taxation; consumption comes second with more than thirty per cent, and "capital" comes only third (OECD 2014). In fact, corporate taxes are "not a major revenue raiser in OECD countries" today (Genschel and Schwarz 2013, p71). Their share as a revenue source has not increased, even though "their share of corporate income [...] in national income has risen continuously since the 1980s" (Genschel and Schwarz 2013, p70).

Comparing the different tax regimes, it may be surprising that the US, for a good part of the twentieth century, "taxed capital at higher rates, and labor and consumption at lower rates, than the welfare states of Europe, including egalitarian outposts like France and Sweden" (Martin et al 2009, p15). In fact, the American welfare state is centred on progressive income taxation, which is a highly "visible" tax, whereas in Europe indirect consumption taxes play a greater role. These have been essential to keep revenue levels high in times of increasing tax competition from the 1980s onwards. Another response by the Nordic countries was to introduce a dual income tax system with "flat rates" for mobile capital income and higher, progressive rates for less mobile labour income (Christensen 2013, p14).

Overall, international tax competition is most effective in corporate taxation and certainly relevant also in capital income taxation, while it plays a more limited and more selective role in the taxation of labour income and consumption (Genschel and Schwarz 2011, pp351, 358). In other words, "tax base mobility" affects savings and investment patterns and the distribution of profits in multinational firms more than employment and consumption patterns (Genschel and Schwarz 2011, pp347–51). The result of this structural asymmetry is a redistribution of tax burden "from mobile to immobile tax bases" and "from capital to labour and consumption" (Genschel and Schwarz 2013, p73). From the perspective of fiscal democracy, this is problematic to the extent that such "regressive" effects on the revenue side of the welfare state are not compensated by "progressive" effects on the expenditure side.

In the European context, a period of "integration through tax harmonisation" until the late 1970s was replaced with "integration through the removal of tax obstacles" from the 1980s onwards (Menéndez 2015). Hence, the Europeanization of taxes came to be furthered by means of negative integration, that is, by making national tax systems compatible with the principle of free movement, instead of positive integration, that is, by unifying national tax laws. This shift is in line with the overall pattern of development – of increased tax base mobility and tax competition – that turned the "social and democratic tax state", which is synonymous with the classic welfare state, into a "market enabling tax state" (Menéndez 2015, pp15, 40).

Since the standard economic model of utility maximization seems insufficient to explain actual levels of tax compliance, scholars have come to resort to the concept of "tax morale". If this is defined as the "intrinsic motivation to pay taxes which arises from the moral obligation to pay taxes as a contribution to society" (Doerrenberg and Peichl 2013, p294), it can be equated with Leroy's socio-political understanding of taxation as "contribution tax". Interestingly, cross-national studies based on the World Value Survey see the US highest in tax morale (Alm and Torgler 2006, p239). However, in this case, tax morale is operationalized by the question item whether "[c]heating on tax if you have the chance is [1 = never … 10 = always] justified" (Alm and Torgler 2006, p239), which is less specific and does not necessarily mean that the US would also score highest in terms of the "contribution tax". Drawing on the moral-economy approach, we will use a different indicator to explore changes in the public perception of taxes in the last four decades: anti-tax protests.

Arguably, the moral economy of taxation may find expression in tax revolts as much as the moral economy of debt finds expression in debt riots (cf. Graeber 2011, p8). What is at stake, in both cases, is the defence of accustomed rights, or vested interests. One of the foundational claims of liberal democracies, which favourably combines civil and political rights, is "no taxation without representation". This slogan was coined 250 years ago, when American Colonies stood up against the British Crown in what was one of the most famous tax revolts in history (cf. Ross 2004, pp231–2). Among the unwanted taxation measures that got the ball rolling was the Sugar Act of 1764, which foresaw strict enforcement of customs duties on foreign sugar imports: a protectionist measure that harmed trade and production, and therefore caused protest in the colonies, which had relied on cheap sugar imports from outside the British Empire before.

Welfare democracies differ from liberal democracies in that social rights come into play, in addition to civil and political rights. If we focus on the trade-off between civil rights and social rights, the fiscal contract links citizens as taxpayers to citizens as welfare recipients. In principle, these are not distinct groups of people, but only different aspects of citizenship. However, in concrete circumstances, taxpayers may mobilize against welfare recipients in the hope of reinforcing or restoring property rights against social rights. Indeed, tax policy has an immediate impact on property rights:

> It determines the degree to which states take profits from firms and earnings from individuals, thus impinging directly on rights of private property ownership and appropriation. It also affects the investment strategies of firms and individuals and, as a result, how they use their property.
>
> (Campbell 2009b, p258)

From a "libertarian" point of view, taxation literally means the "confiscation" of private property. Under this premise, the development from the minimal to the interventionist tax state in the twentieth century appears as an outgrowth of "state-supportive ideologies for stabilizing and increasing their exploitative grip on a population" (Hoppe 2006 [1990], p64).

Such rhetoric forms part of the neo-liberal anti-tax discourse that started in the 1970s and allowed Ronald Reagan and Margaret Thatcher to come to power (Campbell 2009b, pp259–60). Even though the American welfare state is built on "visible" income taxes, taxation was not much politicized in the US before the 1970s, when "elected officials began discussing taxes publicly at much greater rates, and the issue of taxes became more prominent in the public mind" (Campbell 2009a, p49). This anti-tax rhetoric successfully mobilized conservative voters, which allowed president Reagan and his successor in office, George H. W. Bush, to enact a number of tax reforms in the 1980s and 1990s (Campbell 2009a, p62). There is even talk about a "permanent tax revolt" in the US, which shaped politics from the 1970s onwards (Martin 2008). In the UK the precise notion of a tax revolt is less connected with the neo-liberal anti-tax movement that helped to bring Thatcher into power, than with the respective counter-movement that helped to take her down. When a poll tax for local services was introduced in 1989/1990, which everyone had to contribute to at the same rate, this sparked real riots in the streets – not just rhetorical ones (Bagguley 1996).

The anti-tax movement was not limited to the Anglo-Saxon countries; it also took hold in the Nordic countries where respective tax reforms were undertaken in Denmark in 1987, Iceland in 1988, Sweden in 1991, Norway in 1992 and Finland in 1993 (Christensen 2013, p14). In symbolic terms, the "Danish tax revolt" of the early 1970s stands out. This was led by Mogens Glistrup, a tax lawyer who helped companies to avoid income taxes, publicly announced that he did not pay any income tax himself, and later founded a party that aimed to abolish income tax (Christiansen 1984, p22). In the Swedish case, tax reforms were a response to the "traumatic" experience of a protracted fiscal crisis between the late 1970s and early 1990s (Streeck 2015, p23; including fn. 28). In 1991, a conservative government came to power and "cut marginal tax rates on personal and capital income and closed many tax loopholes" (Campbell 2009b, p259). However, the new taxation policy remained contested and the social democrats returned to power only three years later.

The watchword for the contemporary tax state is "optimal taxation". The neo-liberal message is that "less is more": that cutting tax rates may actually yield more tax revenues. This reasoning is illustrated by the Laffer Curve, which describes two counteracting effects (Laffer 2004): on the one hand rising tax rates mean rising revenues; on the other hand, they also decrease the "incentive" to engage in the taxed activities, which ultimately reduces revenues. Popularization of the Laffer Curve helped to sell "supply-side" economics and shape public opinion in favour of tax reductions. At the same time, the model is far too simple to explain actual tax behaviour in complex and dynamic fiscal regimes, and neglects its non-economic dimensions (Mathew 2010, pp48–9, 59).

Not only are the recent tax reforms inspired by the economics of taxation, but economic discourse has also shaped the moral economy of the taxpayers and undermined the socio-political concept of taxation. Among the "anti-tax commonplaces" shaping the new, economic morality are the following: taxpayers have a rational aversion to taxes; present tax rates are too high, hinder economic growth and further tax evasion; globalization requires governments to reduce taxes and cut expenditure (Leroy 2011, p181). Moreover, tax advantages that originally served social purposes are now regarded as "irrational" or "distortionary", which means that taxes are increasingly stripped of their regulatory and redistributive function (Mathew 2010, p71). In short, the "exchange tax" crowds out the "contribution tax".

A neo-liberal tax morale leaves less room for unconditional social rights. Economically minded taxpayers are not content to contribute to the common good or to redistribute market income unconditionally; they want to get something in return. This is not necessarily a concrete good or service; it can also be a commitment by welfare recipients to do something in return, such as improving their "employability" in order to no longer depend on welfare. In the neo-liberal mind-set, taxpayers eventually picture at the other end of the fiscal contract beneficiaries who likewise respond to economic incentives. This is reflected in the expectation that "welfare recipients should seek to become active and responsible managers of their lives and seek to enhance their economic independence" (Jayasuriya 2002, p310). In this sense, the economic morality of taxation also informs the morality of "the new welfare contract", which places certain behavioural conditions on the recipients of social benefits (Jayasuriya 2002, p311; reference omitted).

Who owes? The expenditure side of the welfare state and the moral economy of debt

The restrictions on the revenue side of the welfare state also affect the expenditure side, or the question of who gets – or loses – what. Tax state and welfare state, as they developed in the twentieth century, are two sides of the same coin. However, this budgetary point of view neglects the regulatory function of the welfare state, which likewise engages in economic governance, that is, the active management of the economy. This function cuts across various policy fields, including "[f]iscal and monetary policies; labor law and labor market policies; corporatist agreements between management, labor and government; prices and incomes policies; farming and food subsidies" (Garland 2014, p344). While the objectives of governing the economy may have changed, the basic "technology" – the "specific set of rationalities and techniques [...] employed to govern the nation's economy and its population in the interest of economic growth and social security" (Garland 2014, p335) – has survived the transformation of welfare capitalism. At the same time, we can witness a reorientation in the principles and practices of economic governance, which does have implications for accustomed social rights, both of a material and a moral nature.

A major theme in recent social policy research has been the change of emphasis "from welfare to workfare", which aims at the "activation" of welfare recipients in the labour market. As an analytical category, the distinction between "(Keynesian) welfare state" and "(Schumpeterian) workfare state" originates from critical political economy (Jessop 1993), but it has also become a common reference in the comparative analysis of the different worlds of welfare capitalism (Vis 2007). Whereas the standard paradigm in welfare state research was, in line with Esping-Andersen's approach, mainly concerned with the "old, passive politics of the welfare state", that is, social insurance (or income maintenance) programmes covering the risk of lost earnings due to unemployment, sickness, or old age, the "new, active politics of the welfare state" focuses, first of all, on the prevention and containment of employment-related risks (Powell and Barrientos 2004, p87). More specifically, "active labour market policies" seek to "improve the access by the inactive or unemployed to the labour market, investment in skills, and generally the functioning of the labour market" (Powell and Barrientos 2004, p88). Against this backdrop, some scholars have come to speak of a "social investment state", which likewise furthers "active employment and social participation – especially in the labour market" (van Kersbergen and Hemerijck 2012, p476). This notion draws on the economic rationale behind the reforms of the welfare state, which is to "ensur[e] that the returns to social expenditures are maximised" (van Kersbergen and Hemerijck 2012). While this includes "negative" measures of welfare retrenchment regarding benefit levels or benefit duration, eligibility criteria or coverage of benefits (van Kersbergen and Hemerijck 2012, p479), the concept of social investment can also be understood in more "positive" terms. The idea is not simply to cut public social spending but to target it differently in order to produce better results.

Our aim here is not to analyse how the different worlds of welfare capitalism perform under the new premises of labour market activation and social investment (cf. Powell and Barrientos 2004; van Kersbergen and Hemerijck 2012), but to explore a related transformation of the welfare state, which has been described as a turn "from welfare to debtfare". This requires dealing with the other attributes of the old welfare state and the new workfare state, which relate to their respective forms of economic governance. When Jessop (1993) contrasted the classic "Keynesian welfare state" with the emerging "Schumpeterian workfare state", the references to Keynes and Schumpeter captured alternative ways to govern the economy. In the case of the Keynesian welfare state macro-economic steering was meant "to promote full employment in a relatively closed national economy primarily through demand-side management"; in the case of the Schumpeterian workfare state, the aim of economic governance is "to promote product, process, organizational, and market innovation and enhance the structural competitiveness of open economies mainly through supply-side intervention" (Jessop 1993, p9; Jessop and Sum 2006, pp107, 109). Using Keynes and Schumpeter as "emblematic" figures has richer connotations than the mere distinction between a "demand-side welfare state" governing a relatively closed national economy and a "supply-side welfare state" adjusting to more open or integrated economies (Jessop 1993, p17). However, this latter distinction suffices to illuminate the political-economic context of both the turn from welfare to workfare and the turn from welfare to debtfare. The "supply-side welfare state" namely uses "individual (dis)incentives" as a lever for economic governance, which means that social provision becomes more market-based or, at least, more "market-compatible" (Obinger and Starke 2014, p19).

The "debtfare state" is, just as the workfare state, all about market activation: "it similarly acts to reinforce the work ethic whilst increasing market dependency and discipline" (Soederberg 2013, p499). However, in this case activation – the transformation of social rights into economic incentives – is less targeted at the labour market than at the credit market. To understand the link between the two, we have to go back to the "crisis of the tax state". This was already debated in the early twentieth century (Leroy 2011, pp52–7), but it gained new topicality towards the end of the golden era of the welfare state (Streeck 2015, pp1–3). What one could observe in the OECD countries from the mid-1970s onwards was "steeply and steadily" rising public debt, which can be seen as the result of "an enduring inadequacy of government revenue compared to government spending" (Streeck 2015, p2). As Streeck suggests, this was indeed a crisis of the tax state and not of the welfare state, which was "caused less by an increase in citizen entitlements than by a general decline in the taxability of democratic-capitalist societies" (Streeck 2015, p4). The mismatch between government revenue and government spending turned the tax state into a "debt state" (Streeck 2015, p3): public debt became an ever greater source of revenue, for which not only present but future taxpayers would be liable. If the decline in taxability of capital and labour in increasingly integrated and competing political economies was a cause, or at least a background condition, of the fiscal crisis, the latter had to be solved "not by raising revenue but by cutting expenditure" – that is, by a politics of austerity (Streeck 2015, p10).

This is the essence of the "consolidation state" of today, which is, according to Streeck, committed to a different, transnational constituency than the classic national welfare state: not to the "people of the state" (*Staatsvolk*), that is, domestic citizens with their civil, political, and social rights, but to the "people of the market" (*Marktvolk*), that is, international creditors and investors with their respective claims, interests, and expectations (Streeck 2015, pp11–12). In the consolidation state, "*commercial market obligations* take precedence over its *political citizenship obligations*" (Streeck 2015, p12; original emphasis). Put differently, we can, again, speak of a trade-off between different subjects of rights: members of a national polity and participants in transnational markets. As above, this is not necessarily about different groups of people, but about different aspects of citizenship, broadly understood, which "constitute" both welfare states and financial markets. The reorientation from domestic citizens to market citizens naturally entails a loss of entitlements for the former. If we leave the rights of voters – the hollowing-out of democracy through market imperatives – aside, it is not difficult to specify the resulting conflict, again, as one between social rights and property rights, which means, in this case, the rights of (domestic) welfare recipients on the one hand and of (transnational) creditors and investors on the other. While this may eventually set one group against the other, the conflict can also be "solved" by turning welfare recipients into creditors and investors, or social citizenship into "financial citizenship" (cf. Kear 2013).

This constellation is furthered by changes in the economic governance function of the welfare state, namely, a shift from Keynesianism to "privatised Keynesianism" (Crouch 2009). Whereas Keynesianism had its heyday in the 1960s and 1970s, that is, in the golden era of the welfare state, "privatised Keynesianism" set off from the "neo-liberal turn" in the 1980s (Crouch 2009, p382). In critical political economy, Keynesianism is conceived as a "mode of regulation" which complements the Fordist "accumulation regime" (cf. Crouch 2009, pp387–8). "Fordism" stands for a technically and economically highly rationalized model of mass production, which also furthers mass consumption. Specialized work and standardized products increase economic efficiency, which leads to lower prices and rising wages, and ultimately results in higher effective demand. The demand-side is also key in Keynesian macro-economic steering, which utilizes public spending as a lever to stimulate the economy in a downturn and to stabilize it throughout the business cycle. Combining the interests of capital and labour – the capitalists' interests in "stable mass consumption" and the workers' interests in "stable lives" – the Keynesian welfare state has become the epitome of democratic welfare capitalism (Crouch 2009, pp389–90).

Turning to "privatised Keynesianism", this is less a political programme than an analytical concept that aims to capture the transformation of welfare capitalism in neo-liberal times. While keeping the focus on aggregate demand, it is fully compatible with a "supply-side" focus on individual incentives. What the concept aims to highlight is that private debt seems to have replaced public debt, at least to a certain extent, in keeping aggregate demand high and the economy running. At the same time, the transmission mechanism that channels this debt-financed demand into the economy changes from "fiscal" citizens, that is, taxpayers and the recipients of social benefits, to "financial" citizens, that is, creditors, debtors and investors, including "consumers of financial services". In other words, the relative retreat of the state from macro-economic steering is compensated by a simultaneous expansion of financial markets. This includes the growth of "credit markets for poor and middle-income people" as well as of "derivatives and futures markets among the very wealthy", which both help to sustain aggregate demand (Crouch 2009, p390). Quite obviously, privatized Keynesianism accentuates the property rights and the respective obligations of market participants, whereas "public" Keynesianism worked, not least, through welfare benefits as a "material" expression of social rights.

The "Keynesian welfare national state" (Jessop and Sum 2006, p106), which flourished in the postwar decades, was premised on the international monetary system of Bretton Woods, which provided for currency exchange stability but also preserved national monetary autonomy. Moreover, the different strategies that western political economies pursued to further economic growth and democratic stability – or to combine "flexibility" with "security" (Crouch 2012) – were premised on specific patterns of international exchange between export-led and demand-driven national economies. Keynesian demand management in "the Scandinavian countries, the UK, Austria and, to a lesser extent, the USA" thus increased not only domestic demand but it also had "important international effects": countries high in consumer demand imported the products of more export-oriented nations (Crouch 2009, p386).

Due to its affinity with the Anglo-Saxon world, privatized Keynesianism has also been referred to as the "'Anglo-liberal' growth model" (Hay 2011, p4). In the European context, this growth model is exemplified by the UK and Ireland, but "elements of it can also be detected in a number of southern and east-central European cases (such as Spain and Hungary, respectively)" (Hay and Wincott 2012, p201). The driving force of Keynesianism are "confident consumers" (Crouch 2012, p6). In its "privatised" form, it eventually came to rely on what has been referred to as "consumer credit capitalism" (Ramsay 2007, p248). While this first developed in the United States, which witnessed a huge expansion of consumer credit after World War II, including home mortgages, car loans, and credit card debt, consumer credit capitalism also took root in European countries from the 1980s onwards. At the same time, export-led and demand-driven economies were increasingly interconnected not only through international trade but also through financial integration and "financialization", both within Europe and across the Atlantic. In this sense, the recent financial crisis – which started as a US subprime mortgage crisis and ended as an EU sovereign debt crisis – is also an effect of the "collapse of privatised Keynesianism" (Bellofiore 2013, p506).

The "crisis of financialisation", as it has also been dubbed (Lapavitsas 2013), was triggered by an underestimation of the "securitised" risk of debt default in a clientele whose creditworthiness was doubtful to begin with. At the same time, the neo-liberal overhaul of welfare capitalism, which found expression in "stagnant real wages and salaries, the commodification of public goods and services, the growing prevalence of low-wage jobs in the service sectors, and the turn to workfare from welfare" (Soederberg 2013, p498), made this "subprime" clientele susceptible to disputable credit offers by lenders whose main profit was in packaging and trading risks. Even though there is no necessary link between the expansion of consumer credit and the retrenchment of the welfare state, more recent developments suggest that creditors in the US and elsewhere increasingly targeted consumers with little or no income or assets, that is, "the working poor and unemployed and under-employed workers" (Soederberg 2013).

As much as the workfare state wants potential or previous welfare clients to be active in the labour market, the debtfare state wants them to be active in the credit market. This has euphemistically been referred to as "financial inclusion" or even as "democratisation of finance" (Erturk et al 2007). What is meant is increased access to financial markets and services for individuals and households of moderate income. Often enough the result is over-indebtedness: not-so-sophisticated consumers may not only be exploited by not-so-responsible creditors, who want them to "take on the greatest amount of debt at the highest interest rates and fees possible to extract ever higher rates of revenue streams" (Soederberg 2013, p495); they may also be exposed to incalculable market risks, such as the bursting of real-estate bubbles, which undermines the affordability of mortgage lending. In this sense, financial inclusion may eventually lead to an over-inclusion of consumers in the logic of international finance (Micklitz 2013).

The normative quality of debt relations is evident in the distribution of rights, risks, and responsibilities between creditors and debtors. Throughout history, debtors have defended their rights and livelihoods in debt riots. The moral economy of debt developed between the poles of creditor and debtor protection (Graeber 2011). Whereas modern capitalism generally emphasizes the rights of owners and creditors, it seems that the protection of debtors has taken an upturn through the normalization of consumer bankruptcy in recent decades. The ideological benchmark in consumer bankruptcy legislation is the "fresh start" policy of the United States, which means, in practice, that consumers who declare bankruptcy can, after a relatively short waiting period, start anew, with all their commercial debt – that is, debt incurred in the market – being cancelled. In other words, they can return to the credit market "with a clean slate". The American fresh start paradigm differs from the classic approach in continental Europe, where "the idea of economic rehabilitation was not tied to the goal of a quick economic recovery and re-entry to the credit market" (Niemi-Kiesiläinen 1999, p482). This changed with the transformation of welfare capitalism and the proliferation of consumer credit capitalism, which had the effect that "European countries have moved gingerly towards a modified 'fresh start' policy in recent decades" (Ramsay 1997, p269).

It should be evident from the above that an increase in debtor protection through a more generous bankruptcy law does not necessarily mean an improvement in the position of ordinary citizens if it is coupled with a loss of welfare entitlements; in short, if "social citizenship" is turned into "financial citizenship". To the extent that public debt is replaced with private debt, the social contract between taxpayers and welfare recipients is superseded by private contracts between creditors and debtors. In this sense, the new "emphasis on consumer protection", here the protection of consumer debtors, "is part and parcel of a move away from collective and rights-based worker protections towards individualized, market-driven forms of citizenship" (Soederberg 2013, p500). Indeed, the fresh start policy follows an economic rationale: for consumers the debt discharge is an incentive to work and borrow, and to continue doing so despite problems with accumulating debt; for lenders it is an incentive to monitor the creditworthiness of "boundedly rational" consumers. Overall, the fresh start policy furthers an "internalisation" of a potential debt discharge in the price of credit, which means that the costs "are borne by the credit system (i.e., all consumers of credit) rather than the state welfare system" (Ramsay 1997, p275). This is a market-based form of insurance, which is fully in line with the principles of the "supply-side welfare state".

It goes without saying that not all welfare recipients turn into consumer debtors in "financialised" welfare capitalism; social citizenship and financial citizenship continue developing side-by-side. However, recent developments at the "welfarist" core and the "consumerist" margins of the inventory of social rights seem to point in the same direction. One could even claim that the privatization of the social contract in the context of debtfare is the "contractualisation of social policies" in the context of workfare (Bonvin and Rosenstein 2015) taken to its logical conclusion. In fact, the new "welfare contractualism" (Jarasuriya 2002, p311) between state and citizens likewise follows the model of private contracts, even though they may not be enforceable as such (Vincent-Jones 2000, pp332, 345). Again, the common denominator is a morality that incentivizes individual economic actors (Jayasuriya 2002, p312) rather than, say, empowering disadvantaged social groups, which has been one of the aspirations of the democratic welfare state.

Conclusion

This chapter has dealt with the question of how the transformations of the welfare state affect the material and moral substance of social rights. Building on Marshall's three generations of rights, it has been argued that the combination, or even integration, of functions of the capitalist market economy and the democratic welfare state, which is characteristic of modern welfare capitalism, brings about different subjects of rights, which complement each other but which also remain in conflict. The social contract underlying welfare capitalism is ultimately a contract between different right-bearing subjects, which may be, and has been, renegotiated over time. More specifically, the historical compromise between capital and labour rested on a balance struck between the subject of property rights and the subject of social rights. This balance is at issue again in the moral reconstruction of welfare capitalism. What we can observe in the last few decades is that social rights are increasingly connected with, made contingent on, or even replaced by economic incentives in what has become a "supply-side welfare state".

This chapter has illustrated the structural and semantic changes affecting social citizenship both on the revenue side and the expenditure side of the welfare state. On the revenue side, we observed a structural shift redistributing tax burdens between mobile and immobile taxpayers, at the expense of the latter, and a semantic shift from "contribution tax" to "exchange tax", which accentuated property rights. The question "who pays?" can be answered, in the abstract, with the subject of social rights. A loss of commitment by taxpayers, especially those representing "capital", translates into a loss of entitlements for potential welfare recipients, whose interests are generally aligned with "labour". On the expenditure side of the welfare state, we witnessed a structural shift towards austerity and activation, which generally meant reducing welfare benefits and making them more conditional, and a semantic shift from "social citizenship" to "financial citizenship", which put emphasis on creditor-debtor relations. Turning the question "who benefits?" into the negative, it can be shown that there has likewise been a loss of entitlements for holders of accustomed social rights. Under conditions not only of "workfare" but also of "debtfare" this means that welfare recipients may eventually turn into consumer debtors. Whereas welfare recipients symbolically owe to taxpayers residing in the same polity, consumer debtors literally owe to creditors in transnational financial markets. The new morality of economic incentives may thus materialize in very concrete economic obligations. With property rights being reinvigorated, the social contract gains features of a private contract between those who own and those who owe.

References

ALM, J. and TORGLER, B. (2006) Culture Differences and Tax Morale in the United States and in Europe. *Journal of Economic Psychology*, 2006(2). pp224–246.

ASHIAGBOR, D., KOTISWARAN, P. and PERRY-KESSARIS, A. (eds) (2013) Special Issue: Towards an Economic Sociology of Law. *Journal of Law and Society*. 40(1).

BAGGULEY, P. (1996) The Moral Economy of Anti-Poll Tax Protest. In BARKER, C. and KENNEDY, P. T. (eds) *To Make Another World: Studies in Protest and Collective Action*. Aldershot: Avebury, pp7–24.

BELLOFIORE, R. (2013) "Two Or Three Things I Know About Her": Europe in the Global Crisis and Heterodox Economics. *Cambridge Journal of Economics*, 37(3). pp497–512.

BONVIN, J.-M. and ROSENSTEIN, E. (2015) Contractualising Social Policies: A Way Towards More Active Social Citizenship and Enhanced Capabilities? In RUNE, E., KILDAL, N. and NILSSEN, E. (eds) *New Contractualism in European Welfare State Policies*. Abingdon: Routledge, pp47–72.

BRENNER, N., PECK, J. and THEODORE, N. (2010) Variegated Neoliberalization: Geographies, Modalities, Pathways. *Global Networks*, 10(2). pp182–222.

CAMPBELL, A. L. (2009a) What Americans Think of Taxes. In MARTIN, I. W., MEHROTRA, A. K. and PRASAD, M. (eds) *The New Fiscal Sociology: Taxation in Comparative and Historical Perspective*. Cambridge: Cambridge University Press, pp48–67.

CAMPBELL, A. (2009b) Epilogue: A Renaissance for Fiscal Sociology? In MARTIN, I. W., MEHROTRA, A. K. and PRASAD, M. (eds) *The New Fiscal Sociology: Taxation in Comparative and Historical Perspective*. Cambridge: Cambridge University Press, pp256–265.

CHRISTENSEN, J. (2013) Nordisk skattepolitikk mot 2030 (NordMod 2030, delnotat 1). *Forskningsstiftelsen Fafo, Fafo-notat*2013:07. Available from: www.fafoarkiv.no/pub/rapp/10173/10173.pdf. [Accessed 5 November 2016].

CHRISTIANSEN, N. F. (1984) Denmark: End of the Idyll. *New Left Review*, I/144. pp5–32.

CROUCH, C. (2009) Privatised Keynesianism: An Unacknowledged Policy Regime. *British Journal of Politics and International Relations.* 11(3). pp382–399.

CROUCH, C. (2012) Beyond the Flexibility/Security Trade-Off: Reconciling Confident Consumers with Insecure Workers. *British Journal of Industrial Relations.* 50(1). pp1–22.

DOERRENBERG, P. and PEICHL, A. (2013) Progressive Taxation and Tax Morale. *Public Choice.* 155(3). pp293–316.

ERTURK, I. et al (2007) The Democratization of Finance? Promises, Outcomes and Conditions. *Review of International Political Economy.* 14(4). pp553–575.

ESPING-ANDERSEN, G. (1990) *The Three Worlds of Welfare Capitalism.* Cambridge: Polity Press.

FERRAGINA, E. and SEELEIB-KAISER, M. (2011) Welfare Regime Debate: Past, Present, Futures? *Policy & Politics.* 39(4). pp583–611.

FRERICHS, S. (2009) The Legal Constitution of Market Society: Probing the Economic Sociology of Law. *Economic Sociology – European Electronic Newsletter.* 10(3). pp20–25.

FRERICHS, S. (2011) Re-embedding Neo-liberal Constitutionalism: A Polanyian Case for the Economic Sociology of Law. In JOERGES, C. and FALKE, J. (eds) *Karl Polanyi, Globalisation and the Potential of Law in Transnational Markets.* Oxford: Hart Publishing, pp65–84.

FRERICHS, S., (2012) *What Constitutes the Market Society? Studies in the Economic Sociology of Law.* Habilitation thesis, University of Bamberg.

GARLAND, D. (2014) The Welfare State: A Fundamental Dimension of Modern Government. *European Journal of Sociology.* 55(3). pp327–364.

GENSCHEL, P. and SCHWARZ, P. (2011) Tax Competition: A Literature Review. *Socio-Economic Review*, 9(2). pp339–370.

GENSCHEL, P. and SCHWARZ, P. (2013) Tax Competition and Fiscal Democracy. In SCHÄFER, A. and STREECK, W. (eds) *Politics in the Age of Austerity.* Cambridge: Polity Press, pp59–83.

GRAEBER, D. (2011) *Debt: The First 5,000 Years.* Brooklyn, NY: Melville House.

GUILLÉN, A. M. and ÁLVAREZ, S. (2001) Globalization and the Southern Welfare States. In SYKES, R. et al (eds) *Globalization and European Welfare States: Challenges and Change.* Houndmills: Palgrave Macmillan, pp103–126.

HANN, C. (2010) Moral Economy. In HART, K., LAVILLE, J.-L. and CATTANI, A. D. (eds) *The Human Economy.* Cambridge: Polity Press, pp187–196.

HAY, C. (2011) Pathology without Crisis? The Strange Demise of the Anglo-Liberal Growth Model. *Government and Opposition*, 46(1). pp1–31.

HAY, C. and WINCOTT, D. (2012) *The Political Economy of European Welfare Capitalism.* Houndmills: Palgrave Macmillan.

HOPPE, H.-H. (2006 [1990]) The Economics and Sociology of Taxation. In HOPPE, H.-H. *The Economics and Ethics of Private Property: Studies in Political Economy and Philosophy.* 2nd ed. Auburn, AL: Ludwig von Mises Institute, pp33–75.

HOWARD, C. (2009) Making Taxes the Life of The Party. In MARTIN, I. W., MEHROTRA, A. K. and PRASAD, M. (eds) *The New Fiscal Sociology: Taxation in Comparative and Historical Perspective.* Cambridge: Cambridge University Press, pp86–100.

JAYASURIYA, K. (2002) The New Contractualism: Neo-Liberal or Democratic? *Political Quarterly*, 73(3). pp309–320.

JESSOP, B. and SUM, N.-L. (2006) *Beyond the Regulation Approach: Putting Capitalist Economies in their Place*. Cheltenham: Edward Elgar.

JESSOP, B. (1993) Towards a Schumpeterian Workfare State? Preliminary Remarks on Post-Fordist Political Economy. *Studies in Political Economy*, 40 (Spring). pp7–39.

KEAR, M. (2013) Governing Homo Subprimicus: Beyond Financial Citizenship, Exclusion, and Rights. *Antipode*, 45(4). pp926–946.

LAFFER, A. B. (2004) The Laffer Curve: Past, Present, and Future. *Backgrounder – Published by The Heritage Foundation. 1765.* Available from: www.heritage.org/research/taxes/bg1765.cfm. [Accessed: 5 November 2016].

LAPAVITSAS, C. (2013) *Profiting Without Producing: How Finance Exploits Us All.* London: Verso.

LEROY, M. (2011) *Taxation, the State and Society: The Fiscal Sociology of Interventionist Democracy.* Bruxelles: Peter Lang.

MARSHALL, T. H. (1950) Citizenship and Social Class. In MARSHALL, T. H. *Citizenship and Social Class and Other Essays.* Cambridge: Cambridge University Press, pp1–85.

MARSHALL, T. H. (1972) Value Problems of Welfare-Capitalism. *Journal of Social Policy*, 1 (1). pp15–32.

MARTIN, I. W. (2008) *The Permanent Tax Revolt: How the Property Tax Transformed American Politics.* Stanford, CA: Stanford University Press.

MARTIN, I. W., MEHROTRA, A. K. and PRASAD, M. (2009) The Thunder of History: The Origins and Development of the New Fiscal Sociology. In MARTIN, I. W., MEHROTRA, A. K. and PRASAD, M. (eds) *The New Fiscal Sociology: Taxation in Comparative and Historical Perspective.* Cambridge: Cambridge University Press, pp1–27.

MATHEW, S. K. (2010) *Making People Pay: The Economic Sociology of Taxation.* New Delhi: Global Vision Publishing House.

McCLURE, K. M. (1995) Taking Liberties in Foucault's Triangle: Sovereignty, Discipline, Governmentality, and the Subject of Rights. In SARAT, A. and KEARNS, T. R. (eds) *Identities, Politics and Rights.* Ann Arbor, MI: University of Michigan Press, pp149–192.

MENÉNDEZ, A. J. (2015) Neumark Vindicated: The Europeanisation of National Tax Systems and the Future of the Social and Democratic Rechtsstaat. *ARENA Working Paper* 4/2015. Available from: www.sv.uio.no/arena/english/research/publications/arena-working-papers/2015/wp4-15.pdf. [Accessed: 5 November 2016].

MICKLITZ, H.-W. (2013) Access to, and Exclusion of, European Consumers from Financial Markets after the Global Financial Crisis. In WILSON, T. (ed.) *International Responses to Issues of Credit and Over-indebtedness in the Wake of the Crisis.* Farnham: Ashgate, pp47–75.

NIEMI-KIESILÄINEN, J. (1999) Consumer Bankruptcy in Comparison: Do We Cure a Market Failure or a Social Problem? *Osgoode Hall Law Journal.* 37 (1 & 2). pp473–503.

OBINGER, H. and STARKE, P. (2014) Welfare State Transformation: Convergence and the Rise of the Supply Side Model. *TransState Working Papers No. 180.* Available from: www.sfb597.uni-bremen.de/pages/download.php?ID=221&SPRACHE=en&TABLE=AP&TYPE=PDFZ. [Accessed: 5 November 2016].

OECD (Organisation for Economic Co-operation and Development) (2014) *Revenue Statistics 2014.* Paris: OECD Publishing.

PIERSON, C. (2010) Welfare Capitalism. In FITZPATRICK, T. et al (eds) *International Encyclopedia of Social Policy.* London: Routledge, pp1518–1523.

POLANYI, K. (1957 [1944]) *The Great Transformation.* Boston, MA: Beacon Press.

POWELL, M. and BARRIENTOS, A. (2004) Welfare Regimes and the Welfare Mix. *European Journal of Political Research*, 43(1). pp83–105.

RAMSAY, I. (1997) Models of Consumer Bankruptcy: Implications for Research and Policy. *Journal of Consumer Policy*, 20(2). pp269–287.

RAMSAY, I. (2007) Comparative Consumer Bankruptcy. *University of Illinois Law Review*, 2007(1). pp241–273.

ROSS, M. L. (2004) Does Taxation Lead to Representation? *British Journal of Political Science*, 34(2). pp229–249.

SCHELKLE, W. (2012) Collapsing Worlds and Varieties of Welfare Capitalism. In *Search of a New Political Economy of Welfare*. *LEQS Discussion Paper* No 54/2012. Available from: www.lse.ac.uk/europeanInstitute/LEQS%20Discussion%20Paper%20Series/LEQSPaper54.pdf. [Accessed: 5 November 2016].

SCOTT, J. C. (2005) Afterword to "Moral Economies, State Spaces, and Categorical Violence". *American Anthropologist*, 107(3). pp395–402.

SOEDERBERG, S. (2013) The US Debtfare State and the Credit Card Industry: Forging Spaces of Dispossession. *Antipode*, 45(2). pp493–512.

STREECK, W. (2015) The Rise of the European Consolidation State. *MPIfG Discussion Paper* 15/1. Available from: www.mpifg.de/pu/mpifg_dp/dp15-1.pdf. [Accessed: 5 November 2016].

SWEDBERG, R. (2003) The Case for an Economic Sociology of Law. *Theory and Society*, 32(1). pp1–37.

SWEDBERG, R. (2006) Max Weber's Contribution to the Economic Sociology of Law. *Annual Review of Law and Social Science*, 2. pp61–81.

THOMPSON, E. P. (1971) The Moral Economy of the English Crowd in the Eighteenth Century. *Past & Present*, 50(1). pp76–136.

THOMPSON, E. P. (1991) *Customs in Common*. London: Merlin Press.

VAN KERSBERGEN, K. and HEMERIJCK, A. (2012) Two Decades of Change in Europe: The Emergence of the Social Investment State. *Journal of Social Policy*, 41(3). pp475–492.

VINCENT-JONES, P. (2000) Contractual Governance: Institutional and Organizational Analysis. *Oxford Journal of Legal Studies*. 20(3), pp317–351.

VIS, B. (2007) States of Welfare or States of Workfare? Welfare State Restructuring in 16 Capitalist Democracies, 1985–2002. *Policy & Politics*, 35(1). pp105–122.

WEBER, M. (1978 [1922]) *Economy and Society: An Outline of Interpretive Sociology*. Berkeley, CA: University of California Press.

Chapter 8

Social rights and user charges
Resistance or subsumption?

Amir Paz-Fuchs

Introduction

Along with privatization, contracting out and "new" management techniques, one of the important, but less discussed, manifestations of the way neo-liberal ideology and policies have changed social services is through the requirement that individuals pay for those services – services that were once provided free of charge. A parallel method, which should be distinguished, includes the offer of "premium" services in a given sector at a prescribed cost.

In the UK, for example, over 600 individual services impose user charges (Bailey 1994a). It is interesting to note that "social democratic" countries, such as Norway, Finland and Denmark, which have proud public services, are also those with the wider and longer experience of user charges (Emmerson and Reed 2003). As an indication of the importance of the trend, the IMF has recently offered a definition of user charges which is relatively straightforward: "payments made by consumers to providers of government services" (IMF 2007, p132).

While the literature has addressed the imposition of user charges in public sectors, in general, with some focus on utilities, this chapter addresses user charges in the field of *social* services, with a particular emphasis on health and education. The fact that such charges have adverse effects on equal access to services (and thus on equality in general) seems straightforward: their imposition precludes those without the necessary means from accessing the services. But it will be argued that the charges have more profound effects as well. Through these relatively small charges, the relationship between the citizen and the state is transformed. The citizen, we are told, is now the "citizen-consumer", who "expects improved standards from public services, in line with those supplied by the private sector" (Lister 2003, p438). Replicating free market services, such charges are seen as part of an overall strategy to "roll back the frontiers of the state" (Bailey 1994a, p366).

Closely related is the role and, perhaps, the nature, of the relevant rights. This chapter focuses on the relationship between user charges and the rights to health and to education. This may be referred to in two ways. First, the relevant rights should have a role to play when assessing the legitimacy and legality of user charges. Rights, after all, are "especially sturdy objects to stand upon, a most useful sort of moral furniture" (Feinberg 1970, p252; also Holmes and Sunstein 2000). They have the potential, at the very least, to alter the confines of the debate that would have taken place in their absence. A world without the right to freedom of speech, we assume, would be different from a world in which such a right is granted and respected. Focusing on social *services* in general, and on health and education in particular, we therefore need to explore what impact social *rights* may have on the phenomenon of user charges and/or its effects. Second, the direction of the cause and effect may also be reversed. If the nature of services changes, and the relationship between the citizen and state becomes increasingly mediated through market norms, then our understanding of rights – or at least of social rights – should be revisited.

But in doing so, we need to, first, understand the origins and breadth of the trend; to come to terms with the rationales and justifications that drive it; and to offer a tentative typology of user charges in the fields of health and education. The chapter then moves on to inquire whether the right to education and the right to health can, and should, provide the analytical and pragmatic basis for bucking this trend. The chapter concludes with an assertion that social rights' failure to serve as safeguards in the face of increased marketization of the services has consequences not only for the services and their clients, but also for the understanding of the rights themselves.

The origins of the trend, and its rationales

To an extent, paying for services has become quite natural for most of us. Indeed, where services offered on the market are concerned, this has been the case (almost) since the dawn of time. And yet, in many areas, *public* services have been insulated from the reach of market practices. They are paid for, of course, but through general taxation.

This was not always the case. User charges for public services were common in the 19th century, and a harsh critique of their implementation may be found in the 1906 Webbs Minority Report of the Poor Law Commission. They stated that the practice was a "chaotic agglomeration of legal powers conferred on different authorities at different dates for different purposes proceeding upon no common principles" (cited in Judge 1980, p2). Indeed, nationalizing the payment for public, and in particular social, services, was viewed as not only a progressive move that was part and parcel of the development of welfare state institutions, but one guided by concerns of efficiency and effectiveness. And yet, in a lovely historical twist, exactly 100 years later, the British House of Commons Health Committee report on National Health Service (NHS) charges echoed (probably unknowingly) the Webbs indictment, opening with the clear statement: "The system of health charges in England is a mess" (House of Commons 2006, p3). It goes on to note that there is no clear reason why some services are charged while others are not; why one constituency (say, the elderly) receive exemption from one service, while another (say, the disabled) are exempt from charges for a different type of service, and so on.

The case against user charges in social services has not been based solely on efficiency grounds. Perhaps more importantly, it is clearly in *society's interest* (even regardless of its assessment of the individual's rights or, indeed, her inclinations) that individuals access these services. In the economists' terminology, such services have obvious positive externalities. The more educated a population, the more employable they are, and the more competitive a country's economy becomes. The healthier the population, the less chance that epidemics will spread, and the lower the costs to the health services. And so on.

While these rationales have supported the foundation of public services that are free at the point of delivery, they have been met with strong opposition in recent years. The adherence to a neoliberal framework has led to alternative rationales, some of which are set out below, that favour the imposition of user charges:

1   *As a source of income and an alternative to taxation*: the macro-economic rationale suggests that in times of austerity the state should look "outside the box" to other sources of income. As this chapter was in its final stages, the British government made public its intention to charge non-European Union (EU) patients for general practitioner (GP) services, thus saving UK£500 million a year. Bailey noted over 20 years ago that "in almost all countries, there is a clear and consistent trend for user-charge revenues to grow substantially faster than other income sources" (1994b, p746), and since then the trend has not abated (Sjoquist and Stoycheva 2012). Quite cynically, this rationale relies on the inelasticity in the demand for public services. Simply put, people will be willing to pay for health, education, welfare and urban services when they need them (Creese 1991, p311). Charging small sums of money will not deter them, and it may have a positive significant impact on public finances (cf Rose 1990). It should be noted, however, that this rationale requires that the administration of the charges be considered. Significant revenue may be gained if charges are flat rate, simple and universal, but such charges are more prevalent where urban services, such as waste disposal or congestion charges, are involved. They are less justifiable for social services, where costs may restrict access to health, education and welfare. In such cases, administrative costs and wide exemptions will weigh down the budgetary gains significantly (Asato 2006).

2   *To restrict demand and change behaviour*: in times of austerity, on the one hand, and increased desires, on the other, the state simply cannot provide free access to all social services that citizens demand access to. "Principles are priceless", it is said, "but services are not costless" (Bailey 1994b, p752). Despite the similarity, or even partial overlap, with the previous category, this rationale is based on a diametrically opposed logic. Here policy-makers would like (some) people to be deterred from making use of public services that are readily available, thus reducing the need to supply them to the same extent, and consequently saving costs.

3   The British Prime Minister at the time of the establishment of the NHS, Clement Attlee, highlighted (what is now referred to as) the "signalling"

attribute of charges: "a deterrence against extravagance, rather than as an economy" (Eversley 2001, p53). The idea here is to prevent abuse, while also refraining from deterring those who are in need. Thus, if you do *not* charge for a doctor's appointment, people who have nothing better to do will come by, simply to talk to the doctor whilst not deterring those who truly need to see a doctor.

4   *Equity*: while this justification would, intuitively, serve as grounds to *oppose* user charges, it has been employed as an argument in their favour. There are three complementary strands to this argument. First, a moral argument is made that those who wish to gain access to a particular service should pay for it, partially or even in full. Thus, if I, after serious consideration, chose not to have children because (*inter alia*) of the cost of childcare, why should I be asked to pay (through taxation) for other people's childcare? Second, other individuals, who use and support public services, may be willing to pay for them, but do not trust the government to spend tax revenues on the "right" public services. They would therefore prefer "hypothecated", or "earmarked" taxes to general taxation (Le Grand 2006). And, third, a utilitarian justification would suggest that user charges with means-tested exemptions would actually allow *more* people to access social services, while requiring those who are better off to pay their way.

It should be obvious that searching for one rationale across the whole range of services is an exercise in futility. Over 25 years ago, Richard Rose noted that: "The present pattern of hundreds of charges throughout every aspect of British government cannot be explained by a single hypothesis or a single theory" (Rose 1990, p303). Since then, the number of services imposing charges has more than doubled.

User charges in health and education, and the rights involved

Health and education are two central areas of the welfare state that are subject to the recent trend of user charges, also known as user fees, or co-payments. They share some similar traits: both are massive public services that command vast budgets; both serve a very wide range of the population, which are considered worthy of heightened protection: the sick, elderly and disabled, and children; in both, women are the "field level" workers (nurses and teachers) on relatively low graduate salaries. And yet, insofar as charges are concerned, we find an important difference, that may be attributed to the second pillar (in addition to the charges themselves) of this chapter: social and economic rights. Even where the two are present in the same document, a curious (and highly relevant) difference is notable: the word "free". Thus, here are the relevant provisions of the United Nations' International Covenant on Economic, Social and Cultural Rights 1966:

Article 12

1 The States Parties to the present Covenant recognize the right of everyone to the enjoyment of the highest attainable standard of physical and mental health.

Article 13

2 The States Parties to the present Covenant recognize that, with a view to achieving the full realization of this right:

    1 Primary education shall be compulsory and available *free* to all;

    2 Secondary education in its different forms ... shall be made generally available and accessible to all by ever appropriate means, and in particular by the progressive introduction of *free* education;

    3 Higher education shall be made equally accessible to all ... in particular by the progressive introduction of *free* education;

And the European Social Charter uses similar language:

Article 11

... the Parties undertake...

1 to remove as far as possible the causes of ill-health;

2 to provide advisory and educational facilities for the promotion of health and the encouragement of individual responsibility in matters of health; ...

Article 17(2)

... the Parties undertake...

2 to provide to children and young persons a *free* primary and secondary education as well as to encourage regular attendance at schools.

Similar conclusions can be derived from the comparison of Articles 25 and 26 to the UN Declaration of Human Rights; Articles 14 and 35 of the European Charter of Fundamental Rights, and elsewhere. On a national level, section 16(1) of the Constitution of Finland states that "Everyone has the right to basic education *free* of charge"; while section 19(3) states that "The public authorities shall guarantee for everyone ... adequate social, health and medical services and promote the health of the population". Similarly, section 27(4) of the Constitution of Spain prescribes similarly that "Elementary education is compulsory and *free*"; while section 43 only provides that "(1) The right to health protection is recognized; (2) It is incumbent upon the public authorities to organize and watch over public health by means of preventive measures and the necessary benefits and services".

We may prefer to be sceptical about the effect that human rights conventions and constitutional provisions have over policy; and yet, it may not be a coincidence that user charges are used widely in core health services; in contrast, Western capitalist democracies have, by and large, shielded the core of primary and secondary education from such hazards. The caveats in the last sentence may suggest, however, where the provision of free education has suffered some inroads of its own: in tertiary education, in the form of university fees; in the existence of "private", fee-paying primary and secondary schools, as an alternative to the state system; and in the peripheral services in the state system (e.g., school meals and school buses). We turn now to provide a brief outline of user charges in the fields of health and education, while mentioning some of the motivations behind the charges, and a glimpse into their effects.

Health

Healthcare user charges exist in all Organisation for Economic Co-operation and Development (OECD) countries, but not all charges are created alike. For present purposes, three examples highlight different rationales for user charges (see Commission 2014):

1   *Consultation fees*: for sessions with a GP or a hospital visit. The UK is one of only 9 EU countries that does not charge for GP visits and one of 14 EU countries that does not charge for hospital treatment. Against this background, it is not surprising that consideration of the policy is constantly on the horizon. An early BMA research report found, for example, that a £10 GP consultation fee could raise £3.3bn annually (British Medical Association 1997).

2   *Ancillary (non-medical), but necessary, services*: charging for hospital car parking may seem reasonable to some, but in Britain charges have been introduced only recently in some hospitals, and have been rising dramatically in others, forcing the government to introduce a Guidance to regulate the area (Department of Health 2014). The Guidance lists the categories of individuals for which concessions should be available (e.g., people with disabilities; visitors with relatives who are gravely ill), but does not include a cap on charges, thus enabling some hospitals, such as the Heart of England NHS Foundation in England, to rake in UK£4 million in car park charges for the tax year 2013–2014. More controversial are charges for hospital beds – again, not a "medical service" *per se*, but one that is intimately associated to the medical care. And yet, in late 2014, the chief executive of the NHS Confederation stated that if the service's financial crisis is not addressed, hospitals may have to "think the unthinkable" and start charging hospital patients for the "hotel costs", or "bed and board", of their hospital stay (Unauthored 2015).

3   *"Premium" or additional services*: the House of Commons Health Committee on NHS charges noted the "increasing number of charges for clinical services" (House of Commons 2006, p24). These may be services which are provided

by the NHS for free at a basic level, but for which a charge enables a higher level of service at additional cost; or services provided only at cost (i.e., no free service) by NHS personnel. The Jentle Midwifery Scheme at Queen Charlotte's and Chelsea Hospital in London is an example of the first case, as it offers women one-on-one midwife care during the course of the pregnancy and after delivery for UK£4000. Delivery at a private hospital costs between UK£7000 and £10,000. The dermatology clinic run by Harrogate and District NHS Foundation Trust offers a wide array of skin treatments (e.g., removal of moles and warts) that prior to 2003 were provided for free by the NHS, but are now provided by NHS staff at a cost that ranges from UK£85 to £250.

A comparison across OECD countries reveals the breadth of the trend. In 2008, France, a country that has prided itself on a socialist ethos that is far deeper than that of Britain, introduced higher charges for hospital care, as well as new charges for GP appointments and for ambulance services. Italy has introduced, and Ireland has increased, charges for unnecessary accident and emergency (A&E) attendance (Emmerson and Reed 2003).

There are surprisingly few studies of the consequences of user charges in the health sector. However, those that exist seem to agree that charges deter at least some patients from accessing necessary treatment, thus worsening their own situation and potentially (in the case of infectious diseases, for example) harming others. If charges are universal, they will deter those who cannot pay; and if they are means-tested, the administrative costs and the reduced income may render the policy inefficient (House of Commons 2006).

A prominent exception to the scarcity of empirical evidence is the controlled experiment study conducted by the RAND group. The study took place in the US in the 1970s, where 2000 patients were subject to four different charging regimes. It lasted 15 years and is the largest health policy study ever conducted. The study revealed that increasing costs resulted in consistently reduced use of health care services, with particular effect on individuals from lower social and economic groups; and on those with chronic illnesses. Moreover, those who were poor and suffered from health conditions were more subject to hypertension, which resulted in a rise in the annual likelihood of death by 10 per cent. More contemporary studies, which are survey based, conclude that "charges above zero had a serious adverse effect on those who were both poor and suffering from poor health, the poor being defined in this study as those in the bottom 20 per cent of the income distribution" (Commission 2014, p25). Thus, a recent survey of 20,000 individuals in 11 countries found that patients in the UK had the lowest tendency (4 per cent) to forgo meeting a GP or filling in a prescription form when compared to countries, such as the United States (37 per cent), that have far higher user charges. Obviously, when patients defer consulting a GP or purchasing medicine to treat an illness at its early stages, their condition may deteriorate, worsening their personal situation and leading to more expenses for the health services (House of Commons 2006). These are some of the reasons that lead the King's Fund Commission to conclude that "health care should be freely available to those who need it, regardless of income" (Commission 2014, p29).

Education

As noted in the introduction to this section, despite the fact that health and education are often discussed in conjunction, user charges in the field of education have some different attributes, when compared to health. The explicit mention of a duty to provide *free* primary and secondary education in international conventions as well as in national constitutions and statutes imposes (or perhaps reflects) an understanding that paying for education at young ages will link a child's socio-economic background to his or her life chances, thus widening, instead of limiting, inequality.

Against this background, most of the attention of policy-makers and, correspondingly, academics, has been on tertiary education, or as it is commonly referred to – university fees. Interestingly, when compared to user charges in the field of health, here the equity rationale is said to be reversed. That is, the argument is made that while charging for health care is regressive, charging for tertiary education is *progressive* (Johnstone 2004). The reason is that those subject to health care charges tend to be poor, disabled, and socially disenfranchised; while those taking advantage of tertiary education tend to be more privileged. Higher education fees are thus redistributive because of students' backgrounds, and because graduates tend to earn higher salaries. Some suggest that higher education is expected to increase women's pay by 25 to 27 per cent; and men's pay by 18 to 21 per cent. Universities UK refers to research suggesting that the difference is even more pronounced – up to 45 per cent in the UK, and an average of 40 per cent across OECD countries (Universities UK 2013). Therefore, *not* charging for university education would mean that tax payers, including working class families, would be paying for middle class and upper middle class children's free access to a service that would plausibly widen social and economic gaps (Asato 2006; King 2012, p82).

Whether or not this is the case, or even the motivation, it is clear that university fees have gone up significantly over the past decade. The fact that fees in private (non-profit) universities in America have risen by 28 per cent in a decade may surprise few, but perhaps more significant is the fact that public universities increased their fees by 27 per cent over five years, leading the Economist (2014) to conclude that "Universities have passed most of their rising costs to their students".

In England, fees were introduced for the first time in 1998, at a flat rate of UK £1000 per year. They were raised to £3000 in 2006–2007 and then, in 2012–2013, following a significant change in structure, to a maximum of £9000. The change in structure refers to the fact that, with the rise in fees, home students are no longer required to pay the fees up-front, as charges deferred until after graduation (subject to the individual earning above UK£21,000 per annum), with loans available at a reduced (at lower earnings – zero) interest rate.

Charging for education, however, is not limited to tertiary education. Two additional realms of user charges in education are noted: "private" schools and peripheral educational services.

First, we note the existence of "private", fully fee-paying, primary and secondary schools. To an extent, this would mean privatization of the public service. As such, these cases do not seem to fall within the main interest of this chapter, because (as indicated by the OECD definition) charges are not understood as an *alternative* to public service provision, but rather are integrated into the public provision of services. And yet, it is worth questioning whether we should not view "private" education as an extreme case of user charges, rather than as an alternative to the public system. Most schools are on public land and, as charities, enjoy generous tax benefits funded by the public, to the tune of UK£700 million a year, in the UK (Wintour 2014); users of the service often enjoy similar tax benefits, thus suggesting that the state supports the provision of health and education even in the "private" sector.

Second, peripheral but essential services, such as school meals and school buses, are subject to charges. Section 451(2) of the Education Act 1996 prohibits the imposition of charges for education, stating that "Where the education is provided for the pupil during school hours no charge shall be made in respect of it". And yet, the Department of Education reported receipts of £1.3bn for education (Heald 1990; Department for Education 2014). The explanation for this conundrum is that the Education Act opens the door to charging for musical instrument lessons (s.451(3)); for education outside of school hours; and where a governing body is liable to pay a fee in respect of the entry of a student for an examination, and the student fails without good reason to meet any examination requirement (s.453(2)). The Education Act 1996 also proscribes the requirement that a school and local authority may maintain a policy with respect to the provision, classes and description of cases in which they propose to charge (s.455).

Limiting user charges through social rights?

Why is it acceptable to charge for some services, of a more commercialized nature, while serious objections are raised in other cases (use of public parks, or libraries); and what's law got to do with it? The market pricing model assumes that all goods are commensurable. We may agree that insofar as these goods are private (albeit provided by the *public* service) and not collective (Rose 1990), they *can* be commensurable or, perhaps more relevantly, marketable. Moreover, even the paradigmatic lighthouse could be sustained by charging ships arriving at the port or visitors at the sea front (Bailey 1994a). But *should* they?

Barry Schwartz and Anne Alstott separately refer to Michael Walzer's *Spheres of Justice* (Walzer 1984), suggesting that in deciding the relevant principles for the provision of goods and services, the dominant principles should be identified, and distinguished from those prevalent in other spheres (Schwartz 2012; Alstott 2012). Economists sometimes describe goods that *can* but *should not* be marketable as merit goods (Musgrave 1987). However, this has been viewed as "an apolitical way to refer to political values" (Bailey 1994a, p367), or plainly tautological (Rose 1990, p303). So if that is the case, how can we buck the trend? According to Anne Alstott, "If market ideology has a tendency to take over, to spill over into nonmarket spheres where it doesn't belong, then we should consider constructing *legal firewalls* to protect spheres of nonmarket exchange" (2012, p191; my emphasis). In other words, per Alstott, if we cannot rely on market, social or cultural norms, it is for the law to carry the load. But how can the law assist in identifying the boundaries that should be protected?

Increasingly, in our individualized world, when we say "law", we refer to "rights". If that is indeed the case, can rights provide a "legal firewall", or at least a stop-gap measure, to curb the breadth and depth of the tendency to impose user charges? Where civil and political rights are concerned, courts have had no qualms about restricting the government from levying charges on protesters. In a case concerning free speech, the Israeli Supreme Court suggested (and not for the first time) that "setting a price for the implementation of a right means violating the rights of those who cannot afford it".[1]

In contrast, courts are far less willing to accept the argument that substantial user charges violate the right to health, for example. The ECtHR dismissed such claims as manifestly ill-founded (see references in Brems 2007, p141). In Israel, a woman who required surgery so as not to lose her hearing was asked to pay 70 per cent of the cost.[2] In rhetoric that is strikingly different from the one employed in free speech cases, the Israeli Supreme Court stated that when priorities are to be set, the judiciary should defer its judgment to professional committees, such as the one that deliberated the question in this case (Gross 2007).

In light of the above, how are we to identify the role that the rights to health and to education are to play? We may identify two relevant distinctions *en route* to this enquiry.

First, we find the distinction between core and peripheral services. Take the case of an individual who is not given access to a primary education or life-altering health service solely because she cannot afford them. Arguably, this is the strongest case for social and economic rights intervention, and even here courts have failed to give the relevant rights true meaning. The Israeli Supreme Court ruling noted above is a case in point. In addition, although *Roe v. Wade* (1973) is familiar to many as the case that established a woman's right to have an abortion in the United States, far less familiar is the case of *Harris v. McRae* (1980), which denied a woman's right to have an abortion funded, if she cannot afford it. The link between the two was not missed by Justice Marshall, in dissent, who noted (p383) that the policy "den[ies] to the poor the constitutional right recognized in *Roe v. Wade*".

Can we envisage a similar scenario in the field of education: a local government begins to charge fees for primary schools, rejecting children whose parents cannot pay for access to education? The fact that it seems inconceivable (at this stage) is, perhaps, indicative of the fact that, within the realm of social welfare rights, the right to *free* education is perceived by policy makers and the public at large as stronger than the right to health, and less subject to government policy of imposing user charges.

These cases are distinguished from peripheral services. It should be noted that here we refer to peripheral services themselves, and not to their qualities, availability, or peripheral characteristics (to which we turn immediately). Thus, this case refers to the distinction between, for example, cancer treatment, on the one hand, and cosmetic surgery for aesthetic reasons, on the other; and not to matters such as waiting times, the expertise of the physician or the size of the hospital room in which the patient recovers. In education, it may refer to the distinction between primary and tertiary education (and, for that matter, private music or arts lessons), and not to the size of classes. Parker (1980) hypothesizes that charges are more likely to be imposed when a "part of a service can be regarded as marginal".

Of course, a difficulty may, and will, exist as to where to draw the line. Thus, the Canadian Supreme Court denied a claim that behavioural therapy for autistic children must be funded by the government, stating that it is not a core service, and thus not covered by the charter.[3] But drawing the line would be important only if core services should be protected more vigorously than peripheral services. I believe that they should (similarly King 2012, p132). If we are to preserve the importance, integrity and function of the right to education and the right to health, their core and peripheral meanings should be argued for and identified, with the implication that the further we are from the core, the less weight would be carried by the right used to challenge a government that refuses to fund the service. But the opposite is also true: the closer we are to the core, the more courts should be able to review policy decisions that condition the service on ability to pay.

We need not limit ourselves to two categories (core and periphery). Stephen Bailey (1994a) identified four: "need", "protective", "amenity" or "facility" services. According to Bailey's prescription, "need" services would be wholly financed from taxation and so free at the point of use whilst the "facility" services would be wholly financed by charges. In between these extremes, the "protective" and "amenity" services would be financed by a combination of taxes and charges, income from subsidies exceeding charges for the former and the reverse for the latter. The closer we are to the need category, the more vigilant we should be in allowing the right to health and the right to education, if taken seriously, to provide the "legal firewalls" that Alstott referred to. In the intermediate categories, courts would be advised to undertake a proportionality test to assess whether the charges are overbearing, and if the same (legitimate) aim may be achieved through means that are less onerous, or charges that are lower.

The second distinction arises between basic and non-basic elements of a given service. The "basic" elements will be provided free of charge, while non-basic elements will be chargeable at a subsidized rate, or up to full cost. Though a distinct matter, it raises boundary issues that are similar to those in the previous case. But, more importantly, while the focus of the previous category was on access to health or education, this category is mainly concerned with the idea of equality in the provision of the service. So this category will assume that a certain service is governed by the relevant right (cf. the case of behavioural therapy above), but those who are willing to pay receive a more professional service, shorter queues, or simply general amenities (nice room, Wi-Fi connection). Supporters of this two-tiered service argue that allowing some to pay for better services harms no one and, moreover, that money funnelled through this channel will be used to support the free, universal provision, thus being Pareto-superior to the situation which does not allow for such distinctions. In response, opponents argue that when well-resourced users opt out of universal services, the "voice" necessary for their improvement is substantially weakened. The creation of "poor service for poor people" is thereby facilitated. What is the role of social rights in such cases? To be honest, probably quite minimal. As long as access to the core element of the right is provided, courts are likely to be of the view that the right is not violated. The long-term deterioration of the service as a result of the two-tiered structure is likely to be seen as a speculative argument that the court will not entertain.

However, an alternative, and perhaps stronger, avenue is available by arguing that a two-tiered service is a straightforward violation of the right to equality, a well-established constitutional principle which has managed to secure more success for social welfare interests than arguments based on the rights themselves (Gross 2007; Brems 2007). Indeed, the right to equality would seem vacuous if white people would enjoy the right to education, health or housing that is denied to black individuals. Moreover, at times it seems that the right to equality is doing the "heavy lifting", far more than the right to health or the right to education. It is now almost 50 years since Frank Michelman (1969) argued that equality will be the most promising vehicle to secure social welfare rights, and advance the cause of social justice in general. A similar, wide-ranging ambition was presented more recently by Kerry Rittich:

> ... social rights remain fundamentally about distributive justice. They are concerned not simply with the provision of basic needs or a safety net for the most destitute ... they operate as a metric of our commitment to relative social equality.

> (Rittich 2007, p109)

This link between distributive justice and social rights leads us to the most ambitious challenge: that which relates to the possibility that rights will safeguard certain spheres from marketization. In particular, the idea that courts will play a role in constituting, through the language of rights, some spheres as "taboo" (Schwartz 2012; Harrington 2009), not to be tainted with, or mediated by, money. If that avenue were to succeed, challenges based on the right to education and health could be advanced against the support that private schools and private hospitals receive from the public purse. This idea is politically appealing (if private schools and hospitals facilitate inequalities in the provision of health and education, why should the public support them?) but it is not clear what the legal rationale would be. If the existence of such private institutions have deleterious effects on distributive justice, and thus on the provision of the particular right, could a challenge be mounted against their existence in general? Here, we find the aim of social rights is most removed from its core, minimal meaning and assumes a remit that even some of its supporters are not comfortable with (King 2012).

In summary, policy-makers and courts can and should consider social rights when assessing the implementation of user charges. They should ascertain the expected effects of such imposition on equal access to social services. If a detrimental effect is expected, they should assess whether it relates to the basic services and thus, to the core of the rights involved; or whether, alternatively, the detrimental effect affects only peripheral services or ancillary, non-basic elements of the services. It is perhaps worth noting that while courts are justified in awarding more discretion to policy-makers in the latter cases, policy-makers themselves would do well to consider the social effects of differential education, health care or other social services.

User charges and the transformation of social rights

Lawyers tend to focus on the relationship between rights and the world around them in a manner that is uni-directional: rights have, or should have, an impact on decision-making, on policy, on end-states (Dworkin 1977). But one need not be a committed Marxist to appreciate the fact that rights themselves are also the *products* of a social and economic structure. User charges can be seen as part of a process in which the rights that a citizen enjoys no longer independently define the range of activities available to her (Rawls 1999); instead, this liberal concept of citizenship is transformed into one associated with consumerism, or "consumer citizenship" (Carney and Ramia 2002, p16). Foucault, for example, identified the trend with alarming prescience almost 40 years ago: "neoliberalism models the overall exercise of political power on the principles of the market ... and the economic grid *tests action and gauges validity*" (Foucault 2010, pp131, 247; emphasis added). With the benefit of awareness to contemporary developments, Wendy Brown has recently developed this approach, showing how, "As liberty is relocated from political to economic life, it becomes subject to the inherent inequality of the latter and is part of what secures that inequality" (Brown 2015, p41).

This is a crucial insight, with important implications for the role of rights in political discourse and public policy. Rather than providing boundaries and limits to the economic rationale, rights (and social rights in particular) are *reconstructed* as subordinate to the demands of the economy. The consequence of this is that they lose their core function, and are made redundant. If this trend continues, the right to health, for example, will cease to guarantee access to care based on the criterion of need, and will instead become a right to treatment conditional upon payment (Gross 2007, pp311–13; cf. Atria 2015, p603). The internal logic of (social) rights will change. Traditionally, rights are designed to shield individual interests, and in the case of social rights, to provide a strong political and legal argument in favour of guaranteeing access to social goods irrespective of the ability to pay. This is true, it should be made clear, even where the need for user charges is justified by resorting to budgetary constraints. The phrase "rights cost money" should be as applicable in the case of social rights as it is in the realm of civil and political rights. If this is not the case, collective interests – such as budgetary constraints, the need to reduce queues for services or the general effort to change individual behaviour – will be advanced uninhibited, and social rights will provide no barrier. Rights will be no match for the neoliberal rationality which justifies the transformation of political relations (rights governing relations between citizen and state) into economic relations (purchasing services). Moreover, through the mechanism of (social) rights, law itself becomes complicit in disseminating this rationality into constitutive elements of our social and democratic life (Brown 2015, p151).

How does this come to pass? Policies implementing user charges put in place a contractual mechanism that, as Vincent-Jones rightly notes, "both draws upon and reinforces these notions of agency and choice … *contracts render individuals responsible for their predicament* … in ways that differ significantly from the governance of relations by hierarchal authority" (Vincent-Jones 2006, p233; emphasis added). The theme of responsibility is one that is central to the neo-liberal paradigm, and is eerily relevant to the issue at hand. The burdening of individuals with financial responsibility in these spheres is neatly captured by Shamir as "the economization of the political" (Shamir 2008, p1). Brown suggests that it involves:

> … the moral burdening of the entity (individual) at the end of the pipeline … [It] tasks the worker, student, consumer or indigent person with discerning and undertaking the correct strategies of self-investment and entrepreneurship for thriving and surviving; it is in this regard a manifestation of human capitalization.
>
> (Brown 2015, p133)

The point here is not only legal, but moral as well. Since social and economic rights are constantly under contention, there is an ongoing struggle to define their content, and their boundaries (Barak-Erez and Gross 2007). This struggle takes place not only in legal arenas, but also in the moral and political sphere. Now, with the shift in emphasis to a marketized provision of social services, an individual who does not have the means to pay for treatment, or for her child's school trip, is not only legally denied the service itself, but also denied the moral right of protest against an unjust system. This is because the system has redefined not only legal, but, through the law, moral entitlements to social goods as well. The construction thus "cloaks the status quo with an air of legitimacy" (Barry 2005, p40). As a result, the right to education – which would include, say, joining a school trip – has been *redefined*: you have the right to join only if you pay for the trip. If you do not, or cannot afford to, pay, you do not have the right. In a way, you are not even denied your right to education, because that right was *not engaged at all*, that is, according to this new construction of rights.

One may assert at this stage that paying for services is simply an extension of the theme of reciprocity, which is identified in the founding documents of the design of the welfare state. It is true that the Beveridge Report held a central role for the idea of reciprocity, as did John Rawls, in his construction of "Justice as Fairness". Closely related, Rawls's theory is "contractual" in nature, thus interpreting moral and political concepts through the paradigm of the social contract. And contracts, as we know, are reciprocal. They require "something for something". Herein lies the rub: proponents of user charges may reject the presumption that citizens are entitled to health care or to education free of charge on the basis of a philosophical, or moral, approach that there is no "something for nothing". Rather, individuals who are in need of a service, should be expected to give "something" in return, to wit – to pay, for the service. This logic has, as noted, undermined the moral, political and legal role for rights. Here, it is suggested that it also constitutes a manipulation of the idea of reciprocity that Beveridge and Rawls referred to, as well as the concept of the social contract (Paz-Fuchs 2008; Handler and Hasenfeld 2006; Jones and Novak 1999; cf. Wax 2003).

It is readily admitted that contractarian language lends itself to such manipulation. For some, like David Gauthier (1986) and James Buchanan (1975), the reciprocal nature of the social contract is *exemplified* in economic exchange. Rawls explicitly rejects this approach, stating that: "It is sometimes contended that contract doctrine entails that private society is the ideal, at least when the division of advantages satisfies a suitable standard of reciprocity. But this is not so" (Rawls 1999, p458). In particular, the central role that equality holds in Rawls's theory suggests that primary goods, such as health and education, should be distributed equally in society and thus that the relevant rights dictate the limits of the market (Scanlon 1998).

To close the circle, this very idea – equal distribution of rights, irrespective of ability to pay – is accepted insofar as civil and political rights are concerned, as discussed above with regards to freedom of speech. So, yet again, here we find that social rights are different. But why is that the case? To an extent, charging for social services highlights the tensions inherent in social welfare rights as a concept, and brings them to the fore. These tensions derive from the fact that whereas social rights are based in *social* realms, such as health, education, housing and welfare, "rights talk" is traditionally individualistic. But while social rights seek to bridge this tension, enriching the social, collective dimension of rights, charging for access to rights pushes back, militating towards heightened individualization, the "personalization of risk rather than its collective assumption by the state" (Carney and Ramia 2002, p165).

The risk, therefore, is that not only are rights to health and education losing the battle against charging in their respective realms. It is, additionally, that with the marketization of those realms, social welfare rights are subsumed, and marketized, as well.

Conclusion

This chapter has highlighted the serious risks posed by the expanding policy of charging for publicly-funded services in the health and education sectors. It suggests that a carefully constructed legal firewall, in the form of strong rights to health and to education should, at the very least, protect the core elements of those social goods from the intrusion of market norms. In addition, these rights should be used to temper the use of charging as a precondition for access through familiar public law instruments, such as assessing whether charging serves a legitimate aim, and is advanced through proportionate means.

The fact that some courts have not been willing to adopt this position and halt the advance of user charges through a strong interpretation of social rights has resulted in unequal access to the provision of these crucial social services, and may have worrying negative externalities. But the difficulties do not end there. The intrusion of market norms into social realms includes their intrusion into the conceptualization of the relevant rights themselves. And viewing rights as a vehicle to protect budgets or to engineer social behaviour is a very troubling prospect indeed. Doing so by way of charging, thus realistically affecting only the poorest members of society, who rely most on social rights, effectively means the hollowing out of those rights, and denying these members a crucial instrument to protect their basic interests.

Notes

1 HCJ 2557/05 *The Majority Headquarters v. The Israeli Police* [2006], at [16]; See similarly *Fordyce County, Georgia v. The Nationalist Movement* 505 US 123 (1992).
2 HCJ 2974/06 *Israeli v. Committee for the Expansion of the Health Basket* [2006].
3 *Auton v. British Columbia* [2004] 3 SCR 657.

References

ALSTOTT, A. (2012) "A Fine is Not a Price": Insights for Law. In HANSON, J. and JOST, J. (eds), *Ideology, Psychology, and Law*. Oxford: OUP, pp185–193.
ASATO, J. (2006) *Charging Ahead? Spreading the costs of modern public services*. London: Social Market Foundation.
ATRIA, F. (2015) Social Rights, Social Contract, Socialism. *Social & Legal Studies*, 24(4). pp598–613.
BAILEY, S. J. (1994a) Charging for Local Government Services: A Coherent Philosophy. *Public Administration*, 72(3). pp365–385.
BAILEY, S. J. (1994b) User-charges for Urban Services. *Urban Studies*, 31. pp745–765.
BARAK-EREZ, D. and GROSS, A. (2007) Introduction. In BARAK-EREZ, D. and GROSS, A. (eds) *Exploring Social Rights: Between Theory and Practice*. Oxford: Hart, pp1–20.

BARRY, B. (2005) *Why Social Justice Matters*. Cambridge: Polity Press.

BREMS, E. (2007) Indirect Protection of Human Rights by the European Court of Human Rights. In BARAK-EREZ, D. and GROSS, A. (eds) *Exploring Social Rights: Between Theory and Practice*. Oxford: Hart, pp146–167.

BRITISH MEDICAL ASSOCIATION (1997) *Options for Health Care Funding*. London: Health Policy and Economic Research Unit.

BROWN, W. (2015) *Undoing the Demos: Neoliberalism's Stealth Revolution*. New York: Zone Books.

BUCHANAN, J. M. (1975) *The Limits of Liberty: Between Anarchy and Leviathan*. Chicago, IL: University of Chicago Press.

CARNEY, T. and RAMIA, G. (2002) *From Rights to Management: Contract, New Public Management and Employment Services*. New York: Kluwer Law International.

COMMISSION ON THE FUTURE OF HEALTH AND SOCIAL CARE IN ENGLAND (2014) *A New Settlement for Health and Social Care*. London: The King's Fund.

CREESE, A. L. (1991) User charges for health care: a review of recent experience. *Health Policy Plan*, 6. pp309–319.

DEPARTMENT FOR EDUCATION (2014) *Charging for School Activities*, www.gov.uk/government/uploads/system/uploads/attachment_data/file/365929/charging_for_school_activities_October_2014.pdf (accessed 5 April 2016).

DEPARTMENT OF HEALTH (2014) *NHS patient, Visitor and Staff Car Parking Principles*. www.gov.uk/government/publications/nhs-patient-visitor-and-staff-car-parking-principles/nhs-patient-visitor-and-staff-car-parking-principles (accessed 3 January 2016).

DWORKIN, R. (1977) *Taking Rights Seriously*. London: Duckworth.

THE ECONOMIST (2014) *The digital degree*. London: The Economist.

EMMERSON, C. and REED, H. (2003) Use of fees in the provision of public services in OECD countries. In ANDERSEN, T. M. and MOLANDER, P. (eds) *Alternatives for Welfare Policy*. Cambridge: Cambridge University Press.

EVERSLEY, J. (2001) The History of NHS Charges. *Contemporary British History*, 15. pp53–75.

FEINBERG, J. (1970) The Nature and Value of Rights. *Journal of Value Inquiry*, 4. pp243–260.

FOUCAULT, M. (2010) *The Birth of Biopolitics: Lectures at the Collège de France, 1978–1979*. Basingstoke, Hampshire: Palgrave Macmillan.

GAUTHIER, D. P. (1986) *Morals by Agreement*. Oxford: Oxford University Press.

GROSS, A. (2007) The Right to Health in an Era of Globalization and Privatization: National and International Perspectives. In BARAK-EREZ, D. and GROSS, A. (eds) *Exploring Social Rights: Between Theory and Practice*. Oxford: Hart. pp289–339.

HANDLER, J. F. and HASENFELD, Y. (2006) *Blame Welfare, Ignore Poverty and Inequality*. New York: Cambridge University Press.

HARRINGTON, J. (2009) Visions of utopia: markets, medicine and the National Health Service. *Legal Studies*, 29. pp376–399.

HEALD, D. (1990) Charging by British Government: Evidence from the Public Expenditure Survey. *Financial Accountability & Management*. 6(4). pp229–261.

HOLMES, S. and SUNSTEIN, C. R. (2000) *The Cost of Rights: Why Liberty Depends on Taxes*. New York: W. W. Norton & Company.

HOUSE OF COMMONS HEALTH COMMITTEE (2006) *NHS Charges, Third Report of Session 2005–2006*. London: HMSO.

IMF (International Monetary Fund) (2007) *Manual on Fiscal Transparency*. Washington, DC: Glossary.

JOHNSTONE, D. B. (2004) The economics and politics of cost sharing in higher education: comparative perspectives. *Economics of Education Review*, 23. pp403–410.

JONES, C. and NOVAK, T. (1999) *Poverty, Welfare and the Disciplinary State*. London and New York: Routledge.

JUDGE, K. (1980) An Introduction to the Economic Theory of Pricing. In JUDGE, K. (ed.) *Pricing the Social Services, Studies in Social Policy*. London: Macmillan. pp46–66.

KING, J. (2012) *Judging Social Rights*. Cambridge: Cambridge University Press.

LE GRAND, J. (2006) *Motivation, Agency, and Public Policy: of Knights and Knaves, Pawns and Queens*. Oxford: Oxford University Press.

LISTER, R. (2003) Investing in the Citizen-workers of the Future: Transformations in Citizenship and the State under New Labour. *Social Policy & Administration*, 37. pp427–443.

MICHELMAN, F. (1969) On Protecting the Poor through the Fourteenth Amendment. *Harvard Law Review*, 83. pp7–59.

MUSGRAVE, R. (1987) Merit Goods. In EATWELL, J., MILGATE, M. and NEWMAN, P. (eds) *The New Palgrave: A Dictionary of Economics* (vol 3). London: Macmillan.

PARKER, R. A. (1980) Policies, Presumptions and Prospects in Charging for the Social Services. In JUDGE, K. (ed.) *Pricing the Social Services, Studies in Social Policy*. London: Macmillan. pp24–45.

PAZ-FUCHS, A. (2008) *Welfare to Work: Conditional Rights in Social Policy*. Oxford: Oxford University Press.

RAWLS, J. (1999) *A Theory of Justice*. Revised edition. Cambridge, MA: Harvard University Press.

RITTICH, K. (2007) Social Rights and Social Policy. In BARAK-EREZ, D. and GROSS, A. (eds) *Exploring Social Rights: Between Theory and Practice*. Oxford: Hart. pp107–134.

ROSE, R. (1990) Charging for Public Services. *Public Administration*, 68. pp297–313.

SCANLON, T. (1998) *What We Owe to Each Other*. Cambridge, MA: Harvard University Press.

SCHWARTZ, B. (2012) Crowding Out Morality: How the Ideology of Self-Interest Can Be Self-Fulfilling. In HANSON, J. (ed.) *Ideology, Psychology, and Law*. Oxford: Oxford University Press, pp160–184.

SHAMIR, R. (2008) The age of responsibilization: on market-embedded morality. *Economy and Society*, 37. pp1–19.

SJOQUIST, D. and STOYCHEVA, R. (2012) Local Revenue Diversification: User Charges, Sales Taxes and Income Taxes. In EBEL, R. and PETERSON, J. (eds) *Oxford Handbook of State and Local Government Finance*. New York: Oxford University Press.

UNAUTHORED (2015) Non-EU patients "should be charged for GP services". *BBC News*. URLwww.bbc.co.uk/news/health-35007243 (accessed 14 March 2016).

UNIVERSITIES UK (2013) *The funding challenge for universities*. London: Universities UK.

VINCENT-JONES, P. (2006) *The New Public Contracting: Regulation, Responsiveness, Relationality*. Oxford: Oxford University Press.

WALZER, M. (1984) *Spheres of Justice*. New York: Basic Books.

WAX, A. (2003) *Something for Nothing: Liberal Justice and Welfare Work Requirements*. Faculty Scholarship.

WINTOUR, P. (2014). Tristram Hunt warns private schools to help state pupils or lose £700m in tax breaks. *The Guardian*.

Chapter 9

European integration and the transformation of the social state

From symbiosis to dominance*

Fernando Losada

Introduction

This chapter explains how the evolution of the European integration project has transformed its originally symbiotic relationship with the post-war social state into one of dominance under the current economic crisis. It first provides an overview of the distinctive elements of the social state – which traditionally guaranteed social rights through fundamental rights, social policies and public services – and of its legal manifestation, the Social and Democratic *Rechtsstaat*. Using this notion as a conceptual framework, the analysis describes a series of unrelated events which, when combined, explain how European integration affected and transformed the social state by disentangling from each other its three foundational elements: the rule of law, the democratic principle and its responsiveness to social demands. Concisely, during the early stages of European integration the Court of Justice established European Union (EU) law as an autonomous legal order. Its primacy over national legal systems was the starting point of a process that gradually disconnected law from its concrete (national) social context. After the Treaty of Maastricht, and due to constitutionalization, the economic rationale of EU law was imposed over more socially sensitive national law, hence contributing to law's disconnection from the social context – a process fuelled by the increase of EU competences and Member States. More-over, market rules were for the first time applicable to public services, reducing the number of tools available for states to direct the economy and, importantly, to guarantee social rights. Finally, during the recent global economic downturn, the adoption of a set of anti-crisis measures circumvented the European legal order and undermined the democratic principle at both the European and national levels. In sum, the effects of the evolution of European integration on the social state suggest not only a deviation from the classical formulation of the Social and Democratic *Rechtsstaat*, but a new governing rationale at the European level, according to which social rights are not a priority but a secondary objective subjected to financial stability.

The social state and its legal manifestation: the Social and Democratic *Rechtsstaat*

In the aftermath of World War II, European societies witnessed a transformation in the role and functions of the state, whose keyword switched from "liberal" to "social". Whereas in previous decades (and centuries) the state was supposed to refrain from meddling in society, in post-war Europe the main idea was precisely that state and society interact in a horizontal way to the end of not only respecting individual freedoms but of guaranteeing the well-being of citizens too. This explains why the emergence and consolidation of civil and political rights took place during the pre-eminence of the liberal state and why socio-economic rights were only recognized once the social state model was established. The different role of these generations of rights (protecting citizens *from* the state, first; protecting citizens *through* the state, later) also reflects a change in how human dignity, the basic value on which society is based, was understood: the "liberal" state conceived of individual freedom as a consequence of human dignity, while the "social" state reversed the relationship by making human dignity, materialized in socio-economic rights, a precondition of the effective exercise of individual freedom.

Socio-economic rights were originally concrete and specific social measures, reacting to some particular and problematic situation, but gradually turned into a more general and systemic policy. This shift from a "reactive" to a "proactive" social policy (García-Pelayo 2009 [1977], p102) is closely related to a wider change in the role, powers and legitimation mechanisms of the state. The essence of the liberal state, whose main concern was to limit the power of the state by passing acts constraining it, resided in the activity of Parliament and its legislative capacity. The social state, on the other hand, aims to guarantee a minimum of well-being from which citizens can exercise their freedom – as captured in the concept of *Daseinsvorsorge* (Forsthoff 2015 [1963], pp89 ff., 420 ff.). It has to provide some basic goods, and hence its main task can be labelled as managerial. Consequently, executive power and its administration replace legislative power as the model's defining element. The relevant legitimation mechanisms are accordingly adapted: the liberal state, based on Parliamentary activity, requires input legitimacy, whereas the social state, managing social resources, relies on output legitimacy too (Scharpf 1999, p6).

The social state implies a vast increase in the number of social goals (Rubio Llorente 2012, p959) and consequently requires new rationalities and administrative techniques (Garland 2014, p335), but it basically deals with the distribution of public goods through an adequate use of traditional fiscal power. Importantly, its function is not only to monitor the distribution of public goods but also to produce and deliver them. The social state is therefore responsible for the general direction of the economy and, in particular, is inextricably linked to capitalism (García-Pelayo 2009 [1977], pp66–82; Marshall 1972, p18; Garland 2014, pp355–6).

In constitutional terms a new, social dimension accompanies and complements the classical pairing of democracy and the rule of law, typical of the liberal state. The democratic element configures a bottom-up conception of power, only concretized when placed in relation to other organizing principles of public life, solving the tension between the values of liberalism (freedom) and democracy (equality). On the other hand, the rule of law,[1] based on the principle of legality and subjecting public power formally and substantively to law (via judicial control of administrative acts), organizes human life through a coactive legal order. The coupling of democracy and the rule of law constituted the foundation of the "liberal" state. The limits of this pairing became dramatically apparent in the interwar period, but with the advent of the social state in the second half of the 20th century a new element came into the equation and contributed to mitigate these tensions: from then on the input from society modulated the relation between democracy and the rule of law. Since each society has its own values and traditions, the different realizations of the social state led in the medium and long term to varieties of capitalism (Hall and Soskice 2001; Soederberg et al 2005).

To be sure, constitutional law reflected this closer relationship between society and the state. Henceforth, regardless of the formal way they recognize it, political systems throughout Europe subordinate some private interests to a shared, common project in the framework of the nation-state. They do so, for instance, by guaranteeing the socio-economic and cultural conditions required for the exercise of democratic rights, and by developing policies aimed at diminishing economic, cultural or social differences between citizens. Furthermore, if not literally mentioned in constitutions, the social state is *de facto* reflected in clauses at the intersection of the political (democracy) and economic (capitalism) systems. In this respect, provisions recognizing the social function of private property – only acknowledged after the creation of collective insurance mechanisms diminished private property's historical role as the sole guarantor of basic living conditions against unexpected events – are of particular relevance (see Article 14 of the German Basic Law, Article 42 of the Italian Constitution, Article 33 of the Spanish Constitution, or Article 43.2 of the Irish Constitution). But in legal terms the most refined expression of this change is the inclusion of the formula Social and Democratic *Rechtsstaat* in some constitutions – first of all in Articles 20(1) and 28(1) of the German Basic Law.

This constitutional expression captures the combination and interrelation of the now three defining elements of the state, which in post-war Europe is *social*, in addition to *democratic* and *ruled by law*. This tripartite structure assumes a balance between its elements, so if one element is lacking the whole theoretical construct collapses. But, importantly, the resulting concept is different than the mere addition of its three components. As a matter of fact, each element, without prejudice to its own autonomy, is linked to the others through relations of coordination, which on the one hand limit their development and on the other widen their potential for realization (García-Pelayo 2009 [1977], p103). Hence, the social input helps to adapt democracy to the will and interests of the majority, reducing the risk of a mere formal democracy. Social goals, for their part, are hardly compatible with the rule of law since they impose active policies, which fall within the domain of politics and are therefore not easily enforceable via adjudication. The obligation of ensuring that no one harms the ability of citizens to continue making use of the resources they already have is nevertheless still susceptible to judicial review (Bilchitz 2014, pp714–15).

Importantly, although originating from the German constitutional doctrine and thus only being mentioned in constitutions under its influence (Article 3 of the Italian Constitution; Article 1 of the Spanish Constitution), the Social and Democratic *Rechtsstaat* constitutes the legal expression of the foundational elements of all post-WWII Western regimes, regardless of their constitutional tradition. Through this shared set of constitutional values, common to all European countries, post-war nation states integrated political and economic systems as a way of solving, through social justice, problems of inequality inherent in the liberal state. To that end, the social state guaranteed social rights in three different ways: first, as fundamental rights, although with the inherent difficulties attached to their adjudication; second, as policy programmes implemented in ever-increasing legislation and implemented via a strengthened administrative apparatus, thus requiring additional legitimation; and, third, as public services, usually delivered by state-owned companies.

In what follows I will explore the extent to which the European integration process has affected the most important features of that social state emerging in post-war Europe: its ability to command or steer the economy, on the one hand, and its capacity to redistribute the common goods delivered by the economic (capitalistic) system through welfare policies, on the other. In doing so, I will use as an indicator the evolution of the social function of property rights. Instead of severing the link between property and well-being by abolishing private property, as communists advocated, the social state readjusted that relation through two complementary strategies. First, it increased the amount of owners by promoting publicly subsidized home ownership, which not only created jobs in the construction sector, thus contributing to the reactivation of the battered economy, but also sheltered displaced people and improved general health conditions (Sotelo 2010, p258). And, second, it reduced the dependence on private property for well-being by creating compulsory collective insurance mechanisms – which themselves constitute a form of social property (Castel 2003, Ch. 6). Private property constitutes simultaneously a foundational premise of capitalist economies and a potential limitation on the social state, which accordingly subjects its use to public interests. Hence, when examined through a constitutional lens, property rights can reveal how the balance between individual liberties and collective responsibilities (Caruso 2004, p763), and subsequently between the political and economic systems, has been struck in the different national realizations of the social state (Sotelo 2010, p43). Unsurprisingly, social responsibilities demanded from property owners decreased as the economy became gradually disembedded from society. Once detached from most social functions, property rights were thus mainly understood in their individual sense as entitlements to peaceful enjoyment of property. Consequently, I will argue, the social function of private property changed from being an inherent, endogenous feature of property rights to become an exogenous element, a goal (amongst many others) that could be achieved through their invocation in court.

Pre-Maastricht integration: from symbiosis to early symptoms of uncoupling

In post-war Europe, the European integration project contributed to the consolidation of the social state model in two different but related ways. Firstly, this occurred by establishing the foundations on which economic prosperity would develop. Shared management of basic industrial resources (the European Coal and Steel Community, hereafter ECSC) and, later on, sustained increase of commercial exchanges guaranteed by the gradual opening of borders between participating states (European Economic Community, hereafter EEC), together with the impulse generated by the Marshall Plan and other equally relevant international initiatives (Eichengreen 1995), stimulated economic growth. Secondly, European integration helped realign the political, economic and social existence of Europeans in the framework of the nation-state (Milward 1992, p3), within which regional inequalities, inherent to market development (Myrdal 1963 [1957], p41), were avoided by reallocating resources from relatively better off regions and groups to the most disadvantaged ones. The establishment of public services together with a progressive tax system were crucial in implementing such large scale egalitarian policies. The politically and economically cohesive societies of European nation states legitimated the augmented administrative apparatuses required in particular for launching and sustaining those redistributive policies, while the legitimation of European integration relied on the participation of representatives of national sovereignties in the assembly monitoring the activity of, and decisions adopted by, the High Authority (ECSC) or the Council (EEC) – the latter composed of national executives. The relation between the European integration project and its Member States was therefore symbiotic: the European level contributed to economic prosperity, which in turn provided revenue to be redistributed through welfare policies via public services and social rights "at the expense of indulging in nationalistic economic policies" (Myrdal 1960, p119).

As a result of the long process of transformation from the liberal to the social state model, the new role of the state became that of guardian of the interests of society rather than of those of the economy (Berman 2006, p178). Consequently, even though the compromise with capitalism as a shared systemic choice was implicitly but firmly grounded in the European treaties, national governments conceived of integration as a way to control and shape their now open economies to the benefit of their societies. Hence, the inclusion in the treaties of a whole set of provisions regulating competition in order to prevent unwanted outcomes of the free market; or, as already mentioned in the Schumann Declaration, the explicit acknowledgement that integration was not to interfere with national regulation of property (Article 222 EEC), left to states all decisions related to the balance between the economic and political values at stake. This idea seems also to have inspired the coetaneous drafting of Article 1 of the First Protocol to the European Convention on Human Rights (hereafter ECHR) on the right to property, subjecting owners' peaceful enjoyment of their possessions to the state's right to regulate their use according to the general interest. In sum, the liberal spirit of European integration was the core of an extremely interventionist project (Baquero Cruz 2002, p78), leading to a common liberalized market embedded in democratic nation states (Ruggie 1982). Capitalism was thus subjected to democracy.

According to the initial plan, competences on social matters conferred to the supranational level were scarce. Apart from the competence to adopt measures guaranteeing that all employment periods should be recognized when calculating the social benefits of migrant workers (Article 51 EEC), it was assumed that improved labour conditions would be the natural consequence of economic integration and its subsequent harmonization of national social systems (Article 117 EEC; Falkner 1998, p57). Hence, Commission tasks were restricted to promoting "close collaboration between Member States in the social field" by issuing non-binding measures, namely opinions (Article 118 EEC). The only provision of the treaties with substantive content mandated the equal pay of men and women for the same work (Article 119 EEC). However, rather than having a social rationale, this provision aimed at avoiding competitive advantages for countries paying women less than men (*Defrenne vs Sabena (No. 2)*, case 43/75, EU:C:1976:56, para. 9). In institutional terms, a European Social Fund aimed to help national welfare systems with the expenses related to the presumable geographical and occupational mobility of workers in the common market. Finally, as a way of derogation public services were excluded from the observance of those competition rules incompatible with the performance of their task (Article 90 EEC).

The limited and fragmented character of these provisions led some authors to label the first decade of European integration as "neo-liberal" (Nielsen and Szyszczak 1991, pp22–5). However, this categorization relied exclusively on the amount of social rules established at the supranational level and disregarded the fact that European integration is a holistic project, symbiotic with, instead of detached from, its Member States (Fossum and Menéndez 2011). As a matter of fact, integration, by establishing a market regularly providing revenues to be redistributed at national level, critically contributed during its two first decades to the realization of the Social and Democratic *Rechtsstaat* in European nation states. However, things changed in the early 1970s due to the economic instability following the end of the Bretton Woods system and the oil crises: peaking unemployment and inflationary monetary policies – in some cases leading to stagflation – were met with cutbacks on welfare expenses. The subsequent crisis of legitimacy (Habermas 1975; Crozier et al 1975) was aggravated by the increasingly contradictory roles of the state as promoter of capitalist economy and as provider of social services (O'Connor 1973, p6; Offe 1984, p149 ff.). Consequently, the first criticisms of public services and welfare policies (based on efficiency and cost-benefit grounds) were voiced. The rise of neoliberalism in countries such as the United Kingdom, now a member of the EEC, anticipated a widespread change in how the relation between the economic and political systems (namely capitalism and democracy) would be balanced.

Against this background, several Commission initiatives in the social domain were blocked at the Council. Lacking a proper legal basis in the treaties, a few directives were adopted on the grounds of achieving the common market (Article 100 EEC)[2] or by resorting to the subsidiary competence provision (Article 235 EEC).[3] Regardless of this lack of explicit competence at the European level, the Court of Justice emphasized that the aims of integration were not merely economic, but social too (*Defrenne vs Sabena (No. 2)*, EU:C:1976:56, para. 10). However, despite this unequivocal acknowledgement, its action expanding the foundations of the European legal order was detrimental to national social policies in three different ways. First, because consolidating the European legal order through the development of the principles of direct effect and primacy (*Van Gend en Loos*, 26/62, EU:C:1963:1 and *Costa v ENEL*, 6/64, EU:C:1964:66, respectively) led in the long run to the constitutionalization of EU law and the subsequent pre-eminence of its economically oriented rules over the all-encompassing and more socially inclusive national constitutions. In other words, once European law granted market participants subjective rights which they could deploy in court against any national measure – be it of legislative or even constitutional nature – a structural bias promoting the economic rules of the former against the more socially sensitive measures of the latter was established (Grimm 2015, p467).

Secondly, this effect occurred as a result of the way in which the new legal order guaranteed fundamental rights – the right to property among them. Instead of empowering national systems of protection, which could have contradicted each other and thus potentially disrupted the common market, the Court of Justice guaranteed the consistency of the EU legal order by protecting fundamental rights according to its own standards (*Internationale Handelsgesellschaft*, 11/70, EU:C:1970:114, para. 3). These standards were derived from common constitutional traditions of EU members in combination with international law instruments safeguarding fundamental rights, particularly the ECHR (*Internationale Handelsgesellschaft*, EU:C:1970:114, para. 4; *Nold*, 4/73, EU:C:1974:51, para. 13). Therefore, when an individual found a Community measure harmful for her right to property, the Court weighed between the general interest of the Community (*Hauer*, 44/79, EU:C:1979:290, para. 23) and the European (instead of national) fundamental right, according to which its inherent social function is recognized (*Nold*, 4/73, para. 14; *Schräder*, 265/87, EU:C:1989:303, para. 15). However, this balancing was again biased: first, because the Court equated economic integration with the general interest of the Community, as if the latter could be detached from the richer, more plural, interest of its Member States (Utrilla Fernández-Bermejo 2011, pp141, 147); and, second, because instead of leaving discretion to national courts to determine the social function of property, the Court of Justice imposed its own assessment based on the aims of the treaties. This meant the assessment became detached from each state's concrete variety of capitalism. In this regard, the European Court of Human Rights' (hereafter, ECtHR) doctrine of the margin of appreciation is more suitable, for it respects each contracting party's understanding of the social function of property according to their respective national constitutions.

Finally, the Court's activity impaired national social policies by detaching law from politics. In order to promote the common market, the Court of Justice famously ruled that, in the absence of harmonization, products lawfully marketed in one country could be validly commercialized across the whole common market unless very specific conditions related to the protection of public safety, health, or the environment were met (*Cassis de Dijon*, 120/78, EU:C:1979:42). This meant that without an agreement at the Council – a quite unlikely option by then, due to the "Luxemburg compromise" and its *de facto* political blockage of the EEC's decision-making (Teasdale 1993) – members, by default, had to recognize each other's standards regarding product regulation. If we accept that national regulations set mere technical standards, then finding a new standard by mutual recognition would save time and energy in comparison with harmonization. But implications of mutual recognition are different if we instead conceive of national regulations as carrying out a risk assessment according to which a specific balance between conflicting values, social considerations among them, is struck (Weiler 2005, p49). In that case national regulations are an expression of the particular varieties of capitalism corresponding to concrete realizations of the Social and Democratic *Rechtsstaat* and, as such, cannot be replaced by decontextualized value assessments stemming from other countries. It is true that states could still justify restrictions on mutual recognition relying on grounds of overriding public interests ("mandatory requirements", *Cassis de Dijon*, EU:C:1979:42, para. 8), but these are, first, a Court's interpretation of the limits of the common market, thus disentangled from any particular national social context; and, second, always subjected to the principles of proportionality and non-discrimination, which are structurally biased towards economic integration. This is so because national regulations contravening mutual recognition are required to pass a proportionality test and, if their aim is considered acceptable, would only be allowed if a less restrictive measure for the market is not possible. This means that it is ultimately the market and not national (social) regulations that the proportionality test protects, hence the bias.

In short, during European integration pre-Maastricht the intense activity of the Court in developing and consolidating the new European legal order led to a range of subtle changes which first detached some aspects of the *Rechtsstaat* (rule of law) from their (national) social context and then gave them structural priority over the social and democratic components of the social state. The result of this imbalance was the legal imposition of a minimum common denominator for all national realizations of the Social and Democratic *Rechtsstaat* paradigm, disregarding law's context-dependence. In that sense, mutual recognition proved to be an expeditious way to advance the common market via negative integration (Scharpf 1996, p15) – a strategy fully supported by the Commission's "new approach" (Mattera 2005, p13). This, however, came at the price of limiting the regulatory abilities of the nation state. On top of that, the rise of neoliberal thinking, intensively promoted by the UK (Harvey 2005, p55 ff.), not only provided ideological support to these changes but also infiltrated the actual content of the new standards imposed from the European level. Illustrative in this regard was the ECtHR's new interpretation of the right to property, by which a carefully drafted provision explicitly recognizing the ability of states to regulate the use of property (Article 1.2 of the First Protocol) was replaced by a proportionality test balancing between the general interest underlying such measures and the individual's fundamental right (*Sporrong and Lönnroth v. Sweden*, nos. 7151/75 and 7152/75, ECHR 1982). Where previously, due to the political implications of the right to property, the contracting parties had been granted an extensive margin of appreciation beyond the reach of courts, the ECtHR by narrow majority now decided to subject their measures to judicial review (Nicol 2010, pp138–40). When combined, all of these developments contributed to the general detachment of the economy from society ("disembedded liberalism"). Nevertheless, perceived as merely dealing with specific tasks of a technical nature (Milward 1992, p11; cf. Haas 2004 [1958], p29), few critical voices were raised against the integration project before the Single European Act (1985), which included in the treaties not only legal bases allowing the adoption of directives regarding the health and safety of workers (Article 118a EEC) and opening the possibility for a social dialogue at European scale (Article 118b EEC), but also new headings in Economic and Social Cohesion, Research and Technological Development and Environmental Policy (Titles V to VII, respectively). These improvements notwithstanding, integration did not compensate either for the limitation of nation states' competences regarding social policies – although public services did not fall within the scope of EU law, concrete measures of social policy could be considered restrictions to economic freedoms – or for their inability to balance private and collective interests in property rights once the Court provided itself with a new standard of protection detached from national social contexts.

Post-Maastricht integration: the structural predominance of economic integration over national (social) policies

In the following two decades a radical evolution took place in European integration, but this time mainly resulting from political action rather than from judicial activity. A more comprehensive, holistic understanding of the marketplace as inextricably linked to society lay behind the next steps of the European project. Successive agreements (the Treaties of Maastricht, Amsterdam and Nice) amended the original treaties in order not only to deepen economic integration, but also to confer to the European level more competences on socially related areas such as citizenship (Articles 17–21 EC), consumer policy (Article 153 EC), non-discrimination (Article 13 EC), social policy (Articles 136–145 EC), employment (Articles 125–130 EC) and public health (Article 152 EC). Importantly, a new macroeconomic layer was added to the economic constitution, which until then mainly focused on microeconomic integration (Tuori and Tuori 2014, pp35–41; Tuori 2015). An Economic and Monetary Union (EMU) and a common currency were envisaged by 2000, requiring from states first gradual and then permanent coordination of their respective macroeconomic policies. Respect for national sovereignty over economic policy matters was thus articulated with the need for coordination at the European level. On the other hand, and regarding social issues, those inherent to the internal market (related to free movement of workers or undertakings, non-discrimination or consumer policy) were directly conferred to the European level, providing it with decision-making powers under the traditional community method; but those more closely related to macroeconomic policies, such as employment or pension systems, were to be decided according to the Open Method of Coordination (OMC), basically following the main tenets of the coordination of economic policies. Therefore, although in this stage of European integration market and society were indeed considered as interrelated, the con-ferral of competences on social issues from states to the Union corresponded to the layer of the economic constitution (micro- or macroeconomic) to which they refer, confirming again the structural dominance of an economic understanding of society in the design of the treaties.

The changes outlined here were an expression of the radical transformation the European project was undergoing. On the one hand, they confirmed the transfer of the dominant role in integration from France, which conceived of the state as the manager of the economy (dirigisme), to Germany, more prone to limiting the role of the state to guarantor of the free market and competition (ordoliberalism). The economic power of the latter, forged around the Deutschmark as anchor currency since the 1970s, succeeded in influencing the design of the EMU according to its own preferences, codified in the Treaty of Maastricht (Dyson and Featherstone 1999; James 2012). Only then was it possible to address the social concerns voiced by French leaders, particularly in the subsequent revision of the treaties (Treaty of Amsterdam). This evolution proves again that social issues, despite being formally considered in close relation to economic ones, were *de facto* subordinated to the latter. On the other hand, the new powers conferred to the now European Union in a range of different domains, from foreign and security policy to the mentioned coordination of economic and social policies, followed a similar pattern according to which EU members were willing to limit their sovereignty in a European-scale coordinated effort to face the challenges of incipient globalization. It is precisely at this moment when they ceased to be nation states and became Member States (Bickerton 2012; Bickerton et al 2015a, pp708–9), pooling their decision-making powers according to a set of new procedures in which intergovernmental institutions are increasingly prominent (Puetter 2014; Bickerton et al 2015b). These procedures were presumably apt to deal with social policy issues without transferring full competence to the supranational level or agreeing on harmonization strategies potentially damaging for the various (national) social policies, already well established and in several aspects incompatible with each other (Scharpf 2002, p652), even more after the 2004 enlargement, which not only doubled the number of Member States, but exponentially increased their diversity. Provided with these tools the EU was ready to engage in the endeavour of becoming, as the Lisbon Agenda envisaged, "the most competitive and dynamic knowledge-based economy in the world capable of sustainable economic growth with more and better jobs and greater social cohesion" by 2010 (European Council 2000).

Public services were decisive in this respect. The Treaty of Amsterdam formally recognized their role in "promoting social and territorial cohesion", and considered them part of the "shared values of the Union" (Article 16 EC). Importantly, both the Union and Member States, within their respective powers, were in charge of guaranteeing that public services could fulfil their missions. Given this legal framework, and with an eye to the aims of the Lisbon Agenda, it was possible to address their alleged inefficiency by reconsidering for the first time the degree of their exclusion from competition rules (Bauby 2011, p27). Accordingly, "services of general economic interest" (SGEIs) – basically public utilities, including the big network industries, such as transport, postal services, energy or communications – would be liberalized by opening them to competition. On the other hand, principles inherent to public services, like universality, continuity, minimum quality, affordability or consumer protection, had to be guaranteed in any event. Again, this was possible by resorting to a regulated liberalization that opened the market to cross-border competitors and still ensured public service requirements. But liberalization also applied to the provision of economic activities and professional services, where the role of public bodies giving prior authorization and thus monitoring the aptitude of providers according to legal (socially sensitive) requirements was considered an administrative barrier to trade and, therefore, was replaced by the simple requirement of communication by providers.[4] A change in paradigm occurred (Esteve Pardo 2015): instead of being authorized by the state according to social values, these activities were now subject to the market and thus monitored by competitors, consumers and, eventually, the courts.

This liberalization context favoured the doctrine of a more active Court of Justice regarding public undertakings, ultimately discussing the scope of public property in the free market. Originally, competition rules were applicable to all companies regardless of their ownership. When they were given exclusive rights (a common feature of public undertakings in charge of public services) they had a dominant position in the market, so that any exercise of those rights could be considered against competition rules – which forbid the *abuse* of such a position. This breach of EU law could nonetheless be justified on the basis of the social objectives underlying the granting of exclusive rights, in particular when aimed at guaranteeing a universal service through which profitable tasks defray unprofitable ones (*Corbeau*, C-320/91, EU:C:1993:198, para. 17). However, this very same doctrine presented the opportunity to consider open to competition all additional services not offered by the holder of the rights, provided that no harm would result to its financial capacities (*Corbeau*, EU:C:1993:198, para. 19). Publicly owned companies providing public services could then easily be excluded from the application of competition law, though, as a matter of fact, in the following years liberalization and privatization increased. The reasons for this apparently paradoxical development lie in the structural positioning of publicly owned companies as justification for a breach of competition rules, as well as in the competitive pressure exerted by companies offering services additional to the basic ones they provide – something the innovation inherent in capitalist development will exploit, ultimately forcing public companies to adapt and compete in these new sectors.

Simultaneously, capital movements were fully liberalized and became a major source of pressure on public undertakings: as soon as they were open to private shareholders they had to avoid all rules giving state representatives special decision-making powers (usually granted to protect companies considered of strategic interest) as they may deter cross-border investments (*Commission v. Italy*, C-58/99, EU:C:2000:280 and the full *Golden Shares* saga). This case law understood the conflict to be between free movement of capital and the articles of incorporation of privatized undertakings, and ruled in favour of the former. By doing so the Court disregarded the underlying struggle between the shareholder's right to private property and the state's competence to regulate property regimes (in this case of a semi-public undertaking), which should be considered an expression of its own Social and Democratic *Rechtsstaat* and, as such, beyond the scope of EU law – this was the reason behind Article 222 EEC (now Article 345 TFEU). Despite the literal wording of this provision that was not the case. The Court even refused to consider that it could *per se* justify a breach of the economic freedoms, and only recognized that "the reasons underlying the choice of the rules of property ownership adopted by the national legislation" may be capable of justifying those breaches (*Essent and Others*, C-105/12 to C-107/12, EU:C:2013:677, para. 55). A more sensitive line of reasoning could have conceded that when investing in those semi-public undertakings shareholders should know about the attached voting rights. The market could be relied on to assess the limitations that those shares were the object of and to value them accordingly, instead of requiring all shares in the market to give rise to the same rights: ultimately, private property was given priority over the state's ability to regulate property.

In other areas of integration the case law was equally controversial, as in the conflict between fundamental economic freedoms and social policy measures or social rights. This was the case in respect of German labour legislation that promoted fixed-term hiring among older workers, which was considered against the EU principle of non-discrimination for reason of age (*Mangold*, C-144/04, EU:C:2005:709). Even more illuminating were the cases of collective union action against employers' practices regarding the reflagging of ships or posted workers (*Viking*, C-438/05, EU:C:2007:772, and *Laval*, C-341/05, EU:C:2007:809, respectively). While this form of action is protected by fundamental rights (Article 28 of the Charter of Fundamental Rights of the European Union, hereafter the Charter) and thus suitable to justify restrictions on freedom of establishment or free provision of services if able to pass a proportionality test, in the two cited cases, it was found that this test had not been met. By carrying out this test, the Court took the place of national courts in assessing the said practices according to their socio-constitutional context and thus replaced a socially embedded assessment with its own, which was merely based on a socially detached rule of law (Niglia 2016). These cases addressed, from a legal point of view, the politically disregarded implications of an enlargement incorporating countries with less developed social standards and whose only way to compete in an open market was via labour costs.

To summarize, post-Maastricht integration affected the traditional way social rights were guaranteed in two main ways. First, public services were opened to the market and, although social purposes could justify breaches of competition rules, the competitive pressure of companies providing additional services, together with the *Golden Shares* doctrine, reduced the number of means previously available for states to direct the economy. And second, once the Union accepted new members which, because of historical reasons, were mainly concerned with the rule of law and democracy (thus corresponding to the liberal state paradigm), conflicts relating to key practices of social states, like industrial and collective action, could be brought to the Court of Justice and, eventually, considered to be in breach of the economic freedoms. Consequently, the three ways the "social" state traditionally protected social rights – through fundamental rights, social policies and public services – were affected by European integration. On top of that, private property was given priority over the state's competence to regulate public property, leading to a political system in which liberalism was constitutionally protected ("constitutionalized liberalism").

The economic crisis and the final rupture with the Social and Democratic *Rechtsstaat*

It is with the entry into force of the Treaty of Lisbon that the disequilibria in the balance between market and society resulting from European integration are addressed. After adding the social element to the formula, it is recognized for the first time that the Union commits to a "social market economy" (Article 3.3 TEU) primarily based on open market and free competition, but ready to allocate resources through redistributive policies when they better match societal demands (Damjanovic 2013, p1689). In addition, the same provision explicitly enumerates the Union's social aims, requiring the whole *acquis communautaire* to be interpreted accordingly. This more socially-sensitive approach explains why the Union finally acquired competence to legislate on the principles, and economic and financial conditions, under which SGEIs operate (Article 14 TFEU, ex 16 EC). Simultaneously, non-economic services of general interest – a category resulting from the previous application of competition rules by the Commission – were excluded from the treaties' scope of application (Article 2 of Protocol 26). Importantly, the entry into force of the Charter formally anchored social rights in the European legal order. Therefore, the Union was finally involved in the three ways through which states traditionally guarantee social rights: fundamental rights (via the Charter), policy programmes (under the OMC) and public services (establishing the main principles of those with an economic interest). On the other hand, European protection of property rights was reinforced not only through the inclusion of the corresponding article in the Charter (Article 17, with a similar structure to the ECHR one), but also because of the special mention of intellectual property rights (IPR) in its second section. As a matter of fact, the Union acquired competence over the creation and uniform protection of IPRs in Europe (Article 118 TFEU). Because of their strategic relevance in the globalized economy as easily commodified assets of great economic value and, in addition, detached from any particular societal values, establishment of centralized authorization, coordination and supervision mechanisms at the European level did not encounter major resistance. In sum, after the entry into force of the Treaty of Lisbon the Union seemed to be well-equipped to address social and market issues more comprehensively.

But what defines these years is the severe economic crisis, of special significance in Europe because the institutional setting of the EMU not only left Member States with a limited toolkit to address it (currency devaluation or monetary policy were not available anymore), but also because it fostered a market-dependence approach which transferred the various financial problems to the public debt side. Regardless of the underlying reasons, what is relevant now is that austerity was the guideline imposed from European institutions onto national economic policies. Fiscal consolidation was required in order to keep alive the Euro currency and with that aim in mind severe policies were imposed regardless of the opinion of the people. Think about the absolute rejection by EU leaders of the referendum proposed by Greek Prime Minister Papandreu on the second bailout programme; the imposition of a non-elected prime minister – former commissioner Mario Monti – in Italy; or, following the requirement of the European Central Bank's (ECB's) governor Trichet, the amendment of the Spanish Constitution to include the principle of budgetary stability and granting "absolute priority" (Article 135.3 Spanish Constitution) to the repayment of debts among any other expense, social policies included – to name but a few well known examples. The disconnection of economy and politics from society led to overwhelming public demonstrations expressing disaffection with how public policies were run. However, once the traditional activities of the state could potentially hinder the internal market and its role was consequently restricted to mere guarantor of the smooth work of the market (Esteve Pardo 2015), its abilities to commit to fiscal discipline in a contracting economy context were basically limited to reducing expenses – thus leading to the "consolidation state" (Streeck 2014, pp112–16; Menéndez 2016, p116).

The situations of extreme poverty and deprivation which followed the austerity measures imposed from the European institutions soon resulted in social conflicts testing how social rights, now part of EU's *acquis*, would be protected. However, because austerity measures were not agreed according to ordinary EU law but signed in Memoranda of Understanding to which the Commission, ECB, International Monetary Fund (IMF) and concerned state were parties, individuals could not directly oppose those measures by resort to EU fundamental rights (Kilpatrick 2014). Complaints against Commission and ECB involvement in these agreements or against ECB's concrete decisions on monetary policy have so far been consistently rejected (*von Storch*, C-64/14 P, EU:C:2015:300). Procedurally, social rights are very difficult to allege against measures corresponding to the macroeconomic layer of the economic constitution, because states are their addressees and individuals are not (in legal terms) even indirectly affected by them – one of the requirements of active legitimation before the Court. Given these procedural constraints, a constitutional conflict might be an adequate way to obtain a pronouncement of the Court, but precisely because of the constitutional component and its extremely serious economic consequences, nothing except the plain validation of these measures can be expected (*Pringle*, C-370/12, EU:C:2012:756; *Gauweiler*, C-64/14, EU:C:2015:400).

Hence, in order to bring EU law back in, social conflicts had to be reconfigured and reconstructed according to the micro-economic constitution. That has happened in Spain, for instance, where social and economic policies have been traditionally very proactive in favour of making citizens proprietors of their homes. Once the effects of the crisis were evident and unemployment skyrocketed, the number of unpaid mortgages became overwhelming. Due to its serious financial troubles, the banking sector proceeded to massive foreclosures which, according to Spanish procedural rules, were semi-automatic and gave the debtor no opportunity to impugn the terms of the agreement. An extremely serious social problem, resulting from countless evictions and leaving families homeless (and, in accordance to Spanish law, still owing a part of their mortgages), could thus be addressed as a consumer protection conflict (*Aziz*, C-415/11, EU:C:2013:164). Interestingly, neither in this case nor in any of the many which followed (*Banco Popular Español*, C-537/12 and C-116/13, EU:C:2013:759; *Barclays Bank*, C-280/13, EU:C:2014:279) was the right to respect for one's private home – Articles 7 of the Charter and 8 ECHR – invoked. As a matter of fact, the only fundamental right mentioned in these proceedings was the one to have an effective judicial remedy – Article 47 of the Charter – (*Sánchez Morcillo*, C-169/14, EU:C:2014:2099), which again proves how difficult the adjudication of social rights can be. In the ECHR context, the right to property was alleged against the concrete consequence of an austerity measure: the excessive taxation of severance pay (*N.K.M. v. Hungary*, no. 66529/11, ECHR 2013). Social conflicts have thus been reframed in European courts along the lines of market society, of which consumer and property rights are foundational elements. But, simultaneously, the German Constitutional Court recognized for the first time the relation between human dignity and a minimum subsistence amount (*BVerfGE*, 1 BvL 1/09 (9.2.2010), §133), further demonstrated by immigrants' and asylum seekers' entitlement to such a right (*BVerfGE*, 1 BvL 10/10 (18.7.2012)). Doubts arise as to how compatible the individualistic social model corresponding to the European treaties is with this national understanding of human dignity that is traditionally closer to the social state, in particular when considering that market society fosters the replacement of collective social policies by private insurance mechanisms (Frerichs 2016), thus returning to a model in which well-being increasingly depends on private property.

The economic crisis therefore culminated in the divorce of European integration from the Social and Democratic *Rechtsstaat* by uncoupling from each other the three constitutive elements of the social state (the rule of law, the democratic principle and the social dimension). In addition, it reformulated how social problems should be conceived of and, subsequently, addressed: instead of resorting to national (socially sensitive) law, current social problems should be reframed according to market-oriented European law. Recent developments in European integration finally led to a new but still undefined state model guided by fiscal discipline and according to which public expenses have to be reduced in order to repay debts, thus limiting states' abilities to guarantee social rights.

Conclusion: a new governing rationale in European politics after the crisis

During its more than six decades of existence, the relation between European integration and its Member States has evolved significantly. Originally this was one of symbiosis, with each level contributing to the realization of the social state; however, unrelated developments, when combined, transformed that symbiotic relation into one of dominance of the European level over the national one. The first step in this evolution consisted in the pre-eminence of the new, autonomous legal order over national legal systems. However, the constitutionalization of EU law took for granted that the new legal order was itself in line with the rule of law. It is precisely its autonomy, required to guarantee that the market is not fragmented due to dissimilar implementation of EU law, that makes them incompatible: the legality of EU law depends exclusively on autonomous sources and excludes any test according to heteronymous parameters, as proved by the long conflict with national constitutional courts around protection of fundamental rights or the recent rejection of the adhesion to the ECHR (Opinion 2/13, EU:C:2014:2454). This self-referential conception of legality is at odds with the rule of law, according to which legality also depends on substantive, and not merely formal, elements (Kochenov 2015). The constitutionalization of EU law involved both its consolidation as an autonomous legal order and the removal of any external legitimating factor. The consequence was that the autonomous European legal order could overrule national *Rechtsstaats*, which, importantly, were particularly sensitive to their respective (national) social contexts.

The second stage in the evolution refers to the progressive detachment of EU law from any concrete social context. Because of the relative homogeneity of the founding members, this was not a problem during the first decades of integration, but as successive enlargements increased diversity in the Union, the social sensitivity of EU law significantly decreased. If post-war national *Rechtsstaats* were socially sensitive, the new European legal order had to mainly be market-sensitive: when guided by social grounds, its interpretation corresponded to a minimum common denominator for all Member States, by definition diminishing as the number of members increased; but usually it acted according to economic grounds. In those cases the European legal order, through different biases in proportionality tests, gave structural priority to its mainly economic content over national measures, which usually had a broader, all-encompassing rationale. This socially detached European legal order, under the appearance of the rule of law, could justify major legal changes contributing to inclining the balance in the tension between capitalism and democracy towards the former, for instance through the mutual recognition doctrine. Furthermore, the Court matched this trend in its case law on property rights, first by isolating them from their (national) social context, which was replaced by an economic integration-centred and thus self-referential one; and later by giving priority to private over public property, emphasizing the economic performance side of individual property over the social performance of collective property. The social function of the Court of Justice's conception of property corresponds to a neoliberal understanding of society, according to which the functioning of the market is the priority. The autonomous European legal order was therefore followed by its disconnection from any social context.

The final stage in the evolution towards dominance of the European level over the national one began when competences on macroeconomic policies were assigned to the Union. The inherent assumption of some policy choices, when combined with the self-referential and market-based rule of law instead of socially-sensitive rule of law, soon led to doubts regarding the Union's legitimation. In order to address this democratic deficit, the European Parliament was increasingly recognized to have a bigger say in the legislative procedure, to the point of being a co-legislator. Subsequently, institutions were opened to societal input under new forms of governance (European Commission 2001). All these attempts were finally discredited once the economic crisis jeopardized the whole integration project. Resorting to intergovernmental institutions and to non-EU law mechanisms in order to impose austerity measures, EU law detached itself from democracy (excluding the European Parliament) and moved from the (apparent) rule *of* law to a non-democratic rule *by* law – "authoritarian liberalism" (Heller 2015). Thereby a transition from "embedded" to "disembedded", "constitutionalized" and finally "authoritarian" liberalism has been effected.

In each of these three stages, European integration disconnected one of the three elements of the Social and Democratic *Rechtsstaat* from the others: first the rule of law, then the social dimension, finally the democratic principle. An evolution of the social state, whose rationale was to *produce* in order to guarantee *social stability* via *redistribution*, has taken place. The result is a still undefined state model whose rationale is to *produce or reduce costs* in order to guarantee *financial stability* via *payment of debts*. This latter equation reflects the new societal priorities, heavily influenced by economic needs and requirements. In it social rights, whose traditional role was to guarantee social stability and to contribute to wealth redistribution, only figure as an element to be cut off in order to achieve the new – now recognized in the treaties (Article 136.3 TFEU) and by the Court (*Pringle*, C-370/12, EU:C:2012:756, para. 135) – overarching and systemic goal: financial stability.

Notes

* This research is part of the project *The Many Constitutions of Europe*, funded by the Academy of Finland.
1 The concept of "rule of law" used in this chapter corresponds to the translation into English of the German formula *Rechtsstaat*, the Italian *Stato de Diritto* or the Spanish *Estado de Derecho*, which do not fully correspond to the broader common law concept used in English language. Therefore, for the sake of clarity I will use *Rechtsstaat* when possible.
2 Directives on the application of the principle of equal pay for men and women (75/117/EEC), on collective redundancies (75/129/EEC), on employees' rights in the event of transfers of undertakings (77/187/EEC) and on protection of employees in the event of the insolvency of their employer (80/987/EEC).
3 Directive on equal treatment for men and women as regards access to employment, vocational training and promotion, and working conditions (76/207/EEC).
4 Directive on services in the internal market (2006/123/EC).

References

BAQUERO CRUZ, J. (2002) *Between Competition and Free Movement: The Economic Constitutional Law of the Economic Community*. Oxford: Hart.

BAUBY, P. (2011) From Rome to Lisbon: SGIs in Primary Law. In SZYSZCZAK, E., DAVIES, J., ANDENÆS, M. and BEKKEDAL, T. (eds) *Developments in Services of General Interest*. The Hague: T.M.C. Asser Press.

BERMAN, S. (2006) *The Primacy of Politics: Social Democracy and the Making of Europe's Twentieth Century*. Cambridge: Cambridge University Press.

BICKERTON, C.J., (2012) *European Integration: From Nation-States to Member States*. Oxford: Oxford University Press.

BICKERTON, C.J., HODSON, D. and PUETTER, U. (2015a) The New Intergovernmentalism: European Integration in the Post-Maastricht Era. *Journal of Common Market Studies*, 53(4). pp703–722.

BICKERTON, C.J., HODSON, D. and PUETTER, U. (eds) (2015b) *The New Intergovernmentalism: States and Supranational Actors in the Post-Maastricht Era*. Oxford: Oxford University Press.

BILCHITZ, D. (2014) Socio-economic rights, economic crisis, and legal doctrine. *International Journal of Constitutional Law*, 12(3). pp710–739.

CARUSO, D. (2004) Private Law and Public Stakes in European Integration: The Case of Property. *European Law Journal*, 10(6). pp751–765.

CASTEL, R. (2003) *From Manual Workers to Wage Laborers: Transformation of the Social Question*. New Brunswick, NJ: Transaction Publishers.

CROZIER, M., HUNTINGTON, S. P. and WATANUKI, J. (1975) *The Crisis of Democracy: Report on the Governability of Democracies to the Trilateral Commission*. New York: New York University Press.

DAMJANOVIC, D. (2013) The EU Market Rules as Social Market Rules: Why the EU Can Be a Social Market Economy. *Common Market Law Review*, 50(6). pp1685–1718.

DYSON, K. and FEATHERSTONE, K. (1999) *The Road to Maastricht: Negotiating Economic and Monetary Union*. Oxford: Oxford University Press.

EICHENGREEN, B. (1995) Mainsprings of economic recovery in post-war Europe. In EICHENGREEN, B. (ed.). *Europe's Post-War Recovery*. Cambridge: Cambridge University Press.

ESTEVE PARDO, J. (2015) *Estado Garante: Idea y Realidad*. Madrid: INAP.

EUROPEAN COMMISSION (2001) *European governance – A white paper*. COM(2001) 428 final.

EUROPEAN COUNCIL (2000) *Conclusions*. Lisbon European Council, 23 and 24 March 2000.

FALKNER, G. (1998) *EU Social Policy in the 1990s: Towards a Corporatist Policy Community*. London: Routledge.

FORSTHOFF, E. (2015) [1963] *Estado de Derecho en Mutación: Trabajos Constitucionales 1954–1973*. Madrid: Tecnos.

FOSSUM, J. E. and MENÉNDEZ, A. J. (2011) *The Constitution's Gift: A Constitutional Theory for a Democratic European Union*. Lanham: Rowman & Littlefield.

FRERICHS, S. (2016) From Social Rights to Economic Incentives? The Moral (Re)construction of Welfare Capitalism. In Veitch, K. and Kotkas, T. (eds). *Social Rights in the Welfare State: Origins and Transformations*. Abingdon: Routledge.

GARCÍA-PELAYO, M. (2009) [1977] *Las Transformaciones del Estado Moderno*. Madrid: Alianza Editorial.

GARLAND, D. (2014) The Welfare State: A Fundamental Dimension of Modern Government. *European Journal of Sociology*, 55(3). pp327–364.

GRIMM, D. (2015) The Democratic Costs of Constitutionalisation: The European Case. *European Law Journal*, 21(4). pp460–473.

HAAS, E. B. (2004) [1958] *The Uniting of Europe: Political, Social and Economic Forces, 1950–1957*. Notre Dame: University of Notre Dame Press.

HABERMAS, J. (1975) *Legitimation crisis*. Boston, MA: Beacon Press.

HALL, P. A. and SOSKICE, D. (2001) (eds) *Varieties of Capitalism: The Institutional Foundations of Comparative Advantage*. Oxford: Oxford University Press.

HARVEY, D. (2005) *A Brief History of Neoliberalism*. Oxford: Oxford University Press.

HELLER, H. (2015) Authoritarian Liberalism? *European Law Journal*, 21(3). pp295–301.

JAMES, H. (2012) *Making the European Monetary Union: The Role of the Committee of Central Bank Governors and the Origins of the European Central Bank*. Cambridge and London: The Belknap Press.

KILPATRICK, C. (2014) Are the bailout measures immune to EU Social challenge because they are not EU Law? *European Constitutional Law Review*, 10(3). pp393–421.

KOCHENOV, D. (2015) EU Law without the Rule of Law: Is the Veneration of Autonomy Worth It? *Yearbook of European Law*, 34(1). pp74–96.

MARSHALL, T. H. (1972) Value Problems of Welfare-Capitalism. *Journal of Social Policy*, 1(1). pp15–32.

MATTERA, A. (2005) The Principle of Mutual Recognition and Respect for National, Regional and Local Identities and Traditions. In KOSTORIS PADOA SCHIOPPA, F. (ed). *The Principle of Mutual Recognition in the European Integration Process*. Basingstoke: Palgrave Macmillan.

MENÉNDEZ, A. J. (2016) Neumark Vindicated: The Europeanisation of National Tax Systems and the Future of the Social and Democratic Rechtsstaat. In CHALMERS, D., JACHTENFUCHS, M. and JOERGES, Ch. (eds). *The End of the Eurocrats' Dream: Adjusting to European Diversity*. Cambridge: Cambridge University Press.

MENZ, G. (2005) *Varieties of Capitalism and Europeanization: National Response Strategies to the Single European Market*. Oxford: Oxford University Press.

MILWARD, A. S. (1992) *The European Rescue of the Nation State*. London: Routledge.

MYRDAL, G. (1960) *Beyond the Welfare State: Economic Planning in the Welfare States and its International Implications*. London: Yale University Press.

MYRDAL, G. (1963) [1957]. *Economic Theory and Underdeveloped Regions*. London: Methuen.

NICOL, D. (2010) *The Constitutional Protection of Capitalism*. Oxford: Hart Publishing.

NIELSEN, R. and SZYSZCZAK, E. (1991) *The Social Dimension of the European Union*. Copenhagen: Handelshøjskolens Forlag.

NIGLIA, L. (2016) Eclipse of the Constitution: Europe Nouveau Siècle. *European Law Journal*, 22(2). pp132–156.

O'CONNOR, J. (1973) *The Fiscal Crisis of the State*. New York: St. Martin's Press.

OFFE, C. (1984) *Contradictions of the Welfare State*. London: Hutchinson.

PUETTER, U. (2014) *The European Council and the Council: New Intergovernmentalism and Institutional Change*. Oxford: Oxford University Press.

RUBIO LLORENTE, F. (2012) *La Forma del Poder: Estudios Sobre la Constitución* (Vol. II). 3rd Ed. Madrid: Centro de Estudios Políticos y Constitucionales.

RUGGIE, J. G. (1982) International Regimes, Transactions, and Change: Embedded Liberalism in the Postwar Economic Order. *International Organization*, 36(2). pp379–415.

SCHARPF, F. W. (1996) Negative and Positive Integration in the Political Economy of European Welfare States. In MARKS, G., SCHARPF, F. W., SCHMITTER, Ph. C. and STREEK, W. (eds). *Governance in the European Union*, London: Sage.

SCHARPF, F. W. (1999) *Governing in Europe: Effective and Democratic?* Oxford: Oxford University Press.

SCHARPF, F. W. (2002) The European Social Model: Coping with the Challenges of Diversity. *Journal of Common Market Studies*, 40(4). pp645–670.

SOEDERBERG, S., MENZ, G. and CERNY, P. G. (eds) (2005) *Internalizing Globalization: The Rise of Neoliberalism and the Decline of National Varieties of Capitalism*. Basingstoke: Palgrave Macmillan.

SOTELO, I. (2010) *El Estado Social: Antecedentes, origen, desarrollo y declive*. Madrid: Trotta.

STREECK, W. (2014) *Buying Time: The Delayed Crisis of Democratic Capitalism*. London and New York: Verso.

TEASDALE, A. L. (1993) The Life and Death of the Luxembourg Compromise. *Journal of Common Market Studies*, 31(4). pp567–579.

TUORI, K. (2015) *European Constitutionalism*. Cambridge: Cambridge University Press.

TUORI, K. and TUORI, K. (2014) *The Eurozone Crisis: A Constitutional Analysis*. Cambridge: Cambridge University Press.

UTRILLA FERNÁNDEZ-BERMEJO, D. (2011) *Las Garantías del Derecho de Propiedad Privada en Europa: Derecho de la Unión Europea y Convenio Europeo de Derechos Humanos*. Madrid: Civitas-Thomson Reuters.

WEILER, J. H. H. (2005) Mutual Recognition, Functional Equivalence and Harmonization in the Evolution of the European Common Market and the WTO. In KOSTORIS PADOA SCHIOPPA, F. (ed.). *The Principle of Mutual Recognition in the European Integration Process*. Basingstoke: Palgrave Macmillan.

Index

activation: in the credit market 137; in the labour market 45, 112, 137
anti-tax discourse: and Reagan 145; and Thatcher 145; protests 144–6
asylum seekers: social rights of 49, 117, 118, 128–9
austerity measures 3, 148, 153, 159, 188–9, 191
autonomy: political 3; social 99–100, 104–5, 107–11, 113–14

Bailey, S. 167
Beveridge, W. 59–64, 100, 125, 171
Bismarck, O. 100, 114
Bourgeois, L. 102
Brown, W. 169–70

capabilities 91–2, 95–6, 112
Castel, R. 101–2, 107, 178
childcare 88–9, 160
citizenship: and nation 117–123, 129; consumer 169; market 140, 149; social, see Marshall, T. H.
consolidation state 148–9, 188
constitutional social rights: in Finland 23–5, 29, 161; in France 103; in Norway 50; in Spain 161; in Sweden 25–7, 29–30
constitutionalization 16, 48, 53, 175, 181, 190; see also hyper-constitutionalization
contractualism 66, 106, 110, 112, 170
Court of Justice of the European Union 51, 181–2, 185
Crouch, C. 149–50

Dardot, P. and Laval, C. 66–7, 72
debtfare 137, 148
debtfare state 148, 151
Delanty, G. 118, 120–1, 123, 130

dignity 109–11, 176, 189–90
disability allowance in France 107–8, 110, 112
Dworkin, R. 91–2

Economic and Monetary Union 184, 188
economic incentives 137, 140, 146, 148
economic sociology of law 137, 139
egalitarianism 79, 81–2, 84, 89–92, 94–6
Esping-Andersen, G. 15, 88–90, 92, 114, 137–9
European Committee on Social Rights 52
European Convention on Human Rights 30, 50, 52, 180, 189
European Court of Human Rights 35, 50, 182–3
European Social Charter 22, 24, 161
Ewald, F. 19, 22, 104

Foucault, M. 169
Friot, B. 102
fundamental rights 178, 181, 188

Garland, D. 2, 31, 138
Giddens, A. 88, 90–4, 96

Habermas, J. 2–3, 114
health care system: in Finland 17, 21; in Sweden 21
housing policy in Norway 46–7, 51–2
hyper-constitutionalization 27–8

International Covenant on Civil and Political Rights 50, 52
International Covenant on Economic, Social and Cultural Rights 24, 50–1, 129, 160–1
International Labour Organization 24, 99

196 Index

judicial review 35–8, 40–2, 49, 53, 178
juridification 3–4, 16, 27
justiciability of social rights 1–2, 26, 31, 40, 50

Lafore, R. 112
Laroque, P. 101, 113
Leroy, M. 144, 146, 148
liberal state 176–8

Marshall Plan, 179
Marshall, T. H.: on democratic welfare capitalism 84–5, 137, 139; on the duties of citizenship 45, 63–4; on equality 79–84, 87, 96; on social rights and social citizenship 2, 15, 45, 59, 63–7, 70–1, 114, 123, 139
Mill, J. S. 85
moral economy: concept of 140–1; of debt 137, 146, 151; of taxation 144; of taxpayers 146

nationalism: and exclusion 122, 125; and inclusion 124; and post-WWII welfare state 123–6
neoliberalism 35–6, 42, 44, 65, 72–3, 127, 169–70, 191
new egalitarianism 90–2, 94
new nationalism 120, 129–30
new social risks 87–8, 104–5

old-age pensions: in Finland 18–19; in Norway 43; in Sweden 17–18
Open Method of Coordination 106, 184

personalization 110
political liberalism: different forms of 191; in Norway 36, 40
privatised Keynesianism 149–50
property rights: relationship to social rights 137, 140, 145, 149–50; social function of 177–9, 182

Rawls, J. 89–90, 92, 94, 171
Reilly & Wilson case 68–72
revenu de solidarité active 106–7, 109–10, 112–13
revenu minimum d'insertion 3, 106–7
right to education 83, 87–8, 96, 147–8, 151, 161–2, 164, 167
right to health 161, 166–7
Rosanvallon, P. 3, 65, 73–4, 91, 93–5, 105
rule of law 41, 176–8

Sen, A. 91
services of general economic interest 185, 187
sickness insurance: in Finland 20; in France 104; in Norway 43; in Sweden 18, 23
Social and Democratic *Rechtsstaat* 177–8, 182, 186, 190–1
social assistance: in France 103–4, 107, 114; in Norway 45–6, 50–3
social care: in Finland 21; long-term care in France 104–5, 108, 113; in Sweden 22
social contract 127, 138, 142, 151–3, 170–1
social exclusion 87–8, 104–5, 113
social rights: as collective rights 19–20, 35, 51, 53, 171; as individualized rights 20, 25, 35–6, 51–2, 91, 93, 95, 110, 113; marketization of 166–72; as procedural rights 3, 93, 100, 109, 111–13; relationship to civil and political rights 1–3, 26, 31, 35, 58, 139–40, 176; relationship to nation, state and citizenship 119–22; relationship to obligations/duties/ responsibilities 58–9, 62, 64–6, 71–3, 90, 142, 170; social dimension of 58; as social property 102
social risks 99–101; *see also* new social risks
social security system: in Britain 61; in France 101–3, 114
social state 176–8, 190
solidarity: national 118, 121, 123, 126; social 19, 30–1, 61–2, 65–7, 101–3, 107, 109–10, 142
Streeck, W. 145, 148–9
sufficientarism 81–2

tax morale 144, 146
tax state: contribution tax 137, 142, 144, 146; exchange tax 137, 142, 146; obligation tax 142
Thatcherism 126–9
third way thinking 64–6, 68, 88
Thompson, E. P. 140
Titmuss, R. 79, 104, 123–4

unemployment insurance 20–1
user charges: and equality 168–171; and the transformation of social rights 169–71; distinction between core and peripheral services 166–8; in education

164–5; in health care 162–4; IMF definition of 157; in Israel 166; origins of 158; rationales 159–60; in United States 163–4, 166

Weber, M. 112, 142
welfare capitalism: concept of 84–5, 137–8, 141, 150; moral reconstruction of 140, 152; transformation of 151

welfare state: expenditure side of 137, 146, 153; Keynesian 35, 42, 124, 127, 139, 147–50; revenue side of 141, 153; Schumpeterian workfare state 139, 147–8; shifts in subjectivities and the subjects of rights 140, 149, 152; social investment state 79–80, 96, 147
workfare: in Britain 68–72; in France 106; in Norway 45; policy of 67–8, 147–8, 151